MW00674955

ISBN 978-1-934655-22-1

06-017 • COPYRIGHT © 1982 **World Evangelism Press**®
P.O. Box 262550 • Baton Rouge, Louisiana 70826-2550
Website: www.jsm.org • Email: info@jsm.org
225-768-7000

TABLE OF CONTENTS

CHAPTER   **PAGE**

INTRODUCTION 7

1. CHAPTER   1 – The Beginning Of The Gospel 8
2. CHAPTER   2 – A Paralytic Is Lowered Through A Roof And Healed 30
3. CHAPTER   3 – Healing On The Sabbath 42
4. CHAPTER   4 – Jesus Teaches With Parables 56
5. CHAPTER   5 – Jesus Heals A Demon-Possessed Man 70
6. CHAPTER   6 – Jesus' Last Visit To Nazareth 88
7. CHAPTER   7 – Jesus Explains What Defiles 104
8. CHAPTER   8 – Jesus Feeds The Four Thousand 116
9. CHAPTER   9 – The Transfiguration Of Jesus 130
10. CHAPTER 10 – Jesus' Teaching On Divorce 146
11. CHAPTER 11 – Jesus' Triumphal Entry Into Jerusalem 164
12. CHAPTER 12 – The Parable Of The Wicked Husbandmen 176
13. CHAPTER 13 – The Signs Of The End 188
14. CHAPTER 14 – The Chief Priests Plot Against Jesus 198
15. CHAPTER 15 – The Sanhedrin Deliver Jesus To Pilate 220
16. CHAPTER 16 – The Visit Of The Women To The Tomb Of Jesus 233

The Life Of Christ

According To The Gospel Of Mark

The Cross Of Christ Series

THE LIFE OF CHRIST — *According to the Gospel of Mark*

INTRODUCTION

The Gospel of Mark is characterized by fast-moving, dramatic action. The frequent use of the words *"straightway"* and *"immediately"* illustrates the decisive nature of events taking place in the Life of the Lord Jesus Christ.

In this study we have attempted to explain and clarify the actions, accounts, and expressions of the Text. Each event is first presented, followed by a Verse-by-Verse exposition with an in-depth study analyzing the meanings of various words and phrases. Broader understanding results as we go into the original Greek to uncover meanings sometimes confused in translation into English.

As we present this commentary of the Gospel of Mark, we trust it will be a source of special insight in learning more about our Lord — and that your life will be enriched and deepened in Him.

Chapter 1

The Beginning Of The Gospel

SUBJECT	PAGE
THE MESSAGE AND THE MESSENGER	10
THE FORERUNNER'S PICTURE OF THE MESSIAH	13
JESUS IS BAPTIZED	15
THE TEMPTATIONS OF JESUS	15
THE KINGDOM OF GOD IS AT HAND	17
FOUR FISHERMEN BECOME FISHERS OF MEN	18
A MAN SET FREE OF A DEMON SPIRIT	20
JESUS HEALS PETER'S MOTHER-IN-LAW	24
WITH THE FOUR FISHERMEN	25
A LEPER IS HEALED	26

CHAPTER 1

THE BEGINNING OF THE GOSPEL

"The beginning of the Gospel of Jesus Christ, the Son of God" (Mk. 1:1).

The Gospel of Mark is introduced by this statement, which simply says that it is the beginning of the Gospel of Jesus Christ. The word BEGIN-NING — from the Greek word *arche — means *"beginning, origin, the person or thing that commences."* The way the expression is used is somewhere between a title and an introduction.

Mark is stating more here than just the fact that it is the start of *his* account of the Gospel. He shows, from the Prophets, that the Gospel was to *begin* with the sending of a forerunner. This, of course, was John the Baptist.

The other Gospel writers — Matthew, Luke, and John — chose to start at different points. Matthew begins with the ancestry and birth of the Messiah; Luke starts with the birth of John the Baptist; while John begins his Gospel with the preincarnate *"Word of God."* Each of these Gospel writers used a specific point for starting *his* Gospel, as inspired and directed by the Holy Spirit.

OF THE GOSPEL — The Greek word meaning *"good news"* or *"glad tidings"* is *euaggelion.* The Gospel is good news. It is good news for the broken homes restored in Jesus Christ. It is good news for the drunkard made sober. It is good news for *each* of us as we are set free by the supreme Power of Almighty God through Jesus Christ.

OF JESUS CHRIST — When Jesus lived in Israel and walked, talked, healed, and performed miracles upon this Earth, He was known as Joshua. The Greek word translated *"Jesus"* is from *Iesous,* which is transliterated from the word Joshua (Jehoshua). It means *"Jehovah saves."* *Christos* in the Greek is simply transliterated into English as Christ and means *"The Anointed One."* He is the Anointed of God, the Messiah.

In effect, Jesus *is* the Good News. He is the Son of God. He is the Resurrection and the Life. Of course, Jesus brought the world Redemption through Grace, and He is, in essence, the *Good News.*

Jesus is the SON OF GOD. This is implicit in the title *"Christ,"* for He is Anointed of God. The emphasis is on the character or nature of Jesus Christ, in that He is the Son of God by nature. He was with the Father from eternity.

---

* The Greek words are generally given in their basic lexical form in this study. The spelling of the words in the Greek text will be slightly different due to changes in tense, mood, voice, person, case, etc., which affects the spelling.

THE MESSAGE AND THE MESSENGER

"As it is written in the Prophets, Behold, I send My Messenger before your face, which shall prepare your way before you. The voice of one crying in the wilderness, Prepare ye the Way of the Lord, make His paths straight. John did baptize in the wilderness, and preach the Baptism of Repentance for the Remission of sins. And there went out unto him all the land of Judea, and they of Jerusalem, and were all baptized of him in the river of Jordan, confessing their sins. And John was clothed with camel's hair, and with a girdle of a skin about his loins; and he did eat locusts and wild honey" (Mk. 1:2-6).

(1:2) AS — *kathos* — The Greek word translated *"as"* here means *"according as"* or *"just as."* This is a *strong* word emphasizing the unassailable authority of something spoken or written. The statement, then, is exact and guaranteed.

IT IS WRITTEN — *gegraptai* — is in the perfect tense. This can be translated *"it is written in the prophets"* is a quotation from Malachi 3:1 and Isaiah 40:3.

BEHOLD — *idou* — is a word that lends particular emphasis to what is about to be revealed. It demands the reader's attention.

I SEND — *apostello* — literally means *"to send someone off,"* as an ambassador or envoy representing God. This states that John had a most important commission to perform.

MESSENGER — *aggelos* — is a word referring to a messenger on an envoy bearing a message. It is the same root from which our word *"Angel"* is derived.

John was to prepare; that is, to *"furnish, equip, make ready"* the way. The WAY *(hodos)* means *"a traveled way or road."* John was to prepare the hearts of the people (Israel) for their Messiah.

For hundreds of years the Israelites prayed, wept, and discussed the coming of the Messiah. Finally, He *was* coming, and John the Baptist was to prepare the path before Him. How tragic that the nation failed to accept Him, despite the fact that God had sent His Envoy on a commission *"before His Face"* that was to make ready His road by preparing the hearts of the people.

(1:3) John the Baptist was a voice. He was crying (from *boao*, which means to cry aloud or to speak with a high, strong voice). It means more than just speaking out with a *purpose:* it also implies emotion. John preached with great feeling and aroused strong emotions. He was much like a thundering Elijah and was, in fact, the one who came *"like Elijah."*

John was God's P.A. system, crying out in the wilderness — preaching to Israel, God's Chosen People. There was love and entreaty in the message, but it was also uncompromising and stern. It demanded Repentance. He preached IN THE WILDERNESS, (*eremos,* a word signifying a solitary, lonely, uninhabited place). He actually did his preaching in the uncultivated regions of Judaea.

PREPARE — *hetoimazo* — means *"to make ready."* Some feel this figure was drawn from the oriental custom of sending parties ahead to level the roads and make the passage more comfortable for the king. John the Baptist was to prepare the *minds* of men, readying them for acceptance of the Messiah and His Blessings. As John the Baptist sought to prepare the Way of the Lord, it was with strong, direct, straight-from-the-shoulder preaching. His sole ministry was to prepare the people to accept the Messiah.

(1:4) The word *egeneto* is translated *"did."* (John *did* baptize in the. . . .) It is from the Greek root that literally means *"to become,"* and is used in reference to a person's appearing on the stage of history. *"There arose John,"* according to the prophecies mentioned in the two previous Verses. The expression used here clearly indicates that the coming of John the Baptist was not a mere *event* in history, but an epoch — ushering in a new regime of God's dealing with mankind. Perhaps this Passage might have been better translated, *"John **appeared**, baptizing in the. . . ."*

DID BAPTIZE — *ho baptizon* — literally *"the one who baptizes."* This phrase is a *description* of John, who would be *known* as John the Baptist throughout history.

John baptized his converts. The people of Israel, to whom he spoke, were baptized as they repented of their sins. Care needs to be taken in understanding the exact import of this baptism.

Some confusion can be caused by the various possible translations of *eis.* In Matthew 3:11 (where this is also described), *eis* is translated *"unto."* *"I indeed baptize you with water unto Repentance."* This can *seem* to imply that baptism *causes* Repentance. Actually, a better translation would be *"I indeed baptize you with water **because of** your Repentance."* This can be confirmed by referring to Matthew 12:41 where *eis* is translated *"at"*: *"they repented at* (or because of) *the preaching of Jonah."* This approach applies to Acts 2:38, where *eis* is also used.

The clear implication is that Repentance *precedes* and *leads* to baptism. This can be further confirmed in Matthew 3:7-9, where John refused to baptize the Sadducees and Pharisees because they hadn't repented.

Josephus, the great first-century historian, indicated that John taught that the Rite of Baptism did not wash away sins, but was for those who had *already* had their souls purified by Repentance. Water Baptism does not save people. A person submits to the Rite of Baptism because he *is* a Believer and *has* been saved. This is the conclusion of some of the best biblical scholars who have studied the original Text. This does not, of course, minimize the importance of baptism. For those who have had their sins forgiven, have been cleansed by the Blood of Jesus, and are saved — Water Baptism is an *outward* manifestation to the *world* that Jesus has come into their hearts and lives.

Baptism is a marvelously worthwhile ceremony. For those who are in Christ, it declares that they have committed their lives to Christ; have accepted the Death, Burial, and Resurrection of Jesus for *their* lives; and that they are dead to sin and have risen to walk in newness of life.

PREACH — *kerusso* — means *"to herald"* or *"to proclaim after the manner of a herald."* The word suggests formality, gravity, and authority — that which should be heard and obeyed. In general, it means *"to publish"* or *"to proclaim openly."* In the New Testament, it usually refers to public proclamation of the Gospel.

John was a herald delivering an official proclamation. He was proclaiming the coming King, the Messiah of Israel. John is variously referred to as a *"herald"* (*kerusso*), as a *"messenger"* (*aggelon*), and as *"one who is sent"* (*apostello*). *Aggelon* is the root word for *"Angel,"* and *apostello* is the verb from which *"Apostle"* (*apostolos*) is derived.

REPENTANCE — *metanoia* — is a Greek word translated *"Repentance"* and is actually *two* Greek words. In combination they mean *"a change of mind."* The English word *"repent"* implies far more than just to be contrite. An indicted thief is, no doubt, *sorry* for the particular robbery for which he will go to jail, but he has not necessarily *repented* of performing robberies. Repentance implies sorrow, acknowledgement that what was done was wrong, and a firm commitment to never again do so. The Greek word *metanoia* (a turnaround in thinking) illustrates this perfectly.

FOR THE REMISSION OF SINS — This was just covered under the analysis of the word *eis*. Unfortunately, this translation suggests that baptism *brings about the Remission of sins. Properly, as demonstrated above, Remission of sin (through Repentance) brings about baptism.*

(1:5) THERE WENT OUT UNTO HIM — The tense used here denotes a continuing action. It portrays a *stream* of people. Multitudes from the inhabited areas of Judaea and Jerusalem made a difficult journey to the uninhabited places to hear John. They came because of his growing fame and the message he proclaimed. They didn't *chance upon* John — they sought him out despite difficulty — in response to his message.

ALL — Although the translation says *"all"* Judaea came and were baptized, this was a colloquialism. We say *"everyone was there,"* when we mean a *lot* of people, or those pertaining to the event, were there. There are hundreds of times in Scripture when the word *"all"* is used in a limited sense. It is used as a figure of speech (called *synecdoche*) in which a whole really represents a part. It doesn't mean everyone in the world or everyone in a particular city, or even in a limited area. It implies a multitude.

BAPTIZED OF HIM IN THE RIVER JORDAN — As people appeared in response to John's message and repented of their sins, they were baptized *in* the river Jordan. They publicly *"confessed their sins."* Baptism is the *outward indication* of Repentance.

The word *"confess"* is from *homologeo*. It is a compound word made up of *lego*, *"to speak,"* and *homos, "the same."* It means *"to speak the same thing,"* or *"to be in agreement with another person."* Confession of sin is more than just *acknowledging* sin in one's life; it is agreeing with God that we *have* sinned and accepting all of its ramifications. It implies viewing sin from God's viewpoint — and thus moving *onward* to root sin out of our lives.

(1:6) CLOTHED WITH CAMEL'S HAIR — Elijah was John's prototype. John came in the spirit and power of Elijah. He consciously patterned his ministry and dress after this great Prophet. His garment was woven of camel's *hair* instead of the skin of the camel because Elijah wore rough sackcloth woven from camel's hair (II Ki. 1:8). John's garment was a rough, camel's-hair cloth, worn as a girdle about his loins.

LOCUSTS AND WILD HONEY — These were the main elements in John's diet. The wilderness about Judaea contained an abundance of wild honey, and some Bedouins made their living by collecting and selling it in Jerusalem.

In addition to wild honey, John ate locusts. Locusts in this area are larger than the ones we are accustomed to seeing and were apparently considered a delicacy. They were fried or baked in the sun, and locust with wild honey was considered a desirable dish.

While this might be considered distasteful to some, there are various foods throughout the world that are locally considered delicacies. Today snails, clams, shrimp, and a number of other dishes cause varying reactions, some even considering rattlesnake meat desirable. Locusts *were* specifically noted as *"clean"* in Leviticus 11:22.

It should be noted that some consider that this refers to the fruit of the locust *tree,* which was, and is, abundant in this area.

THE FORERUNNER'S PICTURE OF THE MESSIAH

"And preached, saying, There comes One mightier than I after me, the latchet of Whose shoes I am not worthy to stoop down and unloose. I indeed have baptized you with water: but He shall baptize you with the Holy Spirit" (Mk. 1:7-8).

(1:7) Preached. Here again the word *kerusso* is used and it refers to a king's *"forerunner,"* which was an imperial herald proclaiming the coming of his sovereign (Lord). For *"one"* John used the definitive article which denotes that it was a distinct, unique, specific person (the One) who was to come. John stated that he was not worthy to stoop down and loose the latchet of this *"One's"* sandals.

In the oriental household it was the task of a slave to take off the guest's sandals and wash their feet as they entered the home. John the Baptist sought to make it abundantly clear that he was simply a herald for the King (Jesus), whom he announced. He was trying to avoid any personal fame or glory, and direct all attention to the coming King.

(1:8) John declared that he would indeed baptize with water, (and of course this was significant), but he said there was One coming (Jesus) who would baptize with the Holy Spirit and fire. Each of the Gospel writers confirms this (Mat. 3:11, Mk. 1:8, Lk. 3:16, and Jn. 1:33).

It must be understood that *Jesus* is the baptizer with the Holy Spirit. The Power of the Holy Spirit imbues the Christian with power (fire) and is imperative for the effectiveness within the Church and the Kingdom of God. The necessity for the mighty infilling of the Holy Spirit cannot be overemphasized. It is something we stress continually in our ministry.

Being baptized (immersed) with the Holy Spirit is not automatic, not a *"side-effect"* of conversion. There is a difference between being *"born of the Spirit"* and being *"baptized with the Spirit."* John is talking here about a person being baptized *with* the Spirit.

In Luke 11:13 there is encouragement to ask the Heavenly Father for the Holy Spirit. He will then give Him to those who ask (see Lk. 11:9-13). Jesus commanded His Followers to *tarry* until they were endued with Power (Acts 1:4-8). The Baptism with the Holy Spirit is promised to all who desire it.

Jesus died for us; and the full benefits of His Atonement — and Promises of God — are ours. The Baptism with the Holy Spirit is for everyone. Jesus died that all men might have this (Gal. 3:13-14). The early churches expected all Believers to receive, and worked diligently to bring this about.

There are several New Testament accounts of persons being baptized (that is, immersed) with the Power and Presence of the Holy Spirit: Acts 8:14-18; Acts 9:17; Acts 19:1-6 all recount such incidents. When Paul met John's disciples at Ephesus, he asked them if they had received the Holy Spirit since they were Believers. They answered that they had not even *heard* of the Holy Spirit. Paul laid hands on them and they experienced the Baptism with the Holy Spirit — and spoke with tongues and prophesied (Acts 19:1-6).

This miraculous and supernatural occurrence is for everyone. It was indicated in this, and other Scriptures, that they spoke in tongues; that is, a language often known somewhere in the world, but unknown to the speaker.

JESUS IS BAPTIZED

"And it came to pass in those days, that Jesus came from Nazareth of Galilee, and was baptized of John in Jordan. And straightway coming up out of the water, he saw the Heavens opened, and the Spirit like a dove descending upon Him: And there came a Voice from Heaven, saying, You are My Beloved Son, in Whom I am well pleased" (Mk. 1:9-11).

(1:9) WAS BAPTIZED OF JOHN IN JORDAN. Some may wonder why Jesus was baptized by John. Obviously, Jesus did not need Salvation. And — as we have already pointed out — Water Baptism *does not save.* Obviously this was *not* the reason for Jesus' baptism.

Jesus approved of John the Baptist, his work and ministry. He therefore came as a Righteous individual — *submitting* to the baptism of John. He was baptized *"in"* (*eis* — literally *into*) the river Jordan. Clearly, immersion is indicated here because the next Verse states that He came up *out* of the water (literally — *"out from within"* the water).

(1:10) THE HEAVENS OPENED. The word used for *"opened"* is *schizo,* which means *"to cleave asunder, to divide by rending."* Literally this could be translated *"split."* Jesus saw the Heavens rent asunder, and the Spirit, like a dove, descending upon Him. Then there came a Voice *"out from within"* Heaven (a place with boundaries) which was divided — split or opened — to Jesus' view.

(1:11) YOU ARE MY BELOVED SON. The pronoun used is *su* which is in the second person, and literally means *"as for you."* This excludes all others. Jesus, the Messiah, is the unique Son of God. Other Believers are *sons* of God, but the relationship is different from that of the Messiah. Jesus was, and is, the completely unique Son of God. The Father said, *"In You I am well pleased."*

THE TEMPTATIONS OF JESUS

"And immediately the Spirit driveth Him into the wilderness. And He was there in the wilderness forty days, tempted of Satan; and was with the wild beasts; and the Angels ministered unto Him" (Mk. 1:12-13).

(1:12) Driveth, *ekballo,* is a very strong word which literally means *"to throw out from within, to cast out, to drive out."* It does not imply any reluctance on the part of Jesus to go into the wild place, but it emphasizes a *strong* moving of the Spirit to *drive* or compel Jesus into the wilderness.

INTO THE WILDERNESS. The exact place where Jesus went is unknown, but tradition fixes it near Jericho. It was an uninhabited area where wild beasts menaced every living thing.

(1:13) TEMPTED BY SATAN. The present-tense participle of

this word reveals *continuing* action. Satan *continuously* tempted the Messiah throughout the forty days. Matthew records three of the major temptations at the end of the forty-day period, but there are obviously many others.

Forty is the number of probation and testing, and is used a number of places in Scripture. Satan expended his every wile, realizing the significance of Jesus' Mission. The designation *"Satan"* is from the Hebrew word meaning *"adversary."* The other name for this fallen Angel is *"the Devil"* (in Greek *diabolos*), which is a noun form coming from the word which means *"to slander, accuse, or defame."* The verb form from which the word *"Devil"* comes has to do with the bringing of false charges against a person, or disseminating the *truth* in a malicious, insidious, and hostile way.

The word *"tempted"* means basically to be *tested,* to see what good or evil lies within a person. It also means: to make an experience of; to pierce or search into; to try intentionally for the purpose of discovering good or evil, or what powers or weaknesses a person possesses. It seems that both ideas are implied in the use of the word in this context. Jesus, the last Adam, was being put to the ultimate test to see if He was *ready* for His Ministry as Prophet, Priest, and King. A royal battle was waged. Great issues were at stake. He was not only put to the test, but was encouraged to do evil by Satan.

WAS WITH THE WILD BEASTS. This wilderness area abounded with such wild animals as boars, jackals, wolves, foxes, leopards, and hyenas. It was a dangerous environment and uninhabited. There were no supplies available, and hunger was obviously a major part of the experience.

Jesus, the last Adam, resisted all temptation despite a vicious and hostile situation. The first Adam fell into sin in a beautiful and perfect environment. The universe was transfixed as this testing took place. God the Father watched with all His Holy Angels. Even the *fallen* Angels and demon spirits watched with bated breath. This was, no doubt, the greatest and most important spiritual battle ever to be waged between the forces of good and evil.

Jesus was tested in a vicious, vile, and completely hostile environment. People today are sometimes exposed to unpleasant surroundings too, such as workplaces where profanity, vulgarity, and obscenity abound. Victory is still possible, however, even in an atmosphere saturated with sin. A husband or wife may be living with an unsaved spouse who spews out slander, ridicule, and venom. The person seeking Righteousness will often encounter persecution, humiliation, and rejection.

Jesus was not isolated within a spiritual vacuum, but ministered totally within the mainstream. He was nakedly exposed to Satan's vilest attacks. Sometimes God exposes us in the same way. He does not wrap

His Children in gauze, but rather sets them right down within life's main intersections. Sometimes He places us in the very midst of darkness so we can serve as the necessary light for that specific, darkened area.

With the Power of the Holy Spirit one can stand against all suggestions and powers of Satan. Jesus' temptation and testing were many times greater than any we will ever endure; yet by His Grace and Power through the Holy Spirit, we can conquer in *our* times of testing. Satan unleashed every demon power of Hell against Jesus, the last Adam, seeking to thwart His Messianic Mission.

As Jesus suffered the temptations in the wilderness, it was as a *man* filled with the Holy Spirit — not as God. He did not use His Godlike capabilities, and He thus became the perfect example for you and me. His passions were exactly as ours. This is why the Bible makes it clear that He was filled with the Holy Spirit *before* entering the wilderness of temptation.

Without Holy Spirit Power, He could not have withstood the onslaught of the enemy. Even as He — by the Power of the Holy Spirit — was victorious, so can we be also.

THE ANGELS MINISTERED UNTO HIM. *"Ministered"* is from *diakoneo*, which means *"to minister to or serve."* The Angels ministered to Jesus without human intervention. Angels were commissioned by God the Father and they carried out His commands regarding the Son. The expression indicates a *continuous* action throughout the forty days.

The Angels did not bring Jesus food, but ministered spiritually to Him, and thwarted Satan's excesses throughout this spiritual onslaught. It is comforting to realize that there *are* ministering Angels waiting to assist us in *our* spiritual battles.

THE KINGDOM OF GOD IS AT HAND

"Now after that John was put in prison, Jesus came into Galilee, Preaching the Gospel of the Kingdom of God, And saying, The time is fulfilled, and the Kingdom of God is at hand: repent ye, and believe the Gospel" (Mk. 1:14-15).

(1:14) NOW AFTER THAT. *Following* the temptation of Jesus, John's ministry continued. He identified Jesus as the Messiah when he said, *"Behold the Lamb of God, which takes away the sin of the world"* (Jn. 1:29). This was, perhaps, at Bethany beyond Jordan.

Around the same time, Jesus selected the first of His Disciples who would be with Him constantly. They went to Cana in Galilee where Jesus performed His first miracle (Jn. 2:1-11).

From there Jesus went to Jerusalem for the feast of Passover and the first cleansing of the Temple (Jn. 2:12-17). It was during this visit to Jerusalem that Jesus had His notable conversation with Nicodemus (Jn. 2:23-3:21). With the ministries of Jesus and John the Baptist taking place simultaneously in the area of Judea, the Pharisees were becoming disturbed (Jn. 4:1-4). Herod the tetrarch, whom John had reproved for his wickedness, imprisoned John (Lk. 3:19-20). Because of this and other developments, Jesus came into Galilee.

(1:14-15) PREACHING THE GOSPEL OF THE KINGDOM OF GOD. As Jesus came into Galilee, He was preaching the Gospel of the Kingdom of God. The word *"preaching"* is from *kerusso* which means *"making proclamation as a herald."* Gospel is from *euaggelion,* or *"the good news."* The *"Word of God"* is in the form that literally means *"the good news that comes from God."* The message is of Redemption through Jesus the Messiah.

He was announcing that the *"time"* was fulfilled. The word for *"time"* is *kairos* which refers to a particular era marked by an epochal event. It is not from *chronos,* which refers to *passing* time. This was a *new* time, a *new order* being ushered in. The Dispensation of the Law was ending and the announcement of the good news from God (later defined as the Kingdom of Heaven) was being announced.

The Kingdom of God is defined as God's Rule, and includes all subjects within His Will. The Angels and all Believers throughout the ages make up the membership of the Kingdom of God. It implies the Rule and Reign of God in the hearts and lives of men.

Jesus said He was preaching the Gospel of the Kingdom, and that the time was fulfilled. In other words, the old Mosaic Law was done away with, and it was now time for the Messiah to usher in the New Covenant. Although He did not use these exact terms, that is essentially what was meant. This was the epochal moment the Prophets had spoken of and had envisioned over the centuries. Now Jesus said the time had come and the Kingdom of God was at hand. The New Covenant was about to begin.

IS FULFILLED. This expression literally means, *"has been fulfilled."* This indicates that the preparation time is completed and the changeover is at hand. Jesus next said they should repent and believe the Gospel. This is the message that comes to man even today: Repent of your sins; believe in Jesus; and accept Him as Lord and Master of your life.

FOUR FISHERMEN BECOME FISHERS OF MEN

"Now as He walked by the Sea of Galilee, He saw Simon, and Andrew his brother, casting a net into the sea: for they were fishers. And Jesus said unto them, Come ye after Me, and I will make you to become fishers of men. And straightway they forsook their nets, and

followed Him. And when He had gone a little farther thence, He saw James the son of Zebedee, and John his brother, who also were in the ship mending their nets. And straightway He called them: and they left their father Zebedee in the ship with the hired servants and went after Him" (Mk. 1:16-20).

(1:16) As Jesus walked *"by"* (*para* — literally *"alongside"*) the sea, He saw Simon and Andrew. They were casting their nets *"to and fro, first to one side and then to the other."* This refers to their fishing with a net — making a cast and then a haul.

(1:17) COME YE AFTER ME. Jesus said, *"Come here."* In construction, this projects the thought of joining one's party.

MAKE YOU TO BECOME. When Jesus said He would *"make"* them fishers of men, it in no way implies force or coercion. It meant He would fashion or transform them. It carries the idea of sculpturing, or molding, into something special. They were to become fishers of men, and this suggests a long, drawn-out process. It didn't infer that the moment they left their ships they would *suddenly* become fishers of men. Their conversion to this new *"occupation"* would continue throughout the three and one-half years of Jesus' Ministry and beyond.

After Jesus' Ascension into Heaven, His Disciples received the mighty Baptism with the Holy Spirit, poured out on the Day of Pentecost, and were finally *fully* prepared to go forth as dynamic witnesses for Christ. When a person is saved, he doesn't immediately become a finished product. Although Salvation as such is complete within itself, the process of working with a person and developing spiritual maturity is accomplished over a long period of time. The Holy Spirit deals with each of us differently and develops or molds us into what we should become.

Some never reach the fullness of their potential because they do not completely respond to the moving of the Holy Spirit. This is not God's failure; it's the failure of the individual who will not heed and respond to the Lord's leading.

Most of us can look back and realize that we could have developed much more quickly — yet most of us can be happy with the progress we *have* made. It does take time for an individual to be fashioned, molded, and sculptured into the truly Christ-like character he should strive to be. His Disciples were told that if they would follow Him, listen to Him, and *obey* Him, He would make them to become fishers of men — that is, soul winners. We have this same opportunity, if only we will be pliable in the Lord.

(1:18) THEY FORSOOK THEIR NETS. It is stated that they *"straightway"* followed Him. They were not concerned with a brief *"test ride"* to see if they would like it, or with determining the ultimate cost. They *instantly* knew their hearts and walked away from their boats without a backward glance. The word *"followed"* means to *"follow with another"* — and implies fellowship, joint-participation and a side-by-side walk. It also implies *"to join one"* as a disciple, or to *"cleave steadfastly to one and to conform to that individual's example in living — and even dying if called upon."* This expression indicates a decisive commitment. They immediately and without hesitation put away their nets and *followed* Him.

(1:19) As Jesus, now accompanied by Peter and Andrew, went along a little further, He saw James and John, who were brothers. They were in a large fishing vessel, not a rowboat, and were mending their nets for further use when Jesus called to them.

(1:20) WENT AFTER HIM. They immediately left their father, Zebedee, and followed Jesus. The expression used shows a final and complete separation. These individuals walked away from their nets, boat, and father — leaving all to follow the Lord.

A MAN SET FREE OF A DEMON SPIRIT

"And they went into Capernaum; and straightway on the Sabbath Day He entered into the Synagogue, and taught. And they were astonished at His Doctrine: for He taught them as One Who had authority, and not as the Scribes. And there was in their Synagogue a man with an unclean spirit; and he cried out, Saying, Let us alone; what have we to do with You, Thou Jesus of Nazareth? Are You come to destroy us? I know You Who You are, the Holy One of God. And Jesus rebuked him, saying, Hold your peace, and come out of him. And when the unclean spirit had torn him, and cried with a loud voice, he came out of him. And they were all amazed, insomuch that they questioned among themselves, saying, What thing is this? What new doctrine is this? for with authority commands He even the unclean spirits, and they do obey Him. And immediately His fame spread abroad throughout all the region round about Galilee" (Mk. 1:21-28).

(1:21) Jesus and His newly selected Disciples traveled to Capernaum. It was on the Sabbath Day and Jesus entered the Synagogue, which was a Jewish place of worship. This was not the great Temple at Jerusalem where all Israel congregated for worship. The Synagogue services consisted of prayer, praise, reading of God's Word, and an exposition of the Scriptures by a capable person.

Immediately upon entering the Synagogue, the Lord began teaching. The word *didasko* indicates that the Lord's Message was a discourse of some length. We observed earlier that Jesus preached, (*kerusso*), which means *"to make a proclamation."* At various times Jesus did either; the place, time, audience, and subject matter determining the format of His Message. It appears that most of the time He *taught* the people, although He began His Ministry by *proclaiming* the Kingdom of God to be at hand.

(1:22) THEY WERE ASTONISHED. The word used is *ekplesso,* which is a strong word indicating *"shock," "astonishment,"* or *"amazement"* at His Preaching. It also indicates an *extended* amazement as it says they were astonished at His Teaching. The word for teaching would indicate that it was His Doctrine, not His teaching *method,* that surprised them. He was teaching as one who had authority. That is, He did not parrot previous teachings, but made bold statements of principle with complete conviction.

The word *"authority"* is from *exousia,* which means literally *"to be out."* It is used to denote authority derived from someone else. It means the *power* of authority and the right to *use* it. This was usually used in connection with a legal practice or delegated authority and was somewhat analogous to our *"power of attorney."*

Within the context of Mark, *exousia* is used of our Lord as having authority *within* Himself, and not deriving it from some other source. The rabbis quoted other rabbis and earlier scholars and made no statements on their own authority. The people quickly noticed the unusual quality in the Messiah, for He was a teacher who spoke on His *own* Authority. The people were literally stunned and couldn't believe what they were hearing. It was so divergent from what the Scribes and Pharisees had been teaching, as they merely echoed the established doctrines of the *"religious"* leaders of the day.

(1:23-24) The Bible says that *"immediately"* upon the Master's completion of His Message, a man arose and began to speak. This man was demon-possessed. And unclean spirit inhabited him and controlled his body. Luke (in Lk. 4:33) speaks of this man as having an *"unclean demon"* (*daimonion*). *Daimonion* denotes *"demon,"* of which there are multitudes; while there is only one *diabolos,* Devil, (or Satan).

The Devil is a fallen Angel and demons constitute a different category of beings. It appears that demons have no rest unless they are residing in a physical body. Perhaps they were deprived of their original bodies because of some Judgment of God. Many believe (and I agree) that demons are disembodied spirits from a pre-Adamic race which inhabited the first perfect Earth (Gen. 1:1). Apparently they followed their leader, Lucifer, into sin and were thus deprived of their physical bodies and their visible residence on Earth at the time of the cataclysm described in Genesis 1:2. This, no doubt, coincided with the fall of Lucifer as described in Isaiah 14:12-17.

There are also the principalities and powers described in Ephesians 6:12. These comprise the kingdom of darkness; that is, the kingdom of Satan within the atmosphere of the Earth (Eph. 2:2). There are various theories on the origin of demons, but this one is widely accepted.

HE CRIED OUT. The word used is *anakrazo,* meaning *"to raise a cry from the depth of the throat, to cry out."* The demon within the man cried out. He was using the man's vocal cords; and it was a deep, throaty, terrible cry. It was characterized by the fear of impending doom because he was facing One much more powerful than he — the Lord Jesus Christ.

This is a startling phenomenon. There are demonic entities existing in members of the human race who speak out through the host's body. This is happening today and it is not uncommon. Almost anyone working in the Lord's service can recount experiences of confrontations with the demon possessed.

WHAT HAVE WE TO DO WITH YOU? This is a rather unusual expression and the literal rendering differs slightly from the King James, but it can be translated, *"What do we demons have in common with you, Holy One of God?"*

The demon recognized and acknowledged the Deity of Jesus Christ, the Messiah. There was no doubt of this. Later the *religious* leaders of Israel were also to *recognize* Jesus as the Messiah — the Son of God — while in their apostasy they *rejected* Him (Mat. 21:37-39).

ARE YOU COME TO DESTROY US? In the Greek Text, this expression is probably more statement than question. They were actually saying, *"You **are** come to destroy us, for we know who You are — the Holy One of God."*

The demon uses the plural expression *"us."* He was referring to himself *plus* the demons associated with him. There are times when a large number of demons may possess an individual as we will see when we reach Mark 5:9. It is interesting to note that the demons realized that Jesus was come to destroy them. A major element in Jesus' Ministry was the removal of the Devil's influence. Satan comes to kill, steal, and destroy, while Jesus came to destroy the works of Satan (Jn. 10:10).

It may seem strange to discuss a *destructive* power in Jesus Christ, but He actually came to *destroy* the demon forces of Hell and the principalities and powers of darkness that cause untold tragedy and sorrow in the world. Doing away with these forces will result in our having *life,* for Jesus came *"That we may have life and have it more abundantly"* (Jn. 10:10).

(1:25) REBUKED. There are two words used in the New Testament which mean to rebuke. The one used here is *epitimao,* which means *"to rebuke another, the rebuke failing to bring the offender to acknowledgement of his sin."* This is an expression used by Mark for Satan, the fallen Angels, and the demons who were incorrigible. They refused to be convicted of their sins and they wouldn't repent.

HOLD YOUR PEACE — *phimoo* — means *"to close the mouth*

with a muzzle." It means to *"stop the mouth, to make speechless, and reduce to silence."* The words *"hold your peace"* really aren't strong enough. According to some scholars, it would be better rendered *"shut up."* So, in essence, Jesus was saying *"shut up and don't say another word."* He then commanded the demon to come out at once.

(1:26) HAD TORN HIM. The word used here is *sparasso,* which means *"to convulse"* or go into spasm. There are other cases in the New Testament where individuals were thrown down. After the man went into spasm, the demon cried out with a loud voice. This does not mean it spoke — Jesus had forbidden it to speak — but rather a shriek or a groan is implied. Demon forces obey the Authority of Jesus Christ. Many demons are cast out of individuals by Christians today when they stand on their God-given right to exercise the Power and Authority of Jesus in such cases.

(1:27) THEY WERE ALL AMAZED. The word used here is *thambeo*. It means *"to be astonished, amazed, terrified, or frightened."* The people were literally terrified in their shock and surprise. To first see a manifestation of demonic power, and then to experience the awesome Power of God, *can* be a terrifying experience for people who do not fully understand what is occurring.

THEY QUESTIONED AMONG THEMSELVES. The word used is *sunzeteo,* which is comprised of two words. It means *"to seek or examine together, to discuss, dispute."* It is used in reference to a group of people inquiring of one another, and here the people were discussing and *"demanding among themselves"* what this all meant. The expression indicates an animated and prolonged discussion. One can picture the murmur running through the crowd as they turned to one another, trying to determine just what had happened.

"What new thing is this?" They were confused about Jesus and His Doctrines. They recognized a quality in His Teaching different from everything they had been taught by their *"spiritual leaders."* Jesus' statements were a dramatic departure from the dry, rabbinical dronings they had always heard. His fresh, new Doctrines were like a dew from Heaven in a dry and dusty land. And His fresh pronouncements were given with authority — an authority able to *command* obedience from unclean spirits. Hallelujah!

The word *"command"* is *epitasso,* and is a military term, which means to draw up in order of battle. Our Lord has the hosts of Satan under His absolute Power. When He commands them, they *must* obey. The crowd at the Synagogue was most shocked by the realization that the demons *obeyed* Him.

(1:28) IMMEDIATELY HIS FAME SPREAD ABROAD. This means that word of His Power and Authority spread almost instantly throughout

SELF-HELP
STUDY NOTES

23

the countryside. It was *the* topic of conversation and gossip. People discussed His Doctrines, His Authority, *and* His Ability to command demonic powers. He became, almost instantly, the most discussed person in all of Galilee and, no doubt, throughout the entire Holy Land.

JESUS HEALS PETER'S MOTHER-IN-LAW

"And forthwith, when they were come out of the Synagogue, they entered into the house of Simon and Andrew, with James and John. But Simon's wife's mother lay sick of a fever, and anon they tell Him of her. And He came and took her by the hand, and lifted her up; and immediately the fever left her, and she ministered unto them. And at evening, when the sun did set, they brought unto Him all who were diseased, and them who were possessed with devils. And all the city was gathered together at the door. And He healed many who were sick of divers diseases, and cast out many devils; and suffered not the devils to speak, because they knew Him" (Mk. 1:29-34).

(1:29) Simon Peter's house was in the middle of Capernaum and situated near the Synagogue. It is a very beautiful place in a peaceful setting. One can see the ruins of Capernaum today and many tourists visit this site. It is located on the northern end of the Sea of Galilee. The sea is beautiful and the entire area emits an aura of peace and relaxation. Peter was married and his mother-in-law, along with his brother Andrew, lived with him. James and John were also with them as they entered into Peter's home.

(1:30) SIMON'S WIFE'S MOTHER LAY SICK WITH A FEVER. The word used for *"lay"* means to *"have laid down, to lay prostrate."* It was used generally in reference to those who were sick, or *"laid up"* with sickness.

Peter's mother-in-law had been sick for some time. The word used for fever is *puresso,* and literally means *"to be sick with a fever."* The Greek root for this word means *"fire"* and implies that she was *"burning up"* with fever.

This was no minor illness that sent her to bed that particular morning. This was more serious and chronic than a *"twenty-four-hour flu."* Luke, who was a trained physician, described her as *"stretched out with a fever,"* and *"taken with a **great** fever"* (Lk. 4:38-39).

(1:31) Jesus came and stood over her. He literally *"stood facing her."* The Great Physician had come to her couch. Luke said, *"And He stood over her"* (Lk. 4:39) — just as a physician would do. Jesus next took her by the hand and lifted her, and immediately — *instantly* — the fever left and she was miraculously cured.

She had been sick for some time; weeks or perhaps even months. The

Scripture doesn't give the time frame, but it is obvious that she was seriously ill. Then, in an instant when Jesus healed her, she rose up and busied herself with household chores with no convalescent period.

We should realize that Mark did *not* waste space scribbling inconsequential gossip or composing background material. Mark's Gospel is the shortest and most terse of the four. He moved rapidly from one miraculous incident to another, and we can conclude that the healing of Peter's mother-in-law was a major healing incident and not just *"background filler"* in the account of Jesus' visit to Peter's house.

In Luke's Gospel, he states that she immediately began to *"minister"* unto them. The word *"ministered"* is *diakoneo*. It means *"to act as a servant; to wait upon; to serve."* This is related to the word from which we get *"deacon,"* which also means to minister.

It is the same word Martha used when she asked Jesus to persuade Mary to help her, rather than letting her serve alone. Peter's mother-in-law not only arose from a sick bed, but was instantly returned to robust health and could spend the rest of the day cooking, serving, and so forth. The verb tense reveals that this was an extended period of serving visitors. Her healing was instant and complete, praise the Lord!

(1:32-33) When evening came, the people began to bring their sick to Peter's house where they knew Jesus was visiting. Because the Sabbath ended at sunset, once the sun went down, they were at liberty to do so.

The Bible says they brought unto Him *all* who were diseased, even many who had to be carried. There was a throng of sick brought to Jesus that Saturday evening. It was a great number and the expression used indicates that they *continued* to come — an ongoing situation. One can picture the crowds milling about Peter's home — not only the sick, but those who brought them, and the merely curious. Obviously, the previously peaceful neighborhood was turned upside down by Jesus' visit.

Some writers point out that there were hot mineral springs nearby at Tiberius, about ten miles away. Because of the purported therapeutic effect of the springs, there were probably a greater number than normal of sick people in the area.

(1:34) JESUS HEALED THE PEOPLE OF ALL KINDS OF DISEASES. Many were blessed that day. The demons clamored to be heard, but they were silenced and individuals were set free — not only from physical diseases but from demonic powers also. Jesus truly is the Healer.

WITH THE FOUR FISHERMEN

"And in the morning, rising up a great while before day, He went out, and departed into a solitary place, and there prayed. And Simon

and they who were with Him followed after Him. And when they had found Him, they said unto Him, All men seek for You. And He said unto them, Let us go into the next towns, that I may preach there also: for therefore came I forth. And he preached in their Synagogues throughout all Galilee, and cast out devils" (Mk. 1:35-39).

(1:35) Jesus gave priority to prayer. It says this was in the morning (*proi*), which was the last watch of the night — from 3 to 6 a.m. It was in the *early* part of this watch — while still dark — that Jesus went away to pray. If God's very own Son found it necessary to pray, we also need time for prayer.

It was Jesus' habit to go to a solitary place to pray. He would often seek the Mind of His Heavenly Father. There is no other way for a Preacher to obtain the anointing of the Holy Spirit. Great men of God have declared that if one does *not* pray he has *no* power — and *little* prayer brings *little* power.

To have *much* power, there must be *much* prayer. The great examples of Faith over the years have been men and women who sought God early and earnestly. There is no victory except through prayer. We go before God, our Heavenly Father, burdened with a heavy heart, seeking His Face, and our loads are miraculously lifted.

For the ongoing work of the Kingdom and for real revival — prayer is imperative. Jesus was urgently concerned about His Work and Ministry. His time was very limited and extremely valuable. The same is true today. We are living in a day of great urgency. True, in-depth, God-seeking prayer is *crucial* in these last days.

(1:36-37) Simon and those with him *"followed"* Jesus. The word used is one that denotes a hunter or chaser and it means *"to pursue."* With the prefix used, it literally means *"they hunted Him out"* or *"they tracked Him down."* The pressure of the crowds waiting in Capernaum led Simon to seek out Jesus. Throngs were awaiting Him there.

(1:38) But Jesus said to them, *"Let us be going, and keep on going."* He was emphasizing that His Mission was to carry on through a long and arduous preaching Ministry. He added that they would have to go to other towns and areas.

(1:39) So Jesus, with His four newly chosen Disciples, went into the Synagogues — the places of meeting and worship for the Jews — throughout all of Galilee. This was the beginning of His first tour of Galilee and they went throughout the area preaching, teaching, and casting out demons.

A LEPER IS HEALED

"And there came a leper to Him, beseeching Him, and kneeling down to Him, and saying unto Him, If You will, You can make me

clean. And Jesus, moved with compassion, put forth His Hand, and touched him, and said unto him, I will; be thou clean. And as soon as He had spoken, immediately the leprosy departed from him, and he was cleansed. And He straitly charged him, and forthwith sent him away; And said unto him, See thou say nothing to any man: but go your way, show yourself to the Priest, and offer for your cleansing those things which Moses commanded, for a testimony unto them. But he went out, and began to publish it much, and to blaze abroad the matter, insomuch that Jesus could no more openly enter into the city, but was without in desert places: and they came to Him from every quarter" (Mk. 1:40-45).

(1:40) THERE CAME A LEPER. The leper came beseeching, (*parakaleo*), which is an urgent appeal — literally, *"I beg of you, please."* The leper appealed to the tenderheartedness of the Master. He said, in essence, *"See the condition I'm in."*

Leprosy ate away various parts of the body, and it was the most abhorred and dreaded disease of the day. His appeal to the tenderness of the Messiah is revealed in the words, IF YOU WILL.

There was certainly nothing wrong in the form of his appeal to Jesus. No doubt, he had heard of Jesus' Ministry, but he had no idea as to whether Jesus would do it. So, he said, if you will, YOU CAN (*dunamai*), which means *"to have power, to be able."* The leper did not doubt the *ability* of the Lord Jesus to heal him; he was declaring that if Jesus were *willing*, He did have the *power* to cleanse him.

In those days lepers couldn't make a living — they wore rags, ate what they could find, and were social outcasts. Being so despised and an outcast, it is not surprising that he wondered whether Jesus would really care. He felt as if he were nothing.

Satan will use his every wile to persuade us that we are worthless in God's sight. This is what Satan *wants* us to believe — but it is not true. God loves each individual. Everyone is special in His sight, and of tremendous value. Though we may fail many times and suffer from guilt and low self-esteem, God loves us and cares for us. His only desire is to save and to redeem. He is in the Redemption *business*. Through the atoning Blood of Jesus, a person can be forgiven anything. Life then takes on new meaning — once redeemed by the Blood of the Lamb.

(1:41) The tragic state of the leper aroused love and concern in our Lord. It is stated that Jesus was *"moved with compassion."* There was no hint of hesitancy in His response because, before He could even complete saying He would, the act of cleansing had begun.

Immediately the leper was cleansed and healed. Levitical law forbade touching a leper, and Jesus lived under this law and obeyed it. This demonstrates that the healing was instantaneous because, by touching him, Jesus demonstrated to the people that the leper was indeed healed.

Suddenly this poor untouchable was made whole. He was now worthy. He had felt the kind, gentle touch of the Son of God. Within the Bible, leprosy can represent sin. The sinner comes crying, *"Unclean, unclean. If You will, You can make me clean."* Jesus is moved with compassion and stretches out His Hand and touches the sinner and says, *"Be thou clean."* This has been the testimony of millions over the centuries and to the present day.

(1:43-44) Jesus was very explicit in His directions to the leper when He bade him go. The word translated *"sent him away"* expresses sternness, sometimes even to the point of anger or indignation. Jesus earnestly admonished, and sternly charged, the man to go. The word translated *"sent him away"* is *ekballo,* which literally means *"to throw out."*

Of course, Jesus was not angry, but was *firmly* charging the man to go to the authorities. It was legally required for him to go to the Priest and to be *officially* pronounced clean. He was also to present an offering, under the Mosaic Law; but primarily it was necessary to have the Priest officially declare him clean.

This priestly certification was important for several reasons. If it weren't done officially, they could deny that he had been a leper who was truly cleansed. Furthermore, under the Mosaic Law, the leper's being officially declared clean would forestall legal problems for Jesus.

(1:45) The leper didn't follow the Lord's specific directions, however. Instead, he began to *"publish"* the matter of his healing about. The word used is *kerusso,* which means *"to make a public proclamation."* In his excitement and joy, he continued to proclaim the matter, and *"blaze abroad"* his account of the healing. Due to the leper's open revelation of his cure — and his neglecting official *recognition* of his cure — difficulties arose. Jewish leaders may have been stirred to envy by the popularity of Jesus, or other reasons may have existed; but there was an abrupt termination of Christ's Synagogue Ministry in the area. Jesus could no longer openly do the things He had previously done.

Suddenly He was forced *"to go underground,"* shifting His Ministry from the *"establishment"* Synagogues to the wilderness, or uninhabited, areas. We have here the type of the latter days when the True Word of God will be shunned by some *"establishment"* of mainline religious organizations, and moved out to previously *"uninhabited,"* or new, spiritual formats.

When our Lord took His Message and Ministry out of the establishment and into the wilderness, the true seekers sought Him out, followed Him, and came into His Truth. The same thing is happening today.

Notes

Chapter 2

A Paralytic Is Lowered Through A Roof And Healed

SUBJECT	PAGE
A TAX COLLECTOR TRUSTS JESUS	33
FEASTING OR FASTING?	36
A SABBATH CONTROVERSY	38

CHAPTER 2

A PARALYTIC IS LOWERED THROUGH A ROOF AND HEALED

"And again He entered into Capernaum after some days; and it was noised that He was in the house. And straightway many were gathered together, insomuch that there was no room to receive them, no, not so much as about the door: and He preached the Word unto them. And they come unto Him, bringing one sick of the palsy, which was borne of four. And when they could not come near unto Him for the press, they uncovered the roof where He was: and when they had broken it up, they let down the bed wherein the sick of the palsy lay.

"When Jesus saw their Faith, He said unto the sick of the palsy, Son, your sins be forgiven you. But there were certain of the Scribes sitting there, and reasoning in their hearts, Why does this man thus speak blasphemies? Who can forgive sins but God only? And immediately when Jesus perceived in His Spirit that they so reasoned within themselves, He said unto them, Why reason ye these things in your hearts? Whether is it easier to say to the sick of the palsy, Your sins be forgiven you; or to say, Arise, and take up your bed, and walk.

"But that you may know that the Son of Man has Power on Earth to forgive sins, (He said to the sick of the palsy,) I say unto you, Arise and take up your bed, and go your way into your house. And immediately he arose, took up the bed, and went forth before them all; insomuch that they were all amazed, and glorified God, saying, We never saw it on this fashion" (Mk. 2:1-12).

(2:1) Jesus came *"again"* into Capernaum. This expression refers back to His departure (1:35) on a preaching tour. It is not known how long He spent on this preaching tour. It is stated, however, that soon after His return *"it was noised about"* that He was there in the house. Jesus had made Capernaum His headquarters and, as this was Peter's home, it may well be that Peter's house served as their headquarters.

(2:2) People came from every direction. It was a phenomenal gathering. Not only was the house filled, but the space around the door was so crowded that it was impossible to gain entry. Jesus spoke to the crowd and the expression used suggests that it was in a conversational tone. There was beauty in His Voice, charm in His manner, and tenderness and love on His countenance. To the sick and weary assembled there, He was a sweet breath from Heaven. Jesus was talking to them about the Word.

(2:3) The Scripture presents a vivid picture of a group *"bringing"* a man. The word for *"bringing"* is *phero,* which means *"to carry a burden"* or *"to move by bearing."* They were *carrying* the man *"sick of the palsy."*

The word for palsy is *paralutikos,* which is made of two words: *luo, "to loose,"* and *para, "alongside."* It means he was suffering from the relaxation of nerves of one side. Our word "paralysis" derives from the same word and the man was obviously paralyzed on one side, perhaps from stroke, injury, or brain tumor. Friends were accompanying him and the ones actually bearing him may have been servants. Their arrival caused quite a stir.

(2:4) They were not able to bring the man to a place *"before Him"* because of the crowd, so they uncovered the roof. Oriental roofs were flat and served as the *"patio"* for the house. This could be reached by outside stairs, which explains their access to the roof.

They uncovered (dug out) the roof. Roofs in this area are composed of mortar, tar, ashes, and sand, firmly compacted with grass growing in the crevices. In some cases (as here), stone slabs were laid across the joists. They, therefore, had to dig through the grass and earth, prying up the tiles — according to reliable expositors. It is obvious that they were determined to get to Jesus.

Their Faith in Jesus was great, and they didn't allow any circumstance to deter them from reaching Him. Faith is not passive, it is *active.* These men didn't just sit at home and *hope* something would happen; they became *involved.* They could have said, *"Well, the crowd is too great and we can't **hope** to reach Jesus."* However, they didn't. No circumstance or problem was going to defeat them.

The person of Faith will not allow demons or difficulties, catastrophes or circumstances to stop him. These men were so determined that they literally tore up the roof and lowered the sick man on his *"thickly padded quilt or mat"* to where Jesus sat. They allowed nothing to interfere with their determination to reach the Master.

(2:5) And Jesus, *"having seen their Faith,"* speaks to the paralytic. *"Their"* refers to the men who brought the paralytic, dug up the roof, and lowered him into the room. Their actions were dramatic evidences of their Faith. So Jesus spoke to the man who was sick of the palsy and said, *"Son, your sins be forgiven you."*

The word (*teknon*) used here is *"child"* rather than the word normally used for *"son."* It was sometimes used as a term of kindly address, even to adults, although the literal meaning is *"child."*

Jesus said, in effect, that the penalty the law required has been satisfied by Divine Justice. On that basis, God has removed the guilt of sin from the believing sinner and clothes him in Righteousness. Jesus forgives sins immediately and completely.

(2:6-7) When Jesus told the man that his sins had been forgiven (or put away), some of the Scribes that were present began to reason in their hearts. The Scribes were undoubtedly there to spy and to find technical flaws in Jesus' teaching. They were jealous of His popularity and Power, and a hostile atmosphere permeated the room. Jesus was well aware of this.

In their hearts they questioned, *"Why is He speaking thusly? This is blasphemy!"* They were quick to judge Jesus, feeling that for Him to assume this Divine prerogative was indeed blasphemy. On the surface they might be excused for their doubts, but Jesus enjoys a unique relationship with God, and this in itself justified His claim. He is the Son of God and Divine.

(2:8) Jesus knew what they were thinking. He was completely *"tuned into"* their thoughts.

(2:9-11) As the Scribes were reasoning in their hearts, Jesus asked them a question. *"Whether"* literally translates as *"which of the two?"* The word "arise" is *egeire* — which speaks of progressive action and might literally be translated *"be arising." "Take up,"* (aron) means *"to pick up and carry."* It was a form of military command that was to be obeyed at once. The command to walk is one that means *"start walking about and keep on walking."* This means the palsied man had a permanent cure. So, essentially, Jesus asked them whether it was easier to do one or the other.

He indicated that He did this that they might know — absolutely and without doubt — that He possessed the Power to forgive sins. The word used for power is *exousia,* which really means *"delegated authority."* Jesus, as the Son of God, had *Authority from the Father* to forgive sin. The Scribes had been given another demonstration of the Deity of the Messiah.

Then Jesus spoke to the paralytic and told him to *"Go your way."* The man who had been paralyzed arose and took his pallet, and went out before all of them.

(2:12) The people were amazed. The verb is *existemi, literally "to stand out of"*; which is the word from which we get the word *"ecstasy."* The observers were transported beyond their usual manner of viewing things by the wonderful miracle they had witnessed. Their total attention was captured by the marvelous healing, and they were at the point of being almost *"beside themselves."* They had never seen anything like this before.

A TAX COLLECTOR TRUSTS JESUS

"And He went forth again by the seaside; and all the multitude resorted unto Him, and He taught them. And as He passed by, He saw

Levi the son of Alphaeus sitting at the receipt of custom, and said unto him, Follow Me. And he arose and followed Him. And it came to pass, that, as Jesus sat at meat in his house, many publicans and sinners sat also together with Jesus and His Disciples: for there were many, and they followed Him. And when the Scribes *and Pharisees saw Him eat with publicans and sinners, they said unto His Disciples, How is it that He eats and drinks with publicans and sinners? When Jesus heard it, He said unto them, They who are whole have no need of the physician, but they who are sick: I came not to call the Righteous, but sinners to Repentance"* (Mk. 2:13-17).

(2:13) As this next experience was taking place, Jesus was *"by the seaside."* The word *"by"* is *para,* which means *"alongside."* The idea suggests that our Lord not only went to the seashore area, but that He loved to walk along the shore. This would certainly provide rest and solitude and give opportunity to be alone with God, His Father. The fresh air, the soothing influence of the lapping waves, plus the beautiful view across the sea, would certainly be a tonic to the Lord Jesus Christ. He often sought out a solitary place to pray and seek God's Face. It is helpful for every Servant of God to arrange such surroundings for himself from time to time.

But the crowds, the Bible says, kept seeking Him out. It was difficult for Him to find solitude, but each time they came to Him, He taught them. He never turned the crowds away. They were never turned away hungry, sad, sick or discouraged. He fed the hungry; healed the sick; cast out devils; ministered to those in need; and taught them. In this particular account, it says that Jesus taught the multitude.

(2:14) As Jesus was passing by, He saw Levi *"sitting at the receipt of custom."* He was sitting at a tollgate on the Great West Road from Damascus to the Mediterranean. This was also the customs office for the city of Capernaum. It was a landing for ships that traded upon the Sea of Galilee.

Levi was a tax collector who took in tolls for Herod Antipas. The Roman government ruthlessly extracted taxes from its subjects and the Judeans hated and despised the tax collectors, classing them as reprobates and sinners.

Levi was sitting on an elevated platform, or bench, which was the main feature of the toll office. He was a Hebrew who was more concerned with money than he was of the good opinion of his neighbors and countrymen. There has always been a close feeling of kinship among the Hebrews, possibly more than in other races, due to the hardships endured over the centuries.

The fact that Levi could suppress this natural tendency toward brotherhood testifies to the sordid state of his soul. He had forsaken fellowship for gold by becoming a tax collector for the despised Romans. Obviously, he was generally hated. Yet, here was a man the Lord knew He could use.

Apparently this wasn't the first time our Lord had observed Levi. He had, perhaps, watched him for a long time as he sat at the collector's desk. Now he was choosing Levi to become of the Twelve Disciples. What an honor! His name would be eternally inscribed in the foundations of the city of New Jerusalem.

FOLLOW ME. The word used is *akoloutheo,* and it comes from a word that means *"to walk the same road."* It means that one is to follow the one who precedes, joining him as an attendant. It also means to follow as a disciple and become a member of the group.

Much was involved in the Lord's command. It was more than an invitation. The word used is in the imperative mode, which means it was a command. Jesus really wasn't asking Levi a question or extending an invitation. Jesus was speaking as a king — a sovereign — giving a royal command.

Levi recognized this. This was a wonderful call, parallel to the call to Salvation. The one called must respond through an act of free will, and Levi immediately stepped down from his collector's desk. He was drawn by the loving power of the Master. It would mean poverty instead of the affluence and luxury to which he had been accustomed. He had, no doubt, acquired great wealth, but Jesus told him to *"follow with Me."* Jesus didn't merely command Levi to become a *Follower,* but He welcomed him as His companion. It was a side-by-side walk and it is this same blessed fellowship that is available to every Believer in the Lord Jesus Christ.

(2:15) *"And it came to pass"* is a vivid presentation of a present reality. Jesus *"sat at meat"* in Levi's house. The word for sat is *katakeimai,* and it more literally means to *"lie prostrate, to have lain down."* They ate, in those days, in a reclining position on couches rather than sitting upright on chairs. The end of the couch was at the table and it extended out lengthwise from the edge of the table. It was probably an oblong room with sand strewn on the floor and with recesses in the plaster walls for lamps. It was here that they sat *"at meat"* — the word used for meat simply meaning *"food"* in those days.

Levi made a great feast for the Lord and many sat (or reclined) together with Him. These were Levi's friends, the publicans and sinners of the area. This was a group Jesus couldn't contact through the Synagogue. Apparently tax collectors were excluded from the Synagogue. Levi, having committed his life to Christ, provided the opportunity for his fellow tax collectors to meet his newfound Saviour.

Some, perhaps, came who weren't invited. But they soon found themselves captivated by this new *"miracle worker."* Because He had, in a sense, defied the religious leaders by choosing Levi as a Disciple, many of them were sympathetically drawn to Him. Thus the tax collectors and sinners swarming the trade marts of Capernaum wanted to know more of Jesus. Many of them undoubtedly, ended up becoming Believers.

HIS DISCIPLES. The word used for Disciples is *mathetes,* and it means *"one who learns."* It is used here of the Disciples of our Lord, whom He had called to be His Helpers. They were with Him when the group of sinners and publicans joined in the feast at Levi's house.

(2:16) THE SCRIBES AND THE PHARISEES. Some of the best Greek Texts write this: "the Scribes of the Pharisees"; indicating that they were Scribes who belonged to the sect of the Pharisees. One writer calls them *"young theologues."* They would be referred to today as divinity students. These Scribes and Pharisees followed Jesus and His Disciples into the room where they were eating with Levi and his friends. They looked down on the publicans and sinners and questioned Jesus' association with them.

(2:17) Jesus declared to them that they who are whole do not need a physician, but those who are sick. The word for sick is *kakos,* and it is sometimes translated *"diseased."* Literally it means *"they who are having it bad"* physically. The word for whole, *ischuo,* means *"to be strong."* So Jesus was saying that there was *"no need for a doctor among those who are strong, but only among those who are sick."*

Jesus didn't dine with this group simply for enjoyment. He was there to minister Salvation to them. In His sensitive Spirit, Jesus certainly abhorred the evil committed by these individuals, but at the same time He loved them; for He loves sinners and came to seek and save those who are lost.

FEASTING OR FASTING?

"And the disciples of John and of the Pharisees used to fast: and they come and say unto Him, Why do the disciples of John and of the Pharisees fast, but Your Disciples fast not? And Jesus said unto them, Can the children of the bridechamber fast, while the bridegroom is with them? as long as they have the bridegroom with them, they cannot fast. But the days will come, when the bridegroom shall be taken away from them, and then shall they fast in those days. No man also sews a piece of new cloth on an old garment: else the new piece that filled it up takes away from the old, and the rent is made worse. And no man putts new wine into old bottles: else the new wine does burst the bottles, and the wine is spilled, and the bottles will be marred: but new wine must be put into new bottles" (Mk. 2:18-22).

(2:18) This is yet another event in which the Messiah was brought into conflict with the accepted religious practices of His day. Both the disciples of John and the Pharisees observed fasts. Even though John, who was in prison at the time, was less devoted to Jewish observances, his disciples followed some of those ceremonial and ritual practices. However, some of his disciples agreed with the Pharisees on this matter. Although John had called the Pharisees a brood of vipers, his disciples sided with the Pharisees in criticizing Jesus this time.

(2:19) CHILDREN OF THE BRIDECHAMBER. The word used here is *huios* and is properly translated *"sons."* These were not the groomsmen, but they were friends of the bridegroom — some of the invited guests of the wedding. Jesus takes John's own metaphor (Jn. 3:29) and substitutes the sons of the bridechamber for the *"friend of the bridegroom"* — an expression John used of himself in relationship to the Messiah. A marriage scene is, of course, no place for mourning.

Jesus gave three Parables: the bridegroom, the mended cloth, and the new wineskins — all to illustrate and defend His conduct in attending the feast at Levi's house.

When Jesus spoke, it usually perplexed the religious leaders. They could not comprehend His spiritual emphasis — being steeped only in ritual and ceremony. They never looked deeper to God's Purpose *behind* the rituals they loved, and when Jesus emphasized the spiritual values, they despised Him for it.

Jesus went on to say (2:20) that the time would come when the bridegroom would be taken away. He was referring to His Crucifixion. When that happened, it would be a time of deep mourning, and a fast would then be appropriate.

(2:21) A PIECE OF NEW CLOTH ON AN OLD GARMENT. The word for *"piece"* is *epiblema,* which really refers to a patch. If a new, *agnaphos* (unfulled, unmilled, undressed), piece of cloth were used to patch an old garment, it would tear away. Reference here is to the fuller's trade in which a new piece of cloth was made usable through a process of cleansing, shrinking, and thickening. This was accomplished through moisture, heat, and pressure. *"Old"* suggests a garment that was used or worn out, weakened by age. It would not prove strong enough to bond successfully to a patch of unfulled cloth.

The parallel Jesus was drawing was that the Messiah's *new* type of Ministry and Preaching could not be patched onto the Pharisaic religion. Jesus was proclaiming Grace as opposed to the outmoded Sacrificial Ceremonies. These were an old garment, ready to be set aside.

Even today, there are those who would try to retain aspects of the Mosaic Law and then *add* to it God's great Doctrine of Grace and Mercy, as a little patch. Attempting to mix Law and Grace was a problem in New Testament days as well as today. Paul, writing to the Galatians, addressed the doctrines of the Judaizers who were trying to *keep* the Law — while adding Mercy and Grace. This won't work. Salvation is by Grace — through Faith in Christ — and not by the Law. The New Covenant is not a patch on the old Law.

(2:22) Jesus used a third illustration to make His point. He said, new wine is not put into old bottles. The word translated *"bottles"* is literally the word for *"wineskins."* These containers were made of animal skins. If the fruit of the grapevine were put into old wineskins (which were weakened and inelastic with age), they could easily burst as pressure built up as it fermented. Once again, the usage for old is *"worn out,"* referring to the wineskins (and the Law). You cannot mix Law with Grace. Jesus was ushering in a New Covenant of Mercy — with Redemption by Grace through Faith. The two just don't mix. It is doubtful that the *"religious"* understood what He was telling them.

A SABBATH CONTROVERSY

"And it came to pass, that He went through the corn fields on the Sabbath Day; and His Disciples began, as they went, to pluck the ears of corn. And the Pharisees said unto Him, Behold, why do they on the Sabbath Day that which is not lawful? And He said unto them, Have you never read what David did, when he had need, and was hungry, he, and they who were with him? How he went into the House of God in the days of Abiathar the High Priest, and did eat the shewbread, which is not lawful to eat but for the Priests, and gave also to them which were with him? And He said unto them, The Sabbath was made for man, and not man for the Sabbath: Therefore the Son of Man is Lord also of the Sabbath" (Mk. 2:23-28).

(2:23) AND IT CAME TO PASS. The conjunction *"and"* does not connect this incident with the previous one in a temporal sense. It is merely referring to another case of conflict. Jesus and His Disciples *"went through the cornfields."* *"Went through"* is from *paraporeuomai,* which means *"to journey alongside."* It is a word which *combines* the ideas of going through and alongside. He was walking through a grainfield on a footpath that had plants growing on both sides. As they passed, they plucked some of the grain.

The word translated *"ears of corn"* is *stachus,* from which we derive *"stalk."* It means an *"ear of corn or growing grain."* There were several types of cereal grains cultivated in Palestine and sometimes the word corn was used figuratively for the entire vegetable produce of the field. It was undoubtedly some type of grain they plucked, as they walked through the field, to sustain themselves. Actually, corn as we know it developed in the western hemisphere and did not exist in the Holy Land in Jesus' day.

(2:24) It would hardly seem to be a problem, even based on Old Testament Law, for the Disciples to merely take and eat some grain. But the Scribes and Pharisees had added countless interpretations to the laws and developed traditions filling volumes. The people were oppressed with all types of shibboleths, legalisms, and traditions, many of which had no basis whatsoever in the Word of God.

THE PHARISEES SAID — *elegon* — This implies that they Pharisees *persisted* in discussing this matter. They didn't just *mention* it to Jesus, they harassed Him — badgering Him in a condemnatory manner. Jesus was a target for opposition whenever He did anything that technically deviated from their traditions and the many laws imposed upon the people. The Scribes and Pharisees were anxious to discredit Jesus because they were threatened by this awesome new concept. He was pointing out that motivation and attitude were the crucial factors, not ceremony. It was a situation where the age-old argument over *"the **Spirit** of the Law or the **letter** of the Law"* was finally to be confronted.

(2:25) The Pharisees knew the Old Testament Scriptures well. When Jesus referred to David's action in eating the shewbread, it was a rhetorical question and it required an affirmative answer. David had satisfied his hunger by eating the bread from the table in the Holy Place. This bread was only for the Priests, yet David ate it. Jesus was justifying His actions, and those of His Disciples, by the fact that they were hungry just as David had been. Obviously, what He and His Disciples did was of far less import than David's eating of the bread from the table in the Holy Place.

(2:26) Jesus then refers to Abiathar, who was High Priest at the time of the shewbread incident (I Sam. 21:1-6). Jesus pointed out that Abiathar had *given* the bread to David, thus stamping the authority of the High Priest's office on the actions of David and his followers.

(2:27) Jesus then continues by pointing that the Sabbath is made for man. The word used here is not for the male individual, but is *anthropos,* meaning mankind. The Sabbath was made for the *good* of man. The rabbis, however, had made so many petty and foolish rules regarding the Sabbath that they made it appear that man was a slave to the Sabbath Day.

As Jesus talked to them, He knew they couldn't understand for two reasons. First, their minds were so warped with ecclesiasticism and so deeply grounded in man-made traditions, that they had lost all sight of the true importance of the Word of God.

Secondly, they didn't *want* to hear because the New Covenant preached by Jesus created a threat to their positions, not only as *religious* leaders, but as social and political leaders as well. Jesus posed a threat to not only the spiritual darkness that had overtaken the spiritual structure of Judaea, but to the entire political structure as well. The Scribes and

Pharisees had insidiously constructed their political framework and influence over the years.

So Jesus found Himself embroiled in a never-ending series of confrontations involving minor technicalities within the accepted religious framework. It is very easy for religious people to lose themselves in a maze of complicated doctrines, rules, and regulations. Of course, there are many things that are clearly wrong, and these obvious errors should be avoided. But, all too often, people in places of power in the Churches make innumerable rules concerning minor technicalities. They seem to delight in making Christianity burdensome.

Christianity is not a new *law* — it is a new *life*. Obviously, the Christian is not to steal, participate in immorality, or accept the evils of alcohol, drugs, and so forth. But, all too often, there are volumes of rules concerning all the minute details of matters most people don't even concern themselves with. Actually, this is a matter more of individual taste and reflects the Pharisaical approach of concentrating on minutia, while ignoring the matters of true importance.

(2:28) Jesus declared that *"the Son of Man is Lord also of the Sabbath."* Jesus, the Son of God, was manifested in human flesh and He identified with mankind. He often referred to Himself as the Son of Man.

He declared that He was Lord of the Sabbath. The word for Lord is *kurios,* and it means *"he to whom a person or thing belongs."* Jesus is Owner, or Lord. He is the Lord of Creation and also the Lord of the Sabbath — which He created for the sake of mankind.

Jesus was no Sabbath breaker. He did, however, declare Himself against the prevailing attitudes on Sabbath observance — such as restrictions against charity toward a fellow human being when it involved what the traditionalists called *"work."* Healing on the Sabbath was a case in point. While the Scribes and Pharisees *"strained at a gnat and swallowed a camel"* (Mat. 23:24), Jesus tried to put matters into proper perspective. He was, as a watchman on the wall, exposing the faulty spiritual focus of the religious community. Not surprisingly, the Scribes and Pharisees condemned Jesus for doing good on the Sabbath. They had a callous disregard for the needs of the people and they tenaciously sought to enforce the binding and burdensome traditions that had become superimposed upon the Law.

Notes

Chapter 3

Healing On The Sabbath

SUBJECT   PAGE

JESUS TEACHES BY THE SEA OF GALILEE 46
JESUS CHOOSES TWELVE DISCIPLES 48
A BLASPHEMOUS ACCUSATION IS MADE 51
JESUS' MOTHER AND BRETHREN WANT TO TAKE HIM HOME 54

CHAPTER 3

HEALING ON THE SABBATH

"And He entered again into the Synagogue; and there was a man there which had a withered hand. And they watched Him, whether He would heal him on the Sabbath Day; that they might accuse Him. And He saith unto the man which had the withered hand, Stand forth. And He said unto them, Is it lawful to do good on the Sabbath Days, or to do evil? To save life, or to kill? But they held their peace. And when He had looked round about on them with anger, being grieved for the hardness of their hearts, He said unto the man, Stretch forth your hand. And He stretched it out: and his hand was restored whole as the other. And the Pharisees went forth, and straightway took counsel with the Herodians against Him, how they might destroy Him" (Mk. 3:1-6).

(3:1) It was Jesus' custom to attend the Synagogue on the Sabbath Day, Saturday — the last day of the week on our calendar. According to Old Testament Law, the Israeli Nation took its day of rest and worshipped God in the Temple on the last day of the week. When Jesus again entered the Synagogue on the Sabbath, there was a man there with a withered hand. Luke, the Greek physician, says in his account that it was his right hand. This is an indication of Luke's accuracy in reporting details of the incidents he covered.

(3:2) AND THEY WATCHED HIM. *"They"* refers to the Scribes and Pharisees. *"They"* were the people who were trying to catch Him in a technical religious error. They had dogged His steps on countless Sabbaths. They continued to watch Him — being committed to finding Jesus in error regarding His manner of Sabbath observance. They were not concerned about the man's withered hand. They were the watchdogs of the Jewish religious structure, and they had to discredit Jesus' claim to Messiahship. Their only interest in the situation was to find error in Jesus' observance of *their* rules.

This is also true today, for there are many who are not interested in what God is doing. They are so interested in doctrinal nuances that they don't even see the miracles performed before their eyes. They are so obsessed with promoting *"their religion,"* and building up their little empires, that they miss God's whole great picture.

An outstanding missionary was preaching many years ago and God began to move. Lives were changed, souls were being saved, drunkards were made sober, prostitutes became pure — and broken homes were restored. Great things were happening as God moved.

But anger flared against him. Could you guess by whom? It was the hierarchy of religion — the establishment Churches. They managed to have him put in jail. He was held for over a week, and if the Church instigating this were revealed, it would startle many Christians. These people were not interested in the Work of God — nor the mighty move taking place by His Spirit — they were concerned only that he was not a member of *their* Church and that he was preaching a doctrine slightly different from the one they followed.

The *results* of this great man's ministry seemed unimportant and the Redemption of countless drunkards was of no concern to them. The Church responsible for stopping this move of God had great needs within its own body of *"Believers."* Some of the most blatantly immoral people in town were members of this Church.

What a sad example we see in this factual incident where *"religious"* people could ignore lives being changed under a little tent where the Gospel was being proclaimed. The same devilish deceits from the powers of darkness are just as commonplace today as they were two thousand years ago, when Jesus Christ walked the Earth.

The ancient Pharisees trailed Jesus, spying on Him, trying to find any *"fault"* they could manufacture so they could condemn Him and nullify His influence. They watched Him — not because they were awed by the spectacular power He displayed, but they watched Him because they were filled with bitterness and hate. The foul venom of darkness corroded their souls. Terrible attitudes and reactions can masquerade under the names of religion.

Religious prejudices are among the most powerful influences. Demonic spirits often work to direct religious activities and often do so within the organized Churches. Organized religions and organized Churches have, at times, seriously impeded the moving and operation of the Holy Spirit. Some great revivals have taken place *despite* the actions of Preachers and Churches. The same spirit that nailed Jesus to the Cross is operating today, exactly as it existed in religious circles in *that* day.

The Pharisees of Jesus' day were determined to find something in Jesus' activities that appeared to contradict the accepted Pharisaical law. His interpretation of Sabbath observation seemed to present them with the best opportunity. So they doggedly persisted in hope of finding some excuse to accuse and condemn Him.

The word for accuse is *kategoreo,* which means to *"formally accuse before a tribunal, to bring a charge publicly."* They had harassed Him for an extended period — spying on Him in an effort to find *any* deviation from accepted Pharisaical practice through which they could entrap Him.

(3:3) Jesus was well-aware of this and He said to the man with the withered hand, *"Stand forth."* Literally, He told the man to *"Step into the midst of the people so all can see you."* Jesus was going to *openly* demonstrate the Power of God to the spying Pharisees.

(3:4) Jesus then asked the crowd if it was lawful *"to do good on the Sabbath days, or to do evil."* He was demonstrating the difference between His theology and that of the Pharisees. They revered theory without practice and religious observance without benevolence. They had divorced the Divine from the human.

To fail to do good when it is within your power, is to do evil. After Jesus asked this question, there was silence. No one dared to speak, because they couldn't answer the question that so clearly defined the opposing positions. It was all out in the open. They looked only at the legalistic side, while Jesus considered the spiritual and human consequences. Their tongues were silenced because Jesus' question forced them to look at their own position.

(3:5) Jesus directed a *"swift, sweeping glance"* about Him. This glance, the expression indicates, took them all in and it implies that He regarded them *"with anger."* There are three Greek words used in Scripture that denote anger. The first of these is *thumos*, and refers to a sudden outburst of anger that cools off quickly. Another word is *parorgismos*, which denotes anger in the sense of exasperation. This is forbidden in Scriptures. In Ephesians 4:26 it tells us, *"Let not the sun go down on your **parorgismos**."*

The word used for Jesus' anger in the Synagogue is *orge*. This refers to an abiding and settled attitude which would not be present at all times, but which would arise and manifest itself any time a similar situation arose. One would grow angry at the same thing whenever it recurred. This same word is used within Scripture to describe Righteous indignation. Anger can be a justifiable and proper reaction. Scripture not only *condones* anger, there are situations where it is *demanded.*

Matthew 3:7 addresses the matter of the Wrath of God. If a person is to love good, he must hate evil. There is a Righteous anger which Righteous men *must* feel. We would be in a sorry state indeed if we were to lose our ability to become angry with sin. Anger has been described by one writer as *"the sinews of the soul."* Another writer proposes that anger against immoral acts is a sign of moral health. People definitely should hate evil. There are so many dirty, degrading, obscene, and filthy elements in our society today that should be dealt with. If one truly loves God, one will hate sin. It is impossible to love Righteousness without *hating* unrighteousness.

It states that Jesus grieved *"for the hardness of their hearts."* His anger was tempered by grief. Jesus — the Man of sorrows — experienced continuing grief over the sins of the people. His look of anger was fleeting, while His feeling of sadness at the hardness of men's hearts was continuous. The word *"hardness"* is a translation of *porosis*. The verb form of this word means *"a hard skin, a hardening."* The word used by Mark means *"obtuseness of mental discernment, dull perception."* The Scribes and Pharisees were incapable of spiritual understanding because of their willful hardening of their hearts.

How this must have grieved the Master. Christ's command to the man to stretch forth his withered hand brought instantaneous healing. The hand was restored — the man was suddenly whole. The word *"restored"* is from *apokathistemi*, which means *"to restore to its former state."* It was suddenly *"like new,"* or as it had formerly been.

(3:6) As soon as the man had been healed, the Pharisees — the champions of orthodox Sabbath observance — made an immediate exodus. They were filled with wrath because the Sabbath had been *"broken"* again. It irritated them greatly that it had been broken by a miracle that exalted Jesus' stature and added to His fame.

The Pharisees then went to the Herodians, who were a Jewish party of the time who were partisans of the royal family of Herod. The Pharisees normally held the Herodians in great distaste because of their support of the royal family and of the Romans. Now, though, these antagonistic forces united. The Pharisees were so opposed to Jesus that they were willing to accept the assistance of people they despised — in order to gain influence in the court. Their one overwhelming obsession was to destroy Jesus.

It is amazing to see the vile efforts of evil men in their attempts to prevent good from being accomplished. The same is true today and it is often done, in subtle ways, by both religious and political leaders.

JESUS TEACHES BY THE SEA OF GALILEE

"But Jesus withdrew Himself with His Disciples to the sea: and a great multitude from Galilee followed Him, and from Judaea, And from Jerusalem, Idumaea, and from beyond Jordan; and they about Tyre and Sidon, a great multitude, when they heard what great things He did, came unto Him. And He spoke to His Disciples that a small ship should wait on Him because of the multitude, lest they should throng Him. For He had healed many; insomuch that they pressed upon Him for to touch Him, as many was had plagues. And unclean spirits, when they saw Him, fell down before Him, and cried, saying, You are the Son of God. And He straitly charged them that they should not make Him known" (Mk. 3:7-12).

(3:7) JESUS WITH HIS DISCIPLES. The exposition of this Verse demonstrates that the words *"with His Disciples"* have an emphatic position. This clearly indicates that they have assumed prominence. They are now a significant part of His effort, His Ministry, and His Work.

GREAT MULTITUDE. The word *"great," polu*, is in an emphatic position. It calls attention to the *exceptionally* large crowd. If apparently took some time for this vast crowd to assemble. The people were coming from many different places and from great distances. Jesus wanted to withdraw with His Disciples to the seashore for a little rest, a time of prayer, and a private conference with the Disciples. But the crowds continued to be drawn to Him.

(3:9) A SMALL SHIP SHOULD WAIT ON HIM. This was a small boat that waited on Jesus. It was not a large fishing vessel, but rather a rowboat; a little dinghy normally attached to a larger fishing boat. The word *"wait"* imparts the idea of being in constant readiness.

THRONG HIM. The word is *thlibo*, and it means *"to press hard upon."* They were pushing up against Him. Jesus was interested in the crowds, and He stayed with them because they needed Him. But He found it necessary to protect Himself from them since they might actually crush Him. He, therefore, had this little boat prepared so He could escape if necessary. The Disciples procured the boat and rowed it near shore, staying close and keeping a watchful eye on their Master.

The word translated *"throng him"* was also used when speaking of pressing grapes to extract the juice.

(3:10) The reason for providing the boat becomes even more apparent in this Verse, as there is an added emphasis on the press of the people. It says they *"pressed upon Him."* The verb is *epipipto*, which means *"to fall upon."* The crowd was pressing upon Him to the extent that it had become dangerous. They were not pushing at Him in anger, but in desperation. They were suffering and in acute need of healing. They were crushing about Him in their eagerness to be healed. It must have been a pathetic sight, and their only motive was to be cured.

PLAGUES. The word used here is *mastix*, which means *"a stroke or a scourge."* The same expression is used for *"a paralytic stroke,"* or *"an influenza scourge."* Jesus had healed the people of many plagues and problems, and of such specific diseases as leprosy. He had healed the blind, the deaf, the dumb — and many had been delivered of unclean spirits. Now He was continuing to heal them of their distressing bodily diseases. They pressed about Him desperately in the hope they could touch Him and thus be healed.

(3:11) Those with unclean spirits fell down before Jesus while the resident spirits cried aloud. It appears that demonized persons were *constantly* falling prostrate before the Lord, according to the word used. It also indicates that the demons were watching Jesus with wary interest.

They knew He was the very Son of God. As they fell before Him, they declared this over and over. With their throaty, raucous voices from the satanic world, they declared Him to be the Son of God.

(3:12) HE STRAITLY CHARGED THEM. Jesus rebuked and reproved them, censuring them severely. He commanded them to *"shut up."* Jesus did not desire the testimony of the demons as to His Deity. This is an interesting incident in the Ministry and Life of the Master. When He charged them to say nothing, there appeared to be the threat of added punishment if they did not obey immediately. They recognized this and obeyed Him.

Demonic forces could not stand against Jesus and — in the Name of Jesus — we too can take authority over demonic forces.

JESUS CHOOSES TWELVE DISCIPLES

"And He goeth up into a mountain, and called unto Him whom He would: and they came unto Him. And He ordained Twelve, that they should be with Him, and that He might send them forth to preach, And to have power to heal sicknesses, and to cast out devils: And Simon He surnamed Peter; And James the son of Zebedee, and John the brother of James; and He surnamed them Boanerges, which is, The sons of thunder: And Andrew, and Philip, and Bartholomew, and Matthew, and Thomas, and James the son of Alphaeus, and Thaddaeus, and Simon the Canaanite, and Judas Iscariot, which also betrayed Him . . ." (Mk. 3:13-19).

It is simply recorded in Mark that Jesus went up into a mountain and there called the Disciples to Him. Luke adds some additional details and also identifies the place, explaining that Jesus went to the mountain to pray. He then adds that He continued *"all night in prayer to God"* (Lk. 6:12).

Once again, we see the importance Jesus attached to prayer and the significance of it in His Life. Jesus regularly separated Himself in a quiet place early in the day to pray (Mk. 1:35). He also spent *longer* periods in prayer before important events in His Life. Before He selected His Disciples, He spent the entire night in prayer.

Just prior to His Crucifixion we see Him agonizing in prayer in the Garden of Gethsemane, and gaining the victory, which enabled Him to endure the ensuing events, which resulted in His triumphant Death on the Cross. Obviously, Jesus considered prayer very important and made it the prime focus of His Life.

He *"called to Himself"* those *"whom He desired."* Jesus made the *choice* of His Disciples. They did not simply volunteer or ask to go with Him. There were many persons interested in the Work and Ministry of

Jesus, and there were many from which to choose His group of Twelve. Jesus selected those who had separated themselves from the world — those willing to become His Disciples and students during His Life. After His Death they would inherit the awesome responsibility of disseminating the Kingdom Message to the world.

(3:14-15) He *"ordained"* these men to serve. The word for ordained is *poieo*, which means *"to make."* Again, *"make"* does not imply coercion or force; it means rather to mold, sculpt, or fashion.

These were to remain with Him throughout His three and one-half years of Ministry. They would learn to minister, teach, pray, and render many services, in addition to the fellowship they afforded the Master. Primarily they were to be molded into vessels to carry the Gospel Message.

Of course, there would be others involved in preaching, teaching, and the spreading of the Gospel. But these men were to be the primary group, with yet a smaller, more intimate circle composed of Peter, James, and John. The Apostle Paul was to come later. It was a marvelous calling accepted by these twelve men.

He ordained them that they should be with Him to receive His training and subsequently to be sent forth. The verb is *apostello*, and this means to sent someone from you — with credentials and a commission — to be one's representative and to accomplish a mission. The noun form is *apostolos*. From this comes our word *"Apostle,"* which means one who is sent, an envoy, or ambassador.

The Apostles were to preach. The word here is *kerusso*, which means to make a grave, *authoritative*, public proclamation, which is to be heeded. They were also to heal the sick and cast out devils. It states that they were to have *"power"* to heal illnesses and to cast out demons. The word translated power is *exousia*, and it literally means *"delegated authority."* The literal word for power is *dumanis*. The Disciples were equipped with the *authority*, as Jesus' representatives, to heal the sick and cast out demons.

(3:16) The first Disciple mentioned is Simon, whom Jesus surnamed Peter. Peter seems to have been the most vocal of the group. *"Surname"* means *"to place upon."* Jesus therefore *"placed upon"* Simon the additional name of Peter, which was to become descriptive of his character (as the Holy Spirit later came to control his life) for he became a rock.

The name Peter comes from the Greek word *petros*, which actually means *"a detached fragment of stone."* In Matthew 16:18, Jesus said, *"you are Peter, and upon this Rock I will build My Church; and the gates of Hell shall not prevail against it."*

He was saying to Peter, *"You are Petros"*; which means he was a rock-like man. Then Jesus went on to say, *"upon this Rock (petra) I will build My Church."* The word *petra* has reference to a huge, Gibraltar-like rock. Jesus was referring to His *own* Deity, and saying that upon *that* Rock He would build His Church.

He didn't say He was building a Church on Peter. What He was saying was that Peter was a *chip off the block*, but upon the *basic* block (Jesus' Deity) He would build His Church.

(3:17) After giving Simon his additional name, Jesus also surnamed James and John. The surname he *"placed upon"* them was Boanerges, which means *"sons of thunder"* in Syrian, or *"sons of tumult"* in Hebrew. This was also indicative of *their* character, for they wanted to call fire down from Heaven to consume the Samaritan village (Lk. 9:54). The name received by James and John was not perpetuated as was the surname Peter. It may have been something of a title of honor emphasizing their impetuous natures.

Jesus didn't give surnames to the other Disciples. It is interesting to note that the three men surnamed were also the *"inner circle"* — Peter, James, and John. As Jesus chose these men, He knew what they were like and He knew He was going to sculpt and ordain them. He recognized the raw material and the depth of their character, and He knew He could mold, sculpt, and fashion them together with the other Disciples, for their great responsibility and mission. These men had their weaknesses and their problems, but they would be refined — and come out as pure gold.

God chooses individuals who are far from perfect, but there is a purifying process called *"progressive Sanctification"* that takes place. We can grow closer to Him every day and be changed, precept upon precept, and line upon line, from Glory to Glory in His Image.

(3:18) The next Disciple named is Andrew. Though used by the Jews, the name Andrew is of Greek origin and comes from the word *aner*, which means *"manly."* Philip is a Greek name which means *"fond of horses."* The name Matthew is Hebrew meaning *"a gift of God."* Thomas is Hebrew and means *"a twin."* Thaddaeus is the same individual as Judas of John 14:22. He has been called the good Judas. Simon has been referred to as the Canaanite or more properly the Canaanaean. He is also referred to as the Zealot.

The Zealots were a fierce war party of that day, violently opposed to the presence of Rome in the Holy Land. They were fanatical in their belief of Israel exclusiveness — following the Mosaic Laws strictly. Simon's former activities were in great contrast to his service with the Saviour.

(3:19) The last name mentioned is that of Judas Iscariot. It is a compound name meaning *"the man of Kerioth."* Kerioth was located south of the city of Jerusalem toward the coast of Edom. Judas, of course, became the betrayer of the Saviour. He sold his eternal reward for a handful of coins and became the *"son of perdition"* — despised throughout the centuries and for all eternity.

A BLASPHEMOUS ACCUSATION IS MADE

". . . And they went into an house. And the multitude came together again, so that they could not so much as eat bread. And when His friends heard of it, they went out to lay hold on Him: for they said, He is beside Himself. And the Scribes which came down from Jerusalem said, He has Beelzebub, and by the prince of the devils casteth He out devils. And He called them unto Him, and said unto them in Parables, How can Satan cast out Satan? And if a kingdom be divided against itself, that kingdom cannot stand. And if Satan rise up against himself, and he be divided, he cannot stand, but has an end. No man can enter into a strong man's house, and spoil his goods, except he will first bind the strong man; and then he will spoil his house. Verily I say unto you, All sins shall be forgiven unto the sons of men, and blasphemies wherewith soever they shall blaspheme: But he who shall blaspheme against the Holy Spirit hath never forgiveness, but is in danger of eternal damnation: Because they said, He has an unclean spirit" (Mk. 3:19-30).

(3:19-20) The place where Jesus chose the Twelve Disciples was in a mountainous area. Now He was back in a house, and the sense of the Text is that He had come home from being in the mountains. His Headquarters were in Capernaum, perhaps in the home of Peter, and it is likely that this is where the Lord returned.

After Jesus selected the Disciples, He undoubtedly wanted to spend some time with them. There were unquestionably matters He wished to discuss and He required a time for rest. But the crowds, the multitudes, lingered and simply refused to disperse.

He had spent some time with the Disciples in the mountains, but after their descent, the crowds awaited Him. The throngs wanted to see Jesus and His Disciples. Not only were Jesus and the Disciples unable to find rest and solitude, it is obvious that they couldn't even take food.

(3:21) The term *"His friends"* in this Verse means *"those from His side"* — that is, His kin or family. They had *"heard"* of Jesus' activities — referring to the great Galilean Ministry with its huge crowds and the resulting publicity and excitement. When reports reached them, they realized that rumors often become distorted or twisted in the retelling. They, therefore, feared that Jesus was *"beside Himself."* This has reference to a person being out of one's mind, or being insane. His family, undoubtedly, thought that His concern for the people and His strenuous activities had affected His physical or mental well-being. They obviously came intending to take Him away and restrain Him in an effort to *"get Him back to normal."* The attitude they reflect is again addressed in Mark 6:4 where Jesus said, *"A Prophet is not without honour, but in his own country, and among his own kin, and in his own house."*

The members of His family who were present are not identified. More is later revealed of His half-brother James who wrote the Book of James. He was one of the leaders of the Early Church. At this time, Mary and *some* of His brothers were present.

(3:22) The Pharisees in Galilee had joined with the Herodians, and plans to kill Jesus were taking form. It is probable that word had been sent to Jerusalem to the authorities there, soliciting their help. Scribes had now arrived from Jerusalem and were joined in the plot against Jesus and in the attempt to kill Him.

They accused Him of being in league with Beelzebub — possessed by this prince of devils — and of using *his* power to cast out demons. Beelzebub was referred to as *"the prince of demons,"* but he was also known as *"the god of flies,"* or *"the god of dung, filth, and dirt."* The word translated *"devils"* here is from the Greek word *daimonion*, which has reference to *demons*. Satan is ruler over the demonic forces and they were speaking of Beelzebub as being a prince — one who was in the first order of importance, or power, among the demons.

Here they were in the presence of the greatest Man who ever walked the Earth. They were able to observe with their own eyes some of the greatest miracles to ever occur in the history of man. Jesus was raising the dead, healing people with blinded eyes, and restoring malformed limbs. People eaten away by leprosy were being made whole. It is no wonder that crowds in the thousands tried to reach Him. Awe-inspiring events were taking place.

Yet, these self-blinded religious leaders were unwilling to recognize the Power of God. In fact, their minds were so perverted by their fury, and their hearts so hardened, that they were willing to attribute these tremendous manifestations of God's Power to Satan. This is what is referred to as *"blasphemy against the Holy Spirit"* (Mat. 12:31-32; Mk. 3:28-30; and Lk. 12:10).

(3:23) Jesus addressed the Scribes from Jerusalem because He wanted to document their error. He spoke to them in Parables but first He asked *"how is it possible"* for Satan to cast out Satan? Satan would certainly not be operating against himself.

(3:24-27) Jesus points out to them how false their theory is because a kingdom divided against itself cannot stand, nor can a house divided against itself. If Satan were casting out *himself*, he would certainly be working contrary to his own best interests and the end results would certainly be defeat.

He then went on to say that no one could go and *"spoil"* (that is, to plunder or thoroughly ransack) a house unless the strong man was first bound. Demons belong to Satan and he certainly wouldn't use them *against* himself, as they would not be effective against their leader. Jesus was obviously pointing to Himself as the stronger one who could go into the house and bind those forces and thus control the situation.

(3:28-30) Up to here Jesus spoke in Parables and abstractions to demonstrate the fallacy in their thinking. But now His tone changes and He confronts them directly with a warning. Having demonstrated to them the complete lack of logic in their contentions, He states directly that they have maneuvered themselves into a precarious spiritual position. He points out that the act of attributing the Power of God's Holy Spirit to Satan is blasphemy in fact.

The word blaspheme is from *blasphemeo*, which means *"to speak in a reproachful way, to rail at, or to revile."* It has been defined as a *"malicious misrepresentation."* These men were speaking in an abominable way, without any reverence for God or sacred things. It was obvious that the Lord was performing these miracles by the Power of the Holy Spirit. To deliberately credit them to Satan is blatant blasphemy against the Holy Spirit — which is unforgivable.

The original Text states emphatically that this is *"an eternal sin."* This means there is no forgiveness and guilt is unceasing. It is unthinkable to attribute the mighty moving of God's Holy Spirit to the Devil. Undoubtedly, these men knew better but, in their utter perversion, were blinded by the hardness of their hearts and their obsession to destroy Jesus.

Blasphemy of the Holy Spirit is a serious thing, and it is a matter Satan has used to cause problems and obstacles in the lives of a great many sincere Christians. Satan is the accuser of the brethren and often comes to accuse people, making them feel guilty over previous mistakes. One of the prime tricks of the Devil is to try to convince people that they *have* blasphemed the Holy Spirit. He plants thoughts and ideas and then hurls accusations at the individual as having formed these thoughts himself.

Many Christians have been distressed by this issue. Some have become very disturbed and have even lost their way. Blasphemy against the Holy Spirit involves *willful*, malicious, and slanderous expressions against the Person and Work of the Holy Spirit — and attributing the Work of the Spirit to Satan. The sin is eternal and unpardonable because it is a *willful* rejection of Light and a *deliberate* insult against the Holy Spirit — Who is God's Executive, bringing about the Remission of sin through the Blood of Christ.

Jesus is the Way, the Truth, and the Life. If individuals do away with the only method of forgiveness — the Holy Spirit bringing them forgiveness through Christ — their souls are lost eternally. People who ignorantly and unknowingly insult God and the Work of the Spirit are forgiven.

Blasphemy against the Holy Spirit is a fuller, more *willful*, and *deliberate* action — through words or rejection of the Work of the Holy Spirit. Basically this involves a total perverting of God's Redemptive Plan and Purpose. Anyone sincerely seeking forgiveness and desiring to serve God, shouldn't allow Satan to condemn them with thoughts of having blasphemed the Holy Spirit. If we confess our sins to Christ and trust Him for forgiveness, then He *will* cleanse our sin and forgive us, and cleanse us of all unrighteousness (I Jn. 1:9).

JESUS' MOTHER AND BRETHREN
WANT TO TAKE HIM HOME

"There came then His brethren and His mother, and standing without, sent unto Him, calling Him. And the multitudes sat about Him, and they said unto Him, Behold, Your mother and Your brethren without seek for You. And He answered them, saying, Who is My mother, or My brethren? And He looked round about on them which sat about Him, and said, Behold My mother and My brethren! For whosoever shall do the Will of God, the same is My brother, and My sister, and mother" (Mk. 3:31-35).

(3:31) Earlier in this Chapter, reference was made to Mary and Jesus' brethren arriving to see Him (Vs. 21). They were referred to as *"friends"* and the group may have included some of Jesus' friends, together with the family.

It was mentioned that they thought He was insane or demented. They had heard what was transpiring, perhaps including the possibility of the Pharisees and others trying to kill Him. They, therefore, came to take Him home. The account, begun in Verse 21, was interrupted by the encounter with the Scribes from Jerusalem.

Actually, this Passage of Scripture paints a poignant picture. The mother and half-brothers of Jesus are standing outside the house. The house is filled with people and vast throngs crowd about it. The Disciples sit with Jesus in the room full of people where He is talking and teaching, and where He just finished the exchange with the Scribes and Pharisees. Jesus' mother and brethren are outside but can't gain entrance because of the crush of the crowd. They've come to take Him home, because they think He is *"beside Himself"* or mentally deranged.

(3:32) THE MULTITUDE SAT ABOUT HIM. The word *"about"* is from the word *peri*, which means *"around."* The crowd encircled Him. Someone reports to Jesus that His mother and brothers are standing outside. No mention is made of Joseph. Joseph had probably died some time earlier, with Jesus, as the eldest son, assuming responsibility for the family.

He had, no doubt, cared for His mother, Mary, and helped to care for the other children in the family.

Surely, Mary was a most gracious and wonderful woman; however, she was not perfect. Perfection was not the reason for God's choice of Mary. He chose her because she was a dedicated, sincere person, and God honored *her* by allowing her to become the mother of the Messiah.

Let's not forget this: Mary needed a Saviour just as everyone else does. There is no person born (other than the Lord Jesus Christ) who has not needed a Redeemer. Mary needed a Redeemer — and she praised, worshipped, and magnified her Saviour in Luke 1:47. She is never to be worshipped, personally, as a god. She used the term Saviour (in Lk. 1:47) because she required a Saviour. Also, when the Followers of Jesus went to the upper room, waiting to be filled with the Holy Spirit, Mary was among them. Though not perfect or sinless — Mary was truly a precious person.

(3:33-35) Jesus turned and asked, *"Who is My mother, or My brethren?"* The question seems a bit harsh. Jesus does not rise to go to them. Undoubtedly, He loved His mother very much as He made specific provision for her as He hung dying on the Cross, when He gave her into John's care.

He also loved the other members of His family. But more importantly, He loves *all* men. His Mission on this Earth of preaching and teaching the Gospel, of healing the sick and casting out demons, took *precedence* over His family relationships. This is a great lesson for all of us today. Family ties are important — but God *must* come first!

The reason Jesus asked this rather harsh question was because He knew exactly what they were thinking. He knew why they were there. The account goes on to reveal that He *"looked around Him"* with a sweeping, all-inclusive glance. He looked not with anger, like the Pharisees in the fifth Verse, but with warmth and love. Then He answered His own question. *"Whosoever shall do the Will of God, the same is My brother and My sister and mother."*

It is sometimes difficult to accept that spiritual relationships and responsibilities must supersede family ties. But there are many who feel closer to the Family of God than they do to their own blood relatives. This is not uncommon when a person comes to Christ while the rest of the family remains in the world. For such, there is a wonderful family relationship and limitless kinship awaiting members of the Family of God.

Chapter 4

Jesus Teaches With Parables

SUBJECT	PAGE
THE PARABLE OF THE SOWER	58
THE PARABLE OF THE SEED GROWING BY ITSELF	64
THE PARABLE OF THE MUSTARD SEED	65
OTHER PARABLES	66
JESUS STILLS THE STORM	66

CHAPTER 4

JESUS TEACHES WITH PARABLES

"And He began again to teach by the sea side: and there was gathered unto Him a great multitude, so that He entered into a ship, and sat in the sea; and the whole multitude was by the sea on the land. And He taught them many things by Parables, and said unto them in His Doctrine . . ." (Mk. 4:1-2).

(4:1) Jesus had been teaching the Disciples whom He had called. The word for Disciples is *mathetes,* which means learners. But the crowds kept growing, and Jesus had to resume His teaching of the masses along the shores of the Sea of Galilee. His teachings were very simply and clear and we can regain the Spirit of those precious days by reading *"The Sermon on the Mount"* in Matthew 5-7 and Luke 6:12-49. This is a parallel account of these same times.

ENTERED A SHIP. Sometimes the crowds would grow so great and press about Him so that it was necessary for Jesus to resort to a boat as a refuge. In 3:9 we noted that Jesus went into a small boat because of the crowds, but here He went into a larger vessel (*ploion*). This was a larger fishing boat, apparently moored relatively close to the shore.

The crowds pressing in upon Jesus sometimes grew so large that it was more effective if He retreated to a boat and preached from there. It was certainly safer, and they could probably hear Him better since His Voice would carry well over the narrow strip of water separating the boat from the beach.

A GREAT MULTITUDE. The crowd that had gathered this time was a great multitude. The word for *"great"* is from the word *pleistos,* which means *"much."* The crowd was apparently greater than ever.

SAT IN THE SEA. The expression used here does not mean that He was sitting in the water, but rather located just out a bit into the sea in a boat anchored a short distance from shore.

(4:2) HE TAUGHT THEM. The expression used indicates He was *continually* teaching them. Jesus both taught and preached. The word translated taught is from the word *didasko.* It is from this word that we get our word *"didactic."* He would impart information and carefully unfold the Word of God. The word people often used to identify Him was *"Teacher"* which is *didaskalos* in the Greek, but they more probably called Him *Rabboni* in Hebrew. Either word can be translated as *"teacher, master, or even doctor."* He also preached (*kerusso*) which means *"to make a proclamation."*

57

IN PARABLES. Jesus often taught in Parables. A Parable is a short story told as an analogy, conveying a basic and central truth. He used concrete illustrations to get His Messages across. He sought to relate to His hearers, and used various methods as a master teacher. Despite the fact that Jesus was a master instructor unfolding God's Word in a marvelous manner, His Messages often fell on deaf ears, hard hearts, and people who refused to respond.

THE PARABLE OF THE SOWER

"Hearken; Behold, there went out a sower to sow: And it came to pass, as he sowed, some fell by the way side, and the fowls of the air came and devoured it up. And some fell on stony ground, where it had not much earth; and immediately it sprang up, because it had no depth of earth: But when the sun was up, it was scorched; and because it had no root, it withered away. And some fell among thorns, and the thorns grew up, and choked it, and it yielded no fruit. And other fell on good ground, and did yield fruit that sprang up and increased; and brought forth, some thirty, and some sixty, and some an hundred.

"And He said unto them, He that has ears to hear let him hear. And when He was alone, they who were about Him with the Twelve asked of Him the Parable. And He said unto them, Unto you it is given to know the mystery of the Kingdom of God: but unto them who are without, all these things are done in Parables: That seeing they may see, and not perceive; and hearing they may hear, and not understand; lest at any time they should be converted, and their sins should be forgiven them.

"And He said unto them, Know ye not this Parable? And how then will you know all Parables? The sower sows the Word. And these are they by the wayside, where the Word is sown; but when they have heard, Satan comes immediately, and takes away the Word that was sown in their hearts. And these are they likewise which are sown on stony ground; who, when they have heard the Word, immediately receive it with gladness, but have no root in themselves, and so endure but for a time: afterward, when affliction or persecution ariseth for the Word's sake, immediately they are offended. And these are they which are sown among thorns; such as hear the Word, And the cares of this world, and the deceitfulness of riches, and the lusts of other things entering in, choke the Word, and it becomes unfruitful. And these are they which are sown on good ground; such as hear the Word, and receive it, and bring forth fruit, some thirtyfold, some sixty, and some an hundred.

"And He said unto them, Is a candle bought to be put under a bushel, or under a bed? and not to be set on a candlestick? For there is nothing hid, which shall not be manifested; neither was any thing kept secret, but that it should come abroad. If any man have ears to hear, let him hear.

"And He said unto them, Take heed what you hear: with what measure you mete, it shall be measured to you: and unto you who hear shall more be given: For he who has, to him shall be given: and he who has not, from him shall be taken even that which he has" (Mk. 4:3-25).

(4:3) HEARKEN. Jesus instructed the people to listen. The word used is *akouete,* which means literally *"be listening."* It was commanded of the people that they should listen, but it was done with kindness, humility, and graciousness. He had to get their attention. It seems they were more interested in the healing of the sick and the casting out of devils than they were in the Salvation of their own souls. Jesus wanted to teach them the Divine Truths they needed so desperately.

BEHOLD. The Greek word is *idou,* and means *"to behold, see, lo."* It bids the hearer (or reader) to pay attention to what is being said. Jesus was simply asking them to listen and give attention to His Words.

(4:4) He then tells of the sower going forth to sow seeds. Some fell by the wayside (*hodos* — road). The birds came along and ate up these seeds.

(4:5) Then, some other seeds fell on the rocky ground. It should be noted that the seeds were all of the same kind. It was the condition of the *soil* that was different, and this is what determined the amount and kind of fruit resulting.

The seed that fell among the rocks had very little soil and sprang up quickly, having no real depth. Not having much root, it quickly withered away when the hot sun struck it.

(4:7) Some of the seed fell in the midst of thorns. Growing among the bramble bushes and briers, these tender plants choked. The word used is *sumpnigo,* which means *"to choke utterly, to strangle, suffocate, or to throttle."*

(4:8-9) Some of the seed fell on good ground and it grew — increased and bore fruit — some thirtyfold, some sixtyfold, and some a hundredfold.

(4:10) After the crowd was gone and only those closest to the Lord remained, they began to discuss this Parable. Jesus' Twelve Disciples were there, but it is possible that there were more than the Twelve. Perhaps the larger circle of Disciples — from which the twelve were chosen — were present. There were a number of individuals who were interested and anxious to learn more, and these were the group identified as "His Disciples and Followers."

(4:11-12) THE MYSTERY. The Greek word is *musterion,* and it is from this word that we get our word *"mystery."* As it is used in Scripture, it has reference to the secret counsels of God which are hidden from the ungodly, but which are accepted by truth-seekers as they are revealed to them. A mystery has nothing to do with difficulty of interpretation. However, these mysteries are impossible to interpret until their meaning is revealed — at which time they become obvious.

The Disciples had been taught and introduced to spiritual matters by Jesus, and they could understand spiritual Truths. Much of the essence of the Kingdom of God was being revealed to them, and they were gradually coming into a clearer understanding of Divine Truths. It was *"given"* to them to know these things.

TO THEM THAT ARE WITHOUT. This means those who are *"outside our circle."* This obviously has reference to the Scribes and Pharisees and others with hardened hearts. Spiritual matters were shut out from these because of the hostility of their attitudes and minds. They refused to grasp the spiritual implications conveyed by Jesus, especially when revealed by way of Parables.

There was a purpose in Jesus' use of Parables. It was in order that these blind and hostile critics should not understand. The Pharisees were desirous of proving that Jesus was in league with Satan. They didn't *want* to know the Truth and, by rejecting it, they were in a sense blinding *themselves*. Parables were constructed in such a way that they confused those rejecting truth, while enlightening those willing to accept it. As Pharaoh's heart was hardened when he refused to respond to God (working through Moses), so the Scribes and Pharisees hardened their hearts when they rejected the Message delivered by Jesus.

Jesus went on to say that they should not perceive lest they be converted and forgiven. This is not intended to suggest predestination. The matter of being converted refers to one reversing his position — in free will — from that previously held. The Pharisees *willfully* rejected Jesus with blasphemous accusations.

In their hostile rejection of the Lord and their deliberate blindness to Divine Truth, they continued to be hardened as more was expounded. It only demonstrates that the Scribes and Pharisees were in league with Satan and they had no interest in Truth. Millions today are also blinding themselves as they deliberately reject the teachings of our Lord.

(4:13) Even though the Disciples had been initiated into the mysteries of the Kingdom of God, they did not fully understand this Parable. The gentle rebuke from Jesus implies that He was somewhat surprised at their dullness.

(4:14-20) Jesus then proceeded to explain the Parable. Of course, the seed mentioned is the Word of God. The seed is of paramount importance.

The sower is the Lord Jesus Christ and His Ministers of the Gospel. The seed that is sown by the wayside (alongside the road) is taken away by the enemy. The word in Hebrew from which we get *"Satan"* means *"adversary."* Satan (the evil one) comes along and takes away the seed that is sown in the hearts of men. The Word that finds lodging in the heart of an individual, and which starts to germinate and grow, is snatched away by Satan before it can mature.

The Word of God can produce dynamic and dramatic results in the life of an individual and bring about a glorious change. God's Word can give a person joy, peace, hope, and security. The Word of God is *the* answer to the problems of mankind — but Satan wants to keep the Word from taking root and producing results.

Satan is the evil one who wants only to destroy. In a parallel Passage in Matthew (13:19), he is called *"the evil one."* The Greek word used is *ho poneros,* and this literally means *"the evil one."* Satan wants to drag everyone down into corruption and filth with him. The parallel Passage in Luke (8:12) calls him *ho diabolos,* from which we get *"the Devil."* In the original Greek this means *"the slanderer or false accuser."* Satan will do anything within his power to steal away the Word of God to keep it from transforming a person's life.

A similar method of interpretation is used concerning the seeds that *"fall on stony ground."* It has to do with soil filled with rocks. This refers to the individual who has a *superficial* exposure to Divine Truth — but who has not allowed the Word to penetrate deeply into his soul and spirit. This seed cannot grow, because the ground is too hard and any resulting roots are extremely shallow.

When we receive the Word, Satan comes along with disappointments, problems, and obstacles, and will cause the individual to be assailed by doubts. These individuals may have received the Word with joy, but it lasts for only a short time. Because of the world's afflictions and persecutions, they become unhappy and resentful and soon all is lost.

The seed falling in the midst of thorns illustrates those who hear the Word of God, but because of cares and anxieties within the world, fail to have this seed mature. The word *"cares"* comes from *merimna,* which derives from a word meaning *"to be drawn in different directions."* In other words — to be distracted.

The word *"cares"* is used in the context of anxiety and suggests worry. The cares and anxieties of the world come, together with the deceitfulness of riches and a lust for earthly pleasures. These choke the Word. The word translated *"lusts"* means *"a craving or passionate desire."* It is easy for the riches of the world to encroach on Christian commitment. Satan makes a bid for everyone and everything he can. He proffers riches and other lures, causing the Word of God to become unfruitful and choked off by worldly cares and concerns.

Finally, there is the good ground upon which the seed falls, producing fruitful yields. Hallelujah! Each of us hopes that this is the category *we* will be found in as our time on Earth draws to a close.

(4:21) IS A CANDLE BROUGHT? Jesus talks here about a candle, and candles represent light. Of course He is speaking of the Gospel. The Light of the Gospel is never to be hidden. He has been teaching in Parables, and it was not understood by some; but now He is talking plainly to His Disciples. He asked whether a candle is to be put under a bushel; that is, hidden under some opaque object. The way the question is framed, it indicates a negative answer is expected. No, a candle is *not* to be hidden, but rather placed on a stand to *magnify* its illumination.

Jesus is the Light of the world. Any person who has received the Gospel Message is to let the Light of Christ shine out *through* him. He is to proclaim his testimony of Redeeming Grace, and also share the Word of God, which is pure Light.

(4:22) Everything in the Gospel will be brought out. There are things that are mysteries, but they will be manifested and revealed; and anything hidden will eventually be brought into full view. The word translated *"manifested"* is from *phaneroo,* which means *"to make manifest or visible, to make known what has been hidden or unknown."*

(4:23) The word *"if"* is not used as a conditional expression — or for the unfulfilled, hypothetical condition. The point here is that *"since"* the person has *"ears to hear, let him hear."* It is easy for people to hear *words* — while completely ignoring the import of the thoughts they're imparting. We are exhorted to take heed to *how* we hear.

(4:24-25) Jesus said *"keep a watchful eye on what you are hearing."* He then goes on to imply that a reward will be received in proportion to the virtue, the knowledge acquired, and the intensity of the study of the subject. If a person really commits himself to something, thinking about it and seeking to understand, he will grow in understanding and knowledge. If he neglects the seed, it will be destroyed.

How important it is that Preachers proclaim the *Truth* of God. It is tragic that so many today are taught disbelief in the supernatural manifestations of God — that God does not heal and that the miracles of New Testament days are no longer applicable. A person should seek out a Church where he can *hear* the Word of God proclaimed in truth and power. The Word of God needs to be studied seriously and in depth. It is the Word of God that keeps us physically, spiritually, mentally, and financially strong in every area of day-to-day living.

Acquiring a True knowledge of God's Word is vitally important. Here are several practical suggestions for learning and understanding the Word of God:

1. Seek to improve your understanding of the language you speak, and in which your Bible is printed. If your language is English — try to learn English better.

2. Give the *literal* meaning of words to the language of the Bible — just as you would for any other book you might read. Don't try to spiritualize away the basic statements within Scripture. Chances are, they mean *exactly* what they say.

3. Learn the Bible terminology, manners, and customs, as related to the people in the place and time in which the Bible was written.

4. Acquaint yourself with the geography of Bible lands. When a Preacher says *"from Dan to Beersheba,"* do you know that Dan was one of the northernmost cities while Beersheba was one of the southernmost?

5. Develop a general knowledge of the history of the Bible; its peoples and kingdoms. Seek to understand what general historical events were occurring at the same times.

6. Acquire a general knowledge of the Plan of God throughout the Bible. God will ultimately defeat Satan and restore man's dominion on this Earth. He will rid the Earth of all rebellion and establish His Eternal Kingdom.

7. Recognize the different classes of people dealt with in the Bible: the Israelites, the Gentiles (the nations), and the Church (Christians).

8. You should keep in mind the historical background for each Book and the circumstances under which it was written. For instance, much of Psalms was written by David, King of Israel, about one thousand years before Christ, while he was a fugitive in the wilderness round about Jerusalem.

9. Do not try to change the literal meaning of Scripture when it is *intended* to be literal. There are some statements and Passages intended to be symbolic, but not *everything* is meant to be symbolic, figurative, mystical, ethereal, or spiritual. Even when the basic meaning is *not* literal, there are almost always practical applications. When Jesus said we are the salt of the Earth, He did not mean we are literally *salt*. He was comparing salt — as a preservative — to the Saints of God who are a factor in preserving this Earth and maintaining it. Salt keeps some items from rotting or spoiling, and Christians serve a similar role in the world.

10. You should obtain a complete concordance of the Bible. It can be extremely helpful in several ways — especially in finding reference Scriptures, and in defining the true, basic meanings of words in

confusing Passages. Better concordances have a section giving the meanings and derivations of all words used in Scripture.

11. Be intelligent and fair with the Bible as you study it. Do not seek to *"disprove"* it, but seek to be open to its contents and to view it in continuity, just as you would with any scholarly book. When you do, you will find that apparent *"contradictions"* vanish as God's true meanings suddenly leap out at you from the pages.

12. You must settle in your mind for once and for all that the Bible does *not* contradict itself. All Scripture can be harmonized and understood once we know enough about it. Those who try to discredit the Bible do so from a very shallow Scriptural base, and with absolutely no spiritual motivation. Just as Jesus spoke in Parables *"lest they understand and be converted,"* the Bible is not designed by God for superficial reading by the skeptic. Becoming attuned to God's Scriptural Revelations requires *faithful,* prayerful reading. Only then will the venerable language begin to speak out to you with some of God's freshest concepts. As you faithfully and prayerfully immerse yourself in the Bible, the Spirit of God will guide you in understanding *His* Revelations of the Truth.

The Word of God is of vital importance. It is the seed that can produce great fruit in our lives. Study it. Learn it. Meditate upon it. Then apply it to your life.

THE PARABLE OF THE SEED GROWING BY ITSELF

"And He said, So is the Kingdom of God, as if a man should cast seed into the ground; And should sleep, and rise night and day, and the seed should spring and grow up, he knows not how. For the Earth brings forth fruit of herself; first the blade, then the ear, after the full corn in the ear. But when the fruit is brought forth, immediately he putts in the sickle, because the harvest is come" (Mk. 4:26-29).

(4:26-27) At first glance this Parable may not seem very significant. Jesus is telling His Disciples how the Gospel, when presented, will take root and grow despite anything Satan can do.

There is power in the Word of God. It is felt by some expositors that reference is made here to the Disciples as the fertile ground — where the Lord's first seeds were growing. They were the rich first-fruits of the Lord's Ministry. They were the first of all to hear — and heed — the Gospel. The seed had been sown in their lives — and on that soil there was a promise of much fruit to be produced in the future.

There is a sense of mystery in the planting of a seed, and then watching it grow up out of the ground. Scripture indicates that throughout the routine, monotonous drudgery of life — seeds once sown *will* spring up and grow, and one scarcely understands how. The greatest theologians — the greatest minds — may not be able to explain it, but when the Gospel is presented, God's Word will not return void. Satan may oppose it, but still it will produce. As God's Word goes forth, it will touch millions of lives, and it will grow endlessly.

The Fruit of the Gospel will serve His Purpose despite anything and everything the Devil may do to halt the ongoing movement. God *will* have a people that will follow Him, serve Him, and ultimately reign with Him.

Scripture states that it is beyond man's limited mental abilities to fully comprehend the dynamics of the process — but lives are transformed by God's Word — and fruit is born.

(4:28-29) BRINGS FORTH FRUIT OF HERSELF. The word *automate* is translated *"of herself."* It is made up of *autos "self,"* and *memaa, "to desire eagerly."* The total meaning of the word is, *"self-moved, spontaneously, without external aid, and even beyond external control."* From this word we get our word *"automatic."* The Earth brings forth fruit in just this way. The soil, the weather, cultivation — all these enter in. But it is the secret growth element within the seed itself that advances and develops it from one stage to the next.

Just as in the law and order of nature, there is a progression in the order of Grace within the Kingdom of God. It is God's Word that produces fruit within the *spiritual* segment of the world's population.

WHEN THE FRUIT IS BROUGHT FORTH. The word used is *paradidomi,* which means to *"give over, deliver up, to yield up."* It means that the time of harvest has come, and it goes on to say that the sickle is put in and the harvesting done.

We are living during the harvest time right now. The Word is going out by many means — radio, television, churches, missionaries, pastors, preachers, Bible schools, literature, and through personal witnessing. The seed has been sown and results are being produced. The grain is heavy in the head.

THE PARABLE OF THE MUSTARD SEED

"And He said, Whereunto shall we liken the Kingdom of God? or with what comparison shall we compare it? It is like a grain of mustard seed, which, when it is sown in the earth, is less than all the seeds that be in the earth: But when it is sown it grows up and becomes greater than all herbs, and shoots out great branches, so that the fowls of the air may lodge under the shadow of it" (Mk. 4:30-32).

Jesus asks to what He should liken the Kingdom of God. The verb used for *"liken"* is *homoioo,* which means *"to liken, to compare."* Next,

He asks what comparison could be set forth. Then He says, it is like a grain of mustard seed. The mustard seed is a very small seed, but it grows into a large herb. This is not the small plant some of us are familiar with. There are sources that indicate that there were mustard plants in Israel that grew from six to nine feet and some even higher. They had branches an inch or more in thickness with a wood-like quality. This then was an extremely impressive plant which grew from a very small seed.

The Kingdom of God expands with the simple disclosure of the Gospel (the seed) — to affect the lives of *millions* of people. These swell into a great army that will eventually rule and reign in the Kingdom of God. Despite all the persecutions over the centuries — the attempts of the Roman Caesars to destroy Christianity, the slaughter of thousands of Christians over the years — the Kingdom of God has grown and spread. And the citizens of that Kingdom will reign and rule with the Lord Jesus forever!

OTHER PARABLES

"And with many such Parables spoke He the Word unto them, as they were able to hear it. But without a Parable spoke He not unto them: and when they were alone, He expounded all things to His Disciples" (Mk. 4:33-34).

The word translated *"to hear"* (*akouo*) refers to more than the act of hearing. It basically means this, but it also can express the idea of *understanding*. His Parables were employed to clarify basic principles so they might better understand. Jesus spoke many Parables unto His Disciples and then discussed and explained a wide variety of subjects.

The word *epiluo* is translated *"He expounded."* The basic word *luo* means *"to unloose."* The prefix is the preposition *epi*, and this forms a composite word meaning *"to give additional loosening."* It carries the idea of explaining, making plain, clarifying of the Word of God — even to the point of revelation. He was giving this to His Disciples. It was private, unique, and personal relationship that existed between them. These were not ordinary listeners, but *Disciples,* who were open and anxious to learn. We are also His Disciples, and all this is for our understanding and edification, too.

JESUS STILLS THE STORM

"And the same day, when the evening was come, He said unto them, Let us pass over unto the other side. And when they had sent away the multitude, they took Him even as He was in the ship. And there were also with Him other little ships. And there arose a great

storm of wind, and the waves beat into the ship, so that it was now full. And He was in the hinder part of the ship, asleep on a pillow: and they awake Him, and say unto Him, Master, carest Thou not that we perish? And He arose, and rebuked the wind, and said unto the sea, Peace, be still. And the wind ceased, and there was a great calm. And He said unto them, Why are you so fearful? How is it that ye have no Faith? And they feared exceedingly, and said one to another, What manner of Man is this, that even the wind and the sea obey Him?" (Mk. 4:35-41).

(4:35) THE SAME DAY. It was the same day that the blasphemous accusation had been made against Jesus by the Scribes and Pharisees. It was also the same day on which His mother and brothers had visited Him and tried to take Him home. This was the day when He had left the crowded house by the seashore, and the people had followed Him while He had taught. He had preached, taught, and performed miracles all day.

Now Jesus and His Disciples were on the western shore of the Sea of Galilee. It is a beautiful and refreshing spot. It was not far from Capernaum and relatively close to the place where He fed the 5,000 with the five loaves and two fishes. Apparently He and His Disciples felt they should go over to the eastern shore of the sea where they could rest after a full and exhausting day.

(4:36) THEY TOOK HIM. The word used is *paralambano*. The main word, a verb, *lambano,* means *"to take."* The prefix is a preposition that means *"alongside."* It is the same word that was used by the Angel when he spoke to Joseph and told him to take the young child Jesus, and His mother, and flee to Egypt (Mat. 2:13). Joseph was to *take* the young child and His mother *"alongside,"* or under his protection and care. Here the Disciples took the exhausted Messiah under *their* care. They went into a boat, which was their normal vehicle, many of them being fishermen. The word for boat here is *ploion,* referring to a larger ship, not just a rowboat. So, after they had dismissed the crowd, the Disciples took Jesus under their care, transporting Him to the other side.

(4:37) THERE AROSE A GREAT STORM. Storms can come up suddenly on the Sea of Galilee. It has an elevation of about 682 feet *below* the Mediterranean Sea. Some suggest that a storm fell suddenly from Mount Hermon down into the Jordan Valley. They explain that the hot air at this depth draws the storm with sudden power. This was not a single gust or a strong, steady wind; but an extremely violent storm breaking forth with black thunder clouds and violent gusts. The Greek word used is that of a furious storm, or even a hurricane. This word has also been used of a cyclone revolving from below upwards, in some classic Greek writings. So, it was undoubtedly a storm of violent intensity.

It was Satan who brought this storm about. Events like hurricanes, cyclones, typhoons, and floods are not *"acts of God"* as the media likes to describe them. Satan is the god of this world and the prince of the powers of the air. (Later we will see Jesus rebuke this storm and it will quiet immediately. He would not rebuke anything authored by God.) There is no indication that Jesus ever raised or created a storm. He is the one who *calms* storms and quiets the maelstroms of life.

THE WAVES BEAT INTO THE SHIP. The verb used is *epiballo,* which means *"to throw out."* The waves were violently crashing against the boat. Under the onslaught of the storm, the boat was rapidly filling with water to where it threatened to sink.

SO THAT IT WAS NOW FULL. The word used here is *gemizo,* which means *"to fill full."* It states in this Passage that a great windstorm of hurricane proportions had arisen, and the waves had beaten upon the boat until it was almost filled.

(4:38) Jesus was in the hinder part of the boat. This is from the word *prumna,* the stern or after part of the ship. Jesus was there asleep on *"a pillow."* The word *"pillow"* is from the Greek word *proskephalaion,* and means *"that toward which one puts his head."* It was not a soft luxurious pillow or cushion as we might picture it. Instead, it was the leather cushion of the helmsman, or possibly the low bench on which he sat — and where the captain could rest his head. Jesus had endured a long and arduous day and Luke states that He *"fell asleep."*

MASTER, CAREST THOU NOT THAT WE PERISH? Someone has pointed out that Jesus suggested that they go down to the sea, not to drown — but to pass over to the other side. He was tired and resting, but the Disciples were afraid and anxious. They came to Him, calling Him Master. In the Greek Text this is rendered *didaskale,* which means *"Teacher,"* but they may have addressed Him in Hebrew as Rabboni.

They were calling Him, saying, *"Oh, Teacher, don't You care that we are perishing?"*

They were, in effect, *rebuking* the Lord Jesus because He was sleeping through the storm that threatened them. This is an excellent picture of humanity. Many times individuals are caught by the storms of life and see the waves beating about them. They become discouraged, heartbroken, and depressed. It seems that the devils of darkness scream and attack us whenever possible. As we start the journey of Faith with Jesus toward the Throne of the Kingdom, it is not a journey in which we have to be capsized and drowned beneath the waves of oppression, discouragement, worry, and darkness. There may be difficulties that seem insurmountable, but God is eternally alive and alert.

One may look around at his circumstances and become convinced that there is no hope. The storms may beat, the winds may roll, and the boat may be almost full. While it may appear to be sinking, these are the times to trust in God. Just as suddenly as Jesus quelled the storm, He will subdue and utterly remove our individual storms, if only we will ride them out and maintain our trust in Him. While no one goes through life without *running into* an occasional storm, we will survive them all because we are *His* Children. Praise ye the Lord!

(4:39) PEACE, BE STILL. The word translated *"peace"* is *siopao*. It means to be silent, still, hushed, calm. *"Be still"* is from *phimoo,* which is the word meaning to close the mouth with a muzzle — as used in the muzzling of an ox. Jesus commanded the storm to be calm and to remain so. He can also calm *our* storms with His, *"Peace, be still."*

This is what He is saying to us today: *"Why are you fearful? Why do you tremble? Why is it that you have no Faith? Believe God. Believe Me. Hold My Hand. I am going to bring you through. We are going to make it."*

When Jesus gave His command, *"Peace be still,"* the wind ceased. The verb is *kopazo,* which means *"to cease raging, to cease from violence."* Jesus rebuked the wind and told the sea to be calm — to hush and stay that way. The wind ceased its raging, and there was a great calm.

(4:40) Jesus asked the Disciples why they were fearful. Literally, He said, *"How is it possible?"* The Creator and the Sustainer of the universe was in the boat with them. They had accepted Him as the Messiah — but failed to recognize the full implications of His Power. He asked them why they were timid, fearful, and lacking in Faith.

This is the question He asks us today. *"Why do you fear and tremble? Why do you have no Faith? Believe Me and trust Me,"* He is saying. He will carry us through, *if only we will have Faith.*

(4:41) It here states that the Disciples *"feared a great fear."* They said: Who is this Person? He is one Who can command the very wind and the waves, drive out demons, heal diseases, and speak mysteries and Parables. They wondered!

Ah, but this was *Jesus,* the very Son of God.

Chapter 5

Jesus Heals A Demon-Possessed Man

SUBJECT   **PAGE**

A LITTLE GIRL AND A WOMAN ARE HEALED 78

CHAPTER 5

JESUS HEALS A DEMON-POSSESSED MAN

"And they came over unto the other side of the sea, into the country of the Gadarenes. And when He was come out of the ship, immediately there met Him out of the tombs a man with an unclean spirit, Who had his dwelling among the tombs; and no man could bind him, no, not with chains: Because that he had been often bound with fetters and chains, and the chains had been plucked asunder by him, and the fetters broken in pieces: neither could any man tame him. And always, night and day, he was in the mountains, and in the tombs, crying and cutting himself with stones. But when he saw Jesus afar off, he ran and worshipped him, And cried with a lout voice, and said, What have I to do with You, Jesus, Thou Son of the Most High God? I adjure Thee by God, that You torment me not. For He said unto him, Come out of the man, you unclean spirit. And He asked him, What is your name? And he answered, saying, My name is Legion: for we are many. And he besought Him much that He would not send them away out of the country. Now there was there near unto the mountains a great herd of swine feeding. And all the devils besought Him, saying, Send us into the swine, that we may enter into them.

"And forthwith Jesus gave them leave. And the unclean spirits went out, and entered into the swine: and the herd ran violently down a steep place into the sea, (they were about two thousand;) and were choked in the sea. And they who fed the swine fled, and told it in the city, and in the country. And they went out to see what it was that was done. And they come to Jesus, and see him who was possessed with the devil, and had the legion, sitting, and clothed, and in his right mind: and they were afraid.

"And they who saw it told them how it befell to him who was possessed with the devil, and also concerning the swine. And they began to pray Him to depart out of their coasts. And when He was come into the ship, he who had been possessed with the devil prayed Him that he might be with Him. Howbeit Jesus suffered him not, but said unto him, God home to your friends, and tell them how great things the Lord has done for you, and has had compassion on you. And he departed, and began to publish in Decapolis how great things Jesus had done for him: and all men did marvel" (Mk. 5:1-20).

(5:1) Jesus and His Disciples *"came to the other side of the sea"* — to the southeastern shore of the Sea of Galilee. It was called the country of the Gadarenes. There was a small village there called Gerasa in the area of Gadara. Gadara was fairly well known and the inhabitants were referred to as Gadarenes.

(5:2-5) When they arrived, they encountered a man in a miserable and pathetic condition. Mark gives a graphic description of this man. Matthew and Luke also mention this incident, but Matthew refers to *two* men in describing the incident; which isn't surprising because this was apparently the location where uncontrollable *"lunatics"* were isolated. Mark confines his account to the *"inmate"* most dramatically bound by Satan.

He lived among the tombs, which were considered unclean places because of the corpses and bones throughout the area. This man had come from the city where perhaps he had been a man of means and position who had lapsed into sin, resulting in demonic possession. He was restricted to the area about the tombs, which were carved from the rocks and caves.

The tombs no doubt afforded him shelter — but they were also a filthy environment. Rotting flesh was usually present with its attendant nauseating odor. Satan always brings men down into evil and filth, dirt and degradation, if they follow him. Satan is here only to steal, kill, and destroy.

This man had often been bound with fetters and chains. The word translated *"fetters"* is *pede,* which refers to a fetter, or shackle, for the feet. Individuals under demonic influence often possess superhuman strength, so the fetters did not hold him. The demon-possessed demonstrate superhuman strength today, also.

The demonized man had frequently been bound hand and foot, but he broke the fetters and chains. He could not be restrained or tamed. He cried out, cutting himself with sharp stones. The word translated *"crying"* is from *krazo,* which denotes an inarticulate cry or shriek. This was an ungodly wail, and the people undoubtedly could hear him shrieking in the nearby village.

Because he cut himself with stones, his body was probably covered with scars. It is possible he wore no clothing, his beard filthy, his hair matted and long, and his flesh covered with putrid sores. He was without question a dreadful sight. In our society those with similar demonic afflictions are usually confined to mental hospitals, in padded cells.

(5:6-8) Jesus and His Disciples had just come out of the storm. Jesus had calmed it, thus manifesting His miraculous powers over nature. Now He was about to still the storm in a man's soul.

The man ran toward Jesus. It is possible that his original intent was hostile as he was driven by evil, demonic powers. But as he drew near to Jesus, the overwhelming Power of the Presence of God subdued his controlling demons and they began to shrink back. The word for *"worship"* is *proskuneo,* which means to prostrate one's self — to fall down upon one's knees in reverence. This pitiful creature bent his knee to the Son of God. It may well be, as the demons were bound within him, that the man himself cried out for help. This poor child of Hell, lost and demon-possessed, was able to fall down at Jesus' Feet and worship Him once the demons were stilled.

Our response to the Presence of God should be one of worship. People *need* to worship God in Church. Hindrances to a free spirit of worship should be cast out from our Churches. There is great blessing for the spirit and therapy for the soul when one is truly allowed to worship the Lord. As more and more Churches return to *biblically* oriented worship, we are again seeing individuals being freed from bondage and coming to worship the Lord in Spirit and in Truth. Every person and Church should question whether they *truly* worship God.

As this man knelt and worshipped the Lord, he spoke out saying, *"What is there in common between me and You?"*

Then the demons asked that they be not tormented. The word for torment is *basanizo*. This word refers to the testing of metals by stressing them — a *"torture test."* The demons were trying to put Jesus under oath to prevent His troubling them. They knew He was the Son of the Most High God. The main demon possessing the man was the one crying out as spokesman for them all.

Jesus repeatedly ordered the demons out — and, as a consequence, the demon made an outcry. The very Presence of Jesus tormented the demons. We are not supposed to be tormented by demons or to allow them to gain control over us. Rather, we are to exercise authority over *them* in the Name of Jesus.

Demons fear the Power of God and the Blood of Jesus. We do *not* have to be defeated by the enemy. We can walk in victory. Satan will fight, the demonic forces will contest, but we can stand our ground firmly.

In this particular case — according to the original expression — Jesus *continued* to order the demons to come out of the man. They didn't want to come out; they didn't want to vacate the body they had gained. Ultimately, though, the demonic forces had to flee.

Jesus asked the demon (literally, *"kept on asking him"*) what his name was. The demon responded by saying his name was *"Legion."* A Roman legion was a common sight in this region and was an emblem of irresistible power. Legions were combined to form a larger, untied fighting force. Apparently not just a single demon, but rather a large number of them, had taken up residence in this man's body.

Demons are apparently disembodied spirits and feel compelled to inhabit a body. They may inhabit a human or an animal. Many Bible scholars feel that demon spirits once had bodies. It is felt that they may well have been a pre-Adamic race of beings created by God before Adam and Eve. They fell, way back in the aeons of time past, when Lucifer was God's anointed Cherub and walked the Earth in Righteousness and purity, governing the Earth Righteously. At first there was no sin found in him, but then Lucifer fell. When he did, the Earth became, as described in Genesis, void and without form.

When God creates something, He always does it perfectly and completely. He doesn't create anything void and without from. Adam and Eve — as they were created — were told to replenish the Earth, so obviously it had been occupied before. Apparently when Adam and Eve fell, it was the *second* fall to affect the Earth. We believe the Earth to be very old, for it is stated that *"in the beginning God created the Heaven and Earth"* (Gen. 1:1). All this happened before the revolution in Heaven and before Lucifer fell and became Satan, the incarnation of evil.

Demonic forces and spirits are completely evil — and they are completely *real*. They were not *created* evil, but *became* evil at some point in time. They are *fallen* creatures and their lifelong situation is a terrible one. Demons inhabit the world by the millions. We are, indeed, engaged in constant spiritual warfare (Eph. 6:12).

(5:10) The demons begged Jesus not to send them away. The verb used is a very strong expression which means, *"I beg of You, please."* It comes from the word *parakaleo*. The tense in which it is written is imperfect; it means, *"he persisted in pleading with Him."*

The demon called itself Legion and, as it made its request, it spoke on behalf of all the other demons occupying the possessed man. The demons did not want to be *"sent out of the country."* There are many schools of thought as to what is meant by this reference to *"sending them out of the country."* One viewpoint is that this was the part of the universe where they lived and ruled in the aeons while Lucifer ruled the Earth. From this point of view, they would naturally desire to stay on the Earth which they knew.

Another point of view is that the countryside where this incident occurred, around Decapolis, was inhabited by an apostate group of Jews. These people did not believe in God, nor did they obey Him or His Laws as delivered by Moses. Therefore, these demonic spirits supposedly loved the atmosphere of the area because, as some Bible scholars feel, they would have had more freedom to do as they wished — the Power of God was so little in evidence. Once again, there isn't any real clarification in the Bible and both possibilities carry some merit. It may even be a combination of the two.

There *are* areas in the world which have little evidence of the Power of

God working — they have no free witness of the Lord Jesus Christ. Demon spirits virtually control these areas. Demon spirits have much more freedom where there is little awareness of the Presence of God. Demon spirits, however, also operate where religion is strongly stressed — especially by groups that do not lift up the Lord Jesus Christ. In fact, even where there is some emphasis on our Lord Jesus, there is still strong effort by Satan to deny the supernatural Power of God.

Spiritual forces are very much at work in religious circles and "religious spirits" are certainly much in evidence. There are areas where there is severe demonic oppression hindering the Work of the Gospel. Satan works in subtle ways to influence people, even in the religious community.

(5:11-12) The demons *"besought"* (*parakaleo*) Jesus — without much clarification of detail — to send them into the swine. The demon spirits wanted to indwell *some* type of physical body. If they couldn't enter a man, woman, or child, they would settle for swine.

(5:13) Jesus simply gave them permission to enter the swine.

RAN VIOLENTLY. The Greek word is *hormao*, which means *"to set in rapid motion, to incite, to urge on, to start forward impetuously, or to rush."* As the demons entered the swine, they rushed down the steep bank into the sea and were *"choked."* The word is *epnigo* and was sometimes used for drowning.

Some might question the justice of this since it involved the loss of property for someone uninvolved in the situation. It should be pointed out, however, that Jesus did not *order* the demons into the swine; He simply *allowed* the entrance. There are many things which are permitted in the world, such as wars, which result in great suffering and calamity. God does not originate these events, but *permits* them. He is not the author of problems or of sin.

War, drunkenness, and all of man's follies in this world continue — despite the fact that God does not initiate them. There are demonic forces at work which are allowed to function and operate despite Christ's victory over them on the Cross. Eventually, in God's timetable, all evil forces will be cast into the Lake of Fire.

Another factor that should be noted in reference to the drowning of the swine is that they were considered an unclean animal under the Mosaic Law. The Jewish people were specifically forbidden by God to have anything to do with swine. They were commanded not to eat them, nor keep them as pets. They were simply unclean animals, and the Hebrews were to avoid them.

The large herd of swine, numbering two thousand, plunged one after another into the sea and drowned.

(5:14-15) AND THEY THAT FED THE SWINE FLED. One can

well imagine that the swineherders were frightened. The Bible says they *"fled."* The word used is *pheugo,* which means *"to flee away, to seek safety in flight."* It is apparent that they were filled with terror at what had happened, and the loss of their herds.

They fled from the scene and reported the news to the nearby cities and farms. The people swarmed out to the scene upon hearing it. They had heard about Jesus, of His healings, and of His deliverance powers. Therefore, the owners of the swine herds rushed out to investigate, accompanied by the usual assortment of onlookers and curiosity seekers.

The people came to Jesus to SEE HIM WHO WAS POSSESSED WITH THE DEVIL. The word *theoreo* is translated *"see,"* and it means *"to view attentively, to survey, to consider, to ascertain with keen interest."* They conducted a scrutinizing, critical, searching investigation. They saw the man who had been demon-possessed. They had heard his screams at night and had warned their children against straying near him. Undoubtedly they had stared from afar at this individual with the wild, glaring eyes and the demoniac shriek. And now here they were standing right next to him, and he appeared as sane as they were. Obviously, something dramatic had taken place.

The word *sophroneo* means to *"be of sound mind, to exercise self-control, to curb one's passions."* This wild man was now a quiet, self-possessed individual, free of demonic control and influence. People who are not controlled by Christ are easily *influenced* by demons and controlled *by* them to one degree or another. If he is not careful, any individual can open opportunities in his or her life for demonic forces to influence them.

(5:16-17) TOLD THEM. The verb is *diegeomai.* This word means *"to lead or carry a narration or story through to the end; that is, relate in full."* The swineherdmen gave a complete and full account to their employers. They wanted to ensure that they wouldn't be held responsible for events.

The people in this area cared more for their hogs and loss of property than they did for the healing of the demoniac, *"and they began to pray Him to depart out of their coasts."* They requested and urged Jesus to leave.

The word translated request is *erxanto,* and it indicates that Jesus did not need much pressure or urging to do as they wished. Apparently He withdrew at the first suggestion that He wasn't welcome. God does not stay where He is unwanted, and the Spirit of God never forces the things of God onto those who do not desire them. The sad fact is, the people placed more value on a herd of pigs than they did on the souls of men. Even today, many routinely choose the company of filth and trash in preference to the companionship of God.

(5:18) AND WHEN HE WAS COME INTO THE SHIP. It was while

our Lord was stepping aboard the boat that the delivered man begged to be allowed to accompany Him. This man wanted to be with Jesus who had set him free. Perhaps there was also fear in his heart that the demons might try to come back or the people would turn against him. He stands out in contrast to the others who did not want to have Jesus or His influence on their lives. It is the same today, for there are many who deliberately shun the things of God. This man, having experienced the Power of God and having been delivered, wanted to accompany Jesus and (no doubt) become His Disciple.

(5:19) But Jesus told the transformed man, *"GO HOME TO YOUR FRIENDS."* Jesus told him to go home to his *"own"* people. He was to testify to his flesh and blood — his own family.

The word *apaggello* is translated *"tell,"* and it means to *"bring back tidings."* His home was in the area of Decapolis, the name given to the collection of ten small cities. It was an evil place, and the Lord obviously wanted the man to tell the people of this sinful area what He had done. This man had been cured. He was changed, transformed; the transformation being a completed work within itself. He need have no fear — victory had been won. His cure would be permanent.

It also states that Jesus *"HAD COMPASSION."* The verb used is *eleeo,* and it means *"to feel sympathy with the misery of another."* It has special emphasis in implying sympathy resulting in action — rather than just in words. Jesus felt sympathy and compassion for this man.

After his healing, Jesus told the man to go home and tell his people about it. There were other times when our Lord had *forbidden* those healed to announce their miraculous cures. This was due to the wild excitement and enthusiasm that might have resulted from those situations. Here there was no such danger. To the contrary, the people had begged Jesus to leave, even though they desperately needed to hear the Message concerning the Lord.

Jesus' orders to individuals varied, depending upon circumstances and situations. We should not make general rules to be applied to every situation. There are specific orders and directions for each set of circumstances. Here He wanted the man to remain and recount his experience as a continuing reminder to the people of what they had rejected.

(5:20) This man departed and *"HE BEGAN TO PUBLISH IN DECAPOLIS"* what had happened. The word for publish is *kerusso,* and it means to make *"a public proclamation."* In some contexts, this word is also translated *"preach."* He went to ten cities and gave his marvelous testimony.

The former maniac was whole. Over the years since then, millions of others have been set free from drunkenness, prostitution, drug addiction, gambling, and the oppressive influence of demons.

Jesus sets the captives free! The people of this area marveled, and then rejected Him. We have cause for carefree rejoicing when we see individuals liberated and transformed by Divine Grace.

A LITTLE GIRL AND A WOMAN ARE HEALED

"And when Jesus was passed over again by ship unto the other side, much people gathered unto Him: and He was near unto the sea. And, behold, there cometh one of the rulers of the Synagogue, Jairus by name; and when he saw Him, he fell at His Feet, And besought Him greatly, saying, My little daughter lies at the point of death: I pray You, come and lay Your Hands on her that she may be healed; and she shall live.

"And Jesus went with him; and much people followed Him and thronged Him. And a certain woman, which had an issue of blood twelve years, And had suffered many things of many physicians, and had spent all that she had, and was nothing bettered, but rather grew worse, When she had heard of Jesus, came in the press behind, and touched His garment. For she said, If I may touch but His clothes, I shall be whole.

"And straightway the fountain of her blood was dried up; and she felt in her body that she was healed of that plague. And Jesus, immediately knowing in Himself that virtue had gone out of Him, turned about in the press, and said, Who touched My clothes? And His Disciples said unto Him, You see the multitude thronging You, and You say, Who touched Me? And He looked round about to see her who had done this thing.

"But the woman fearing and trembling, knowing what was done in her, came and fell down before Him, and told Him all the truth. And He said unto her, Daughter, your Faith has made you whole; go in peace, and be whole of your plague.

"While He yet spoke, there came from the ruler of the Synagogue's house certain which said, Your daughter is dead: why troublest thou the Master any further? As soon as Jesus heard the word that was spoken, He said unto the ruler of the Synagogue, Be not afraid, only believe. And He suffered no man to follow Him, save Peter, and James, and John the brother of James. And He came to the house of the ruler of the Synagogue, and seeing the tumult, and them who wept and wailed greatly. And when He was come in, He said unto them, Why do you make this ado, and weep? The damsel is not dead, but sleeps.

"And they laughed him to scorn. But when He had put them all

out, He took the father and the mother of the damsel, and them who were with Him, and entered in where the damsel was lying. And He took the damsel by the hand, and said unto her, Talitha cumi; which is, being interpreted, Damsel, I say unto you, arise. And straightway the damsel arose, and walked; for she was of the age of twelve years.

"And they were astonished with a great astonishment. And He charged them straitly that no man should know it; and commanded that something should be given her to eat" (Mk. 5:21-43).

(5:21) Jesus entered His boat and passed over again to the other side and a great crowd gathered about Him. It is translated *"unto Him"* but the word is *epi,* and in this context and construction means *"after Him."* The people were drawn irresistibly to Jesus. They wanted to see Him and to receive help from Him.

HE WAS NEAR UNTO THE SEA. The word used is *para,* which means alongside the sea. He was at the seashore.

(5:22-23) THERE COMETH ONE OF THE RULERS OF THE SYNAGOGUE. A Synagogue could have a number of rulers (Acts 13:14-15) having various duties which involved selecting the readers and teachers of the Synagogue and also ensuring that customs were maintained according to tradition. Jairus was one of the rulers. This is a Hebrew name which means *"whom Jehovah enlightens."* He fell at Jesus' Feet and *"besought Him greatly."* The word translated *"besought"* here is *parakaleo.* It means, *"I beg of You, please."*

HIS DAUGHTER WAS AT THE POINT OF DEATH. The Greek expression used is *eschatos echei.* The first word means *"lastly."* The thought is that she was *"in the last gasp,"* at the point of death. He wanted Jesus to heal her. The word translated heal is actually a word that means to save. He was interested in saving her life because she was lying at the point of death. He asked Jesus to come quickly and place His Hands on her so she might live.

(5:24) AND JESUS WENT WITH HIM. The original term means that Jesus *"went off with Him promptly"* and *"much people followed Him."* Literally, they *continued* to follow Him.

The people THRONGED HIM. The verb is *sunthlibo.* It means *"to press together, to press on all sides."* Luke uses a slightly different word which means to press or throng someone almost to the point of suffocation — *sumpnigo.* A huge crowd surrounded Jesus, but He followed this man toward his house. There were thousands about with various needs, but Jesus followed this one man because of his sense of urgency and because of his Faith.

He believed and trusted, and it is Faith that accomplishes great things. God responds to our Faith. He will overlook our weaknesses and shortcomings because love covers a multitude of sins. Jesus followed this man because the man sincerely believed that Jesus could save his daughter from imminent death.

(5:25-26) There was a woman in the crowd who had experienced a flow of blood for twelve years and had *"suffered"* much. The word is *pascho,* and it means to suffer pain. She was *"under"* (*hupo*) many doctors and had suffered at their hands. She had spent everything she had but had only grown worse.

The woman is not identified by name. Her name was not important or noteworthy, and the Scripture simply refers to her as *"a certain woman."* Jairus was a leader of the Synagogue, so he was identified by name. However, it is not just the rich and powerful who receive from God. The poor and unknown have equal access to God's bounty and sometimes are blessed more abundantly.

The fact that she had not received help from doctors is not an indictment of the medical profession. There are often limits to what they can do, while of course at other times they can be very helpful. Good physicians are often laborers for the Lord. Of course, man's abilities, whatever his training, are limited. In ancient times the art of medicine was rudimentary at best and bordering on witchcraft at worst. This woman had suffered much and spent all her resources in seeking help but she had only grown worse.

(5:27-28) SHE HAD HEARD OF JESUS. This woman had heard much concerning Jesus. Some scholars feel she may have been a stranger to the area who had just heard about the Master a few days before.

The definite article, appearing before the name Jesus, marks Him in a particular way. The name Jesus, as we use it in English, is a transliteration of the Hebrew Name Jehoshua (or Yahoshua). In English it should be translated *"Joshua"* and is a name that was very common in Palestine. Very often the definite article is used in conjunction with the Name of Jesus, our Lord, to distinguish Him from the many others of the same name.

It is felt by some scholars that the woman with the issue of blood possibly came from Caesarea Philippi. It is also noted that she was not supposed to touch Jesus. According to Levitical Law (Lev. 15:19-27), a woman with an issue of blood would have been considered unclean. It is not stated exactly what this disease was other than that she had had this issue of blood for twelve years. Some feel she might have had a type of cancer of the blood stream — a form of leukemia. Her difficulty has also been theoretically diagnosed as a female disorder. At any rate, she was a very sick woman.

Having suffered for that length of time, she was probably in poor physical condition and in imminent danger of dying. Without doubt she was desperate to see her problem resolved.

This woman was in the crowd and reasoned that if she could but touch

His garment she might be made whole. The word translated *"I shall be made whole"* is *sozo,* which is used in reference to a person being saved either from physical illness or an evil spiritual state.

Even though it was forbidden by the Law, she was so desperate for help that she reached out in Faith and touched the hem of Jesus' garment in the belief that she would be healed.

As she pushed her way through the crowd, she repeated to herself (or to others — Scripture is silent on this), *"If I can just touch Him, if I can just touch Him, if I can get close enough to touch Him."* In a sense this was a prayer to God that was answered.

It was a large crowd, and according to Luke, the press nearly suffocated Jesus. The deaf wanted to hear and the crippled wanted to walk. This woman, in her weakened condition, was trying frantically to just *touch* Jesus. In spite of the seriousness of her action and the possible consequences of doing something forbidden, Faith drove her on.

(5:29) She confidently touched the hem of His garment, declaring that she would be whole, and STRAIGHTWAY THE FOUNTAIN OF HER BLOOD WAS DRIED UP. The word translated fountain is *pege,* and means spring. The hemorrhagic flow was stopped.

In other words, whatever the cause of her difficulty, she was healed instantly and felt the healing course through her body. She was free of *"that plague."* The word for plague is *mastix,* which means *"a whip or scourge."* This expression was commonly used for distressing bodily diseases and afflictions. Her illness had been like an endless whipping, or a scourging, but suddenly she was healed and in a state of perfect health.

(5:30) IMMEDIATLEY KNOWING IN HIMSELF THAT VIRTUE HAD GONE OUT OF HIM, TURNED HIM ABOUT. The word *"knowing"* is from *epiginosko,* which means a personal knowledge gained by experience. The preposition *epi* (the first part of this compound word) magnifies the basic meaning of this verb (*ginosko* — I know)

The word *"virtue,"* *dunamis* in Greek, is the same word translated as *"power."* It carries the idea of overcoming a resistance or causing a change. Jesus felt that power had drained from Him.

(5:31) WHO TOUCHED MY CLOTHES? Jesus asked the question, *"Who touched Me on My clothes?"* With the tremendous press of the multitude about Him, this appeared to be a ridiculous question. The word translated throng is *sunthlibo,* and Mark used the second part of this word in 3:19 (*thlibo*), which means to *"press hard."* It was used for the pressing of grapes in wine-making and suggests, *"to crush."*

Here Mark uses the compound form of the word and adds the prefix *sun* which implies an even more *concerted* pressure on the part of the people. The crowd was even more determined as it pressed upon Jesus.

It was therefore a surprise to the Disciples that Jesus would be aware of the touch of one individual and ask who had touched His clothes.

It was the woman's *Faith* that had made contact with Jesus' Spirit as her great need was met. The Disciples couldn't understand this great sensitivity of the Lord. They weren't aware of the tremendous drain and pressure on Him from both the healings and the great compassion wracking His Heart. There was a tremendous expenditure of energy throughout His Ministry, but there was apparently a *specific* draining of power with the occurrence of healings. At least Scripture documents such as occurring in this specific case.

(5:32) AND HE LOOKED ROUND ABOUT. Jesus looked about for the woman. He ignored the comments of His Disciples and gazed out over the crowd to locate the specific person who had touched Him. There were, no doubt, *many* women in the crush, and all was confusion as they shoved and pushed to reach Him. But the Text suggests there was a dramatic pause as He looked for the *specific* woman. The original expression indicates that it was a woman He was looking for and that He persisted in His effort.

(5:33) The woman was fearful and trembling. She had done that which was forbidden, and she knew what had been done. (The verb indicates a complete and permanent cure.) But she also knew He was looking for her. And since she knew she was healed, she came and confessed.

She gave her testimony. She knew she had disregarded Ceremonial Law and was apprehensive. She fell down before Him and told Him the whole truth. Her condition had been desperate, for no physician could help her. She was on the brink of death. She had desperately *needed* the Divine healing touch and moved forward on Faith to receive it.

(5:34) AND HE SAID TO HER, DAUGHTER. The very first word Jesus expressed was *thugater,* which translates *"daughter"* but refers to a mature woman. His expression was one of great sympathy and delicate expression. Just a moment before, she was *"a certain woman,"* but now she is Jesus' daughter. Those who yesterday were the Devil's nobodies can today be Heaven's somebodies. Praise God!

YOUR FAITH HAS MADE YOU WHOLE. The word used here is *sozo,* and means *"to save."* It is sometimes used for the healing of body, but it is also used for the saving of the soul. It is used in a tense that documents her healing as permanent.

She was told to GO IN PEACE. The preposition used in this expression is *eis,* which literally means *"into."* She was actually told, *"Go into peace."*

The peace referred to here, as some have suggested, is more the idea contained in the Hebrew word *shalom.* It is a beautiful word translated *"peace"* but it speaks of health and wholeness for the body and soul.

Then Jesus said, BE WHOLE OF YOUR PLAGUE. This is given in the form of a command and means *"be continually whole."* It is translated from the word *hugies,* which means to be sound of body. We get our word hygienic from it. The word plague is translated from *mastix,* which means a whip, plague, or calamity, as discussed before.

(5:35) Jesus talked to the woman who had just received life by having been cured of a plague that was a virtual death sentence. She had received Salvation and Heaven in place of her hell. She had been delivered and healed. As Jesus talked to her, the immense crowd watched. You can sense the poignancy of the moment. And at the instant He addressed her, some men came up.

These men were messengers from the house of Jairus. Jairus had not sent them, and he was surprised by their sudden appearance. They declared, YOUR DAUGHTER IS DEAD. The tense in which the message is expressed simply states, *"your daughter died."*

What a stunning impact this must have had on Jairus. He was here beside Jesus because of his daughter's serious illness. But Jesus had stopped for a moment to heal a woman. And now they asked, *"Why troublest thou the Master any further?"* The verb used is *skullo,* and is translated here *"troublest."* It can literally mean "to flay, to vex, to annoy, to distress, to bother, or to worry." The word translated *"Master"* is *didaskalos,* which means *"Teacher."* Jairus had kept close to Jesus during this time. His heart had undoubtedly gone out to the woman in need of healing, yet he must have been anxious and concerned about his dying daughter. Now he was told his daughter was dead. What a cruel blow it must have been.

(5:36) JESUS HEARD. The Greek word is *parakouo.* It means *"to hear alongside"*; or in other words, *"to overhear."* Jesus turned and spoke to Jairus. He used the term which meant to be not afraid. Literally translated it says, *"Stop fearing."*

He told Jairus not to fear anymore, nor to doubt. He commanded him to just believe. Jesus can stop *our* fears. Even death can't stop Him. When it seemed that all hope had gone from Jairus, Jesus simply told him to continue believing.

It is not always easy to believe. There are many obstacles. Sometimes it seems that conditions are impossible and circumstances are beyond reversing. Thus it seemed that day when Jesus said to *"be believing."* These are the times we must stand on the promise of Proverbs 3:5 and *"Trust in the Lord with all your heart, and lean not unto your own understanding."*

(5:37) Jesus now told the crowd and His Disciples to stay where they were. He was going in to where the dead girl lay. Of course, He could have healed her from right where He stood, but He took Peter, James, and John with Him.

These three had become a special inner circle. It was they who were allowed to witness this special miracle. They were being trained along with the other Disciples, but their association with the Lord was more intimate. Perhaps they had a deeper commitment, a little deeper cry in their hearts for Him, or perhaps a greater hunger for the things of God.

The Bible doesn't reveal the reason, but Jesus chose them. Scripture does tell us that if we will draw nigh to *Him*, He will draw nigh to *us*. God will touch those who draw closer to Him, those who have a greater hunger for Him.

(5:38) As Jesus and the Disciples came to the house and entered, they went into a house of mourning.

Coming into the house, Scripture says He *"seeing the tumult."* The word translated *"seeing"* is *theoreo*. It means *"to look on a thing with special interest and purpose, to examine it critically and carefully."*

Jesus saw the tumult (*thorubos*), the noise and uproar of the people who were wailing. There was much weeping and wailing and great confusion throughout the house in response to the death of the little girl. The word translated wail is *alalazo,* and is used to describe the monotonous wailing of hired mourners.

(5:39) Jesus asked them — *"Why all the noise, uproar, and tumultuous wailing?"* He said, *"THE DAMSEL IS NOT DEAD, BUT SLEEPS."* The word for *"damsel"* is *to paidion,* which means *"the little girl."*

Jesus' statement was actually that the child was not to *remain* dead, but was dead in the sense of sleeping. Of course, they didn't understand. Because He *knew* He was going to raise her from the dead, He didn't view death in the way most people do.

Death is the last enemy to be defeated by Christ. There will be a day when death will be universally conquered. Certainly there is severe sorrow at the death of a loved one. But we should not sorrow as those who have no hope. People lose loved ones, and sometimes their grief can be almost unbearable. God wants to help us with that grief. He is touched by the feeling of our infirmities. He knows the sorrows and the heartaches we face.

Those with loved ones who die in Christ are assured they will go to be with Him. As such, we should not be burdened with grief. Rather, we should look on it as their graduation into Glory where we too will someday join them in the mansions above.

Of course grief is infinitely more difficult to bear for those who are not in Christ and who have no hope. We have the blessed hope. There *is* eternal life. Life on this Earth is really very short, but when it is terminated it is still just the beginning. We shall see our Christian loved ones again in the portals of Glory where we live with them forever and forever.

Jesus spoke of the little girl as being asleep. In death the physical body does sleep. It goes back to dust, awaiting the Resurrection. The soul and spirit live on, however. They live with the Lord — and our loved ones are in Heaven at this very moment — in the conscious Presence of Christ. They are in the Presence of God and His Holy Angels, so we can praise God and declare, Glory to God! There *is* going to be a reunion. The dead in Christ *will* rise first, and those of us who are alive and remain shall be caught up together with them in the clouds. With this we can comfort one another (I Thess. 4:16-17).

(5:40) The people knew the little girl had died, and when Jesus said that she was only sleeping, they laughed and mocked Him. The expression THEY LAUGHED HIM TO SCORN is from *kategelao,* which means *"to deride, to jeer at."* They laughed and ridiculed Jesus for speaking as a fool.

BUT WHEN HE HAD PUT THEM ALL OUT. The word used is *ekballo,* which means *"to throw out."* Jesus used some type of force to get the hired mourners to leave just as He drove out those desecrating the Temple, which was the House of God. He drove out these people who were filled with the powers of darkness and disbelief. These were circumstances under which Jesus found it necessary to use force in removing people.

HE TOOK. The word in the Greek here is *paralambano*. The simple verb means *"to take."* With the preposition *para* prefixed, it adds the thought *"alongside."* Jesus took the father and the mother of the girl and His three Disciples with Him into the room where the girl lay. He was completely in control of the situation. The mother and father were grief-stricken and needed someone to guide them.

The Jesus ENTERED IN WHERE THE DAMSEL WAS LYING. The word translated *"entered"* is *eisporeuomai*. This word is often used of a person who is going on a journey. There are simpler words which could have been used to describe the act of walking. Even though it was just a few feet, it was in reality an arduous journey. Peter, James, and John were with Jesus. Jesus was in control of the situation and comforting the grief-stricken parents, mourning because their little twelve-year-old girl was dead. They entered the room where she lay.

(5:41) AND HE TOOK THE DAMSEL BY THE HAND. The verb used is *krateo,* which means *"to acquire possession of, to take hold of, to become master of."* This was, without question, an unusual moment for the Disciples. They must have been consumed with wonder and confusion.

Certainly they had never seen anyone raised from the dead and had probably never dreamed that such an event could take place. They were probably confused as they watched Jesus take the little girl's dead hand in His.

Jesus *confronts* death. He confronts all of the dirt, rot, hell, and grief of death. He is the Firstfruits of the Resurrection; and one day when the trump sounds, *all* the dead in Christ shall be raised. Ultimately, He will totally defeat death. But here, at this moment of sorrow and grief, Jesus took the hand of the little dead girl within His own.

AND HE SAID UNTO HER, TALITHA CUMI. The translation is directly provided within the Passage. He simply tells the child to arise. Literally it reads, *"Little girl, to you I say, be arising."*

(5:42) AND STRAIGHTWAY THE DAMSEL AROSE AND WALKED. The word *"arose"* is from *anistemi,* which means *"to arise, to stand up."* She also walked (*peripateo* — that is, to walk about and continue walking).

There was no doubt that the little girl had been dead. This was an established fact. But now she arose and walked. The Bible says they were astonished and so amazed that they were rendered speechless. The verb used is *existemi,* which comes from two words: *ek,* meaning *"out,"* and *histemi,* which means *"to place or put."* Together they mean *"to put out"* and refer to the removal of a person *"out of his senses."* Our English word *"ecstasy"* is derived from this word. It might well be translated *"amazement."* They were, indeed, *totally* amazed, but this amazement was certainly tempered by emotions of joy and rejoicing.

(5:43) Next Jesus charged them (*diastello* — to order, charge) to tell no man. It may seem strange that Jesus commanded them to tell no one. Surely the crowds would hear about the girl raised from the dead. There were already individuals present mourning her passing. Perhaps Jesus didn't want to publicize it too widely lest throngs appear, requesting that *their* departed loved ones be raised from the dead. He did later raise Lazarus and the widow's son. However, the number raised was small in comparison to the great numbers of other miracles performed.

The concluding comment on this Chapter is the command of Jesus to give the restored child food. This little girl was now alive and well, walking and eating, and at home with her rejoicing parents.

Notes

Chapter 6

Jesus' Last Visit To Nazareth

SUBJECT	PAGE
THE DISCIPLES SENT OUT BY TWOS	91
HEROD ANTIPAS IS AFRAID	93
JESUS WITH THE TWELVE AND THE FEEDING OF THE FIVE THOUSAND	97
JESUS WALKS ON THE SEA	100
A BIG RECEPTION AT GENNESARET	103

CHAPTER 6

JESUS' LAST VISIT TO NAZARETH

"And He went out from thence, and came into His own country; and His Disciples follow Him. And when the Sabbath Day was come, He began to teach in the Synagogue: and many hearing Him were astonished, saying, From whence hath this Man these things? and what wisdom is this which is given unto Him, that even such mighty works are wrought by His Hands? Is not this the carpenter, the Son of Mary, the brother of James, and Joseph, and of Juda, and Simon? And are not His sisters here with us? And they were offended at Him. But Jesus said unto them, A Prophet is not without honour, but in his own country, and among his own kin, and in his own house. And He could there do no mighty work, save that He laid His Hands upon a few sick folk, and healed them. And He marveled because of their unbelief" (Mk. 6:1-6a).

(6:1) AND CAME INTO HIS OWN COUNTRY. Jesus went back to His hometown of Nazareth. The word for *"country"* is *patris,* and it means *"one's native country, place, or city."* Jesus was born in Bethlehem but had not lived there since His birth. Nazareth had been His home for about thirty years. Now He had returned home for the first time since beginning His active Ministry. Some expositors feel this may have been another effort to escape the crowd and find a quiet place of rest.

He had been continuously exposed to a strenuous series of physically exhausting public displays of the Power of God. Jesus taught and preached, healed the sick, and raised the dead. Obviously, He needed rest and physical replenishment. Some might not understand that Jesus grew as weary and exhausted as any mortal would. Although He never ceased to be God, He had become completely man when He took upon Himself our weaknesses and frailties. Certainly, He grew weary; He needed rest.

He also spent much time in prayer and communion with the Father — for spiritual replenishment. As He went to His hometown, His Disciples accompanied Him.

(6:2) HE BEGAN TO TEACH IN THE SYNAGOGUE. When the Sabbath (Saturday) was come, Jesus went to the Synagogue as was His custom. The ruler of the Synagogue perhaps invited Him to speak to the people. No doubt it was filled to overflowing, as many would be curious to view this phenomenon whose Ministry and miracles were the chief topic of conversation. As He spoke in the Synagogue, He began to unfold the things of God with great power and wisdom.

THEY WERE ASTONISHED. The verb used is *ekplesso,* which

means *"to strike out, expel by a blow."* It suggests shock — as in the expulsion of breath accompanying a great physical or emotional blow. Jesus' words struck them so forcefully that they were astonished. His Message was interrupted by a murmur running through the crowd. Some grew angry. In essence, some were asking, *"Who do You think You are?"*

They felt Jesus had no right to make such wise and powerful statements. They were unaware of the anointing of the Holy Spirit and wondered how He, *"a local boy,"* could perform the awe-inspiring miracles they had heard about, and where He had suddenly acquired the great wisdom He was now delivering to them.

(6:3) IS NOT THIS THE CARPENTER? The word for carpenter is *tekton,* and it means *"to beget, create"* as in referring to one involved in a craft or an art. It was used of someone who worked with wood, as a carpenter.

Jesus was known primarily in Nazareth as the son of Joseph, the carpenter. After Joseph's death, He no doubt carried on this same work until He was about thirty years old. This physical activity gave Jesus good physical development and strength — which helped Him during the strenuous years of His Ministry.

The people were offended and no doubt jealous because Jesus was, in their eyes, just one of many Galilean peasants who had long earned their living by the sweat of their brows. And now here He was, suddenly and unaccountably performing miracles and speaking with infinite wisdom. They knew Him as someone who had made plows, beds, tables, and chairs. They were unable to reconcile their *local* image of Him with that held by the rest of the general public.

Even His own family had difficulty in believing and understanding. They joined with the crowd in their disapproval. It says, *"And they were offended at Him."* The word used here is *skandalizo,* which means *"to put a stumbling block or some obstruction in the way, upon which another may trip or fall."* It can also carry the thought of bringing about distrust or of creating an occasion for stumbling, or offense. It further implies that an individual might see something which he disapproves, thus hindering this individual's acknowledgement of the authority displayed.

Since the townspeople could not understand or explain Him, they rejected Him. This is frequently the public's reaction to events they can neither accept nor control.

(6:4) Then Jesus said unto them, *"A Prophet is not without honour, but in his own country."* The Greek word for *"Prophet"* is *prophetes,* which means primarily *"a forth-teller,"* or one who speaks of God's Message. He did, of course, predict future events.

The Greek word for *"honour"* is *time,* which means, *"deference, reverence, honor."* Jesus had already claimed to be their Messiah in John 4:26 and Luke 4:21. He was declared to be the Son of Man with the Power of God in Mark 1:10, Matthew 9:6, and Luke 5:24. He was proclaimed the Son of God in John 5:22. Yet the people of Nazareth could not accept Him as a Prophet, and He was without reverence and honor among His own people and His own kinsmen.

(6:5) AND HE COULD THERE DO NO MIGHTY WORKS. The word translated *"no"* is *oudemian,* which means *"not even one."* There were a few *"sick"* people strengthened. The word for sick is *arrostos,* which means *"without strength, weak, sick."* It really has reference to individuals who might be regarded as having constitutional weakness. They were so unbelieving that they did not even bring their sick to Him for healing, so He did no mighty works. *"Work"* is from *dunamis,* which refers to a miracle in which supernatural power would be involved.

Oh, the tragedy of unbelief. Unbelief can stop God. The people of Nazareth could have brought their sick to Jesus for healing. The captive could have been set free and even the dead raised. He could have performed many mighty miracles, signs, and wonders — but they rejected Him. They willfully refused to believe.

Unbelief is tragic. It is great problem and one plaguing many people. Obstacles arise and, with the first contrary wind, people's Faith dissolves.

There are many forms of unbelief. There are the venomous types that can transport a person to Hell. Failure to believe in Jesus as Saviour and Lord will result in eternal death. And there is also the unbelief that prevents us from entrusting God with our lives and allowing Him to undertake in every circumstance confronting us.

(6:6) HE MARVELED BECAUSE OF THEIR UNBELIEF. Jesus was disappointed with the people of Nazareth, marveling at their unbelief. The last time He marveled, it had been at the *Faith* of a Roman centurion. This Roman army officer had told Jesus to simply speak the word and his servant would be healed. Jesus marveled at this great Faith, and said He had not seen such Faith in all Israel. And now He had come to His own, and His own received Him not (Jn. 1:11).

Jesus stripped Himself of Glory and accepted human limitations with feelings and emotions the same as ours. He was subject to all our disappointments, and Scripture says, *"He marveled because of their unbelief."*

THE DISCIPLES SENT OUT BY TWOS

"And He went round about the villages, teaching. And He called unto Him the Twelve, and began to send them forth by two and two; and gave them power over unclean spirits; And commanded them

SELF-HELP
STUDY NOTES

that they should take nothing for their journey, save a staff only; no scrip, no bread, no money in their purse: But be shod with sandals; and not put on two coats. And He said unto them, In what place soever you enter into an house, there abide till you depart from that place. And whosoever shall not receive you, nor hear you, when you depart thence, shake off the dust under your feet for a testimony against them. Verily I say unto you, It shall be more tolerable for Sodom and Gomorrah in the Day of Judgment, than for that city. And they went out, and preached that men should repent. And they cast out many devils, and anointed with oil many who were sick, and healed them" (Mk. 6:6b-13).

This begins the third tour of Galilee. After instructing the Twelve Disciples, Jesus sent them forth by twos.

(6:6) He first made a tour throughout the countryside about Nazareth, visiting all the villages and teaching the people.

(6:7) Then He called unto Him the Twelve. The word is *proskaleo,* which means to call to one's self. It is the simple verb *kaleo* (meaning to call), with the preposition *pros* prefixed to it. This means *"to, towards, facing."* It is not clear if He called the Disciples in pairs, conferring with them thus and then sending them out, or if He instructed them all in a group and then dispatched them in pairs.

AND BEGAN TO SEND THEM FORTH BY TWO AND TWO. The verb used is *apostello.* As we have seen previously, this means *"to send forth as an ambassador on a commission."* The one sent represents someone else in performing a special task. The word *"apostle"* comes from this word. Literally, *"He began sending them forth as His ambassadors."* They went out by twos and thus were able to encourage one another and expand their testimony and their ministry.

AND GAVE THEM POWER OVER UNCLEAN SPIRITS. The verb is in the imperfect tense which indicates that He *continued* to give them power, or He gave them *continuing* power. The word translated power is *exousia,* meaning delegated authority. They had *authority (exousia)* to command demons, and God's *Power (dunamis)* was with them and ensured that their commands would be obeyed. They had *both* the authority and the power. He *continued* to give them power and authority throughout the duration of their tour.

(6:8-9) As they went on their journey, they were commanded to take only a staff (*rabdos* — walking stick), but no scrip (*pera* — traveling bag or pouch). Jesus also stated that they were to take no provisions (food) or money in their purse. There were other times when they *were* to carry provisions with them. The explicit instructions of Jesus depended on the circumstances and situation of the moment. Here, however, it is clearly demonstrated that the laborer is worthy of his hire.

Normally, a person could not work long enough to earn sufficient money to support himself after setting out to do God's Work. A person called by God to His service is worthy of support. At this point in time they were to depend on the hospitality of those to whom they ministered. They could expect to be granted provisions and shelter as they traveled about teaching and witnessing.

(6:10-11) Jesus told His Disciples that if they went somewhere and were not hospitably received, they should not stay. The word for *"received"* is *dechomai,* and means *"to take by the hand, grant access to a visitor."* It also projects the idea of extending friendship and welcome and not withholding hospitality.

If they were not accepted, they were to *"shake off the dust underfoot"* as a testimony. This was an act of contempt and an indication that further association was withdrawn. It is a very serious matter to reject a God-called, God-anointed minister of the Gospel. Such rejection is not only toward the preacher himself, but it is a rejection of Jesus who sent him, and is basically a rejection of God.

(6:12-13) AND PREACHED THAT MEN SHOULD REPENT. The word for *"preached"* is *kerusso,* which means — as mentioned before — a grave, formal, authoritative proclamation. They were to preach Repentance, God's Kingdom of Righteousness, and the abandonment of sin. The word *"Repentance"* comes from *metanoeo,* and means a change in one's life and method of living. Their way of life was sinful, and a change in attitude was necessary to redirect the course of their lives.

Sin must be dealt with. Preachers must define it if people are to be saved. Those committed to Christ must live clean lives, confess their sins, and ultimately walk in victory.

They also cast out many demons and ANOINTED WITH OIL MANY WHO WERE SICK. In James 5:14 we are told that a sick person can call for the elders and be anointed with oil. Under such anointing great healings took place then — and such are still in evidence today. People were delivered and healed as the Disciples went about proclaiming the Message of Christ.

HEROD ANTIPAS IS AFRAID

"And king Herod heard of Him; (for His Name was spread abroad:) and he said, That John the Baptist was risen from the dead, and therefore mighty works do show forth themselves in him. Others said, That it is Elijah. And others said, That it is a Prophet, or as one of the Prophets. But when Herod heard thereof, he said, It is John, whom I beheaded: he is risen from the dead.

"For Herod himself had sent forth and laid hold upon John, and bound him in prison for Herodias' sake, his brother Philip's wife: for he had married her. For John had said unto Herod, It is not lawful for you to have your brother's wife. Therefore Herodias had a quarrel against him, and would have killed him; but she could not: For Herod feared John, knowing that he was a just man and an Holy, and observed him; and when he heard him, he did many things, and heard him gladly.

"And when a convenient day was come, that Herod on his birthday made a supper to his lords, high captains, and chief estates of Galilee; And when the daughter of the said Herodias came in, and danced, and pleased Herod and them who sat with him, the king said unto the damsel, Ask of me whatsoever you will, and I will give it to you. And he sware unto her, Whatsoever you shall ask of me, I will give it to you, unto the half of my kingdom. And she went forth, and said unto her mother, What shall I ask? And she said, The head of John the Baptist. And she came in straightway with haste unto the king, and asked, saying, I will that you give me by and by in a charger the head of John the Baptist.

"And the king was exceeding sorry; yet for his oath's sake, and for their sakes which sat with him, he would not reject her. And immediately the king sent an executioner, and commanded his head to be brought: and he went and beheaded him in the prison, And brought his head in a charger, and gave it to the damsel: and the damsel gave it to her mother. And when his disciples heard of it, they came and took up his corpse, and laid it in a tomb" (Mk. 6:14-29).

(6:14) KING HEROD HEARD OF HIM. Herod Antipas, a tetrarch, was one of four men ruling Palestine. The word *"tetrarch"* simply means a rule by four. Matthew and Luke speak of Herod as tetrarch, but Mark calls him the king. The title of king was freely applied within the Roman world to all eastern rulers.

Herod was seriously troubled by conscience and was beset by guilt, shame, and fear. He had heard of the fame of the Master and of the miracles He performed — raising the dead, casting out devils, and healing people. From the finest palace to the peasant's hovel, people were talking about this miracle worker.

Jesus was also a prominent subject of conversation in Herod's court. Diplomats and officials discussed Jesus and the impressive manifestations of His Ministry. Herod explained the Lord's miracles by concluding that John the Baptist had risen from the dead. Some expositors point out that Herod was a very troubled man in his conscience, who repeated again and again that John the Baptist had risen from the dead. Herod had killed John in a sordid and senseless act of murder described in the following Verses.

(6:15) While Herod thought it was John the Baptist back from the dead, others said Jesus was Elijah. Still others said He was a Prophet — not necessarily one of the Old Testament Prophets, but one *like* them.

(6:16) Herod, familiar with the various opinions, stubbornly insisted that John, whom he had beheaded, had been raised from the dead. The use of *"I"* in this expression is emphatic. Herod was *certain* that Jesus was John.

(6:17-18) The gruesome story of the death of John the Baptist is told by Mark. Herod himself had given the order for John to be taken to the prison of Machaerus, a grim fortress situated on the barren heights of Moab, above the Dead Sea.

Herod had done this for the sake of his wife Herodias, the daughter of Aristobulus. Aristobulus was one of the sons of Herod the Great with his wife Marianne. Herodias was married to her Uncle Philip, a brother of Aristobulus. Herod Antipas — the ruler spoken of here in Mark's account as Herod — was the half-brother of Philip. Though she was married to another, Herod had taken Herodias unto himself.

Herod Antipas was interested in, and moderately taken with, John's philosophy. However, he feared John, knowing that he was a just and Holy man (Vs. 20). When John the Baptist denounced the scandalous relationship between Herodias and Herod, it caused embarrassment for the king and rage in the queen. John had publicly proclaimed it unlawful for Herod to have his brother's wife.

(6:19) Therefore Herodias was embittered against John. The word *enecho* is translated *"had a quarrel,"* and it means *"to be enraged with, to set one's self against, to hold a grudge against one."* To put it in a popular vernacular, Herodias *"had it in for John the Baptist."* Because this is in the imperfect tense, it indicates that Herodias at no time cooled her anger against John the Baptist. She was consumed with lust for revenge.

(6:20) HEROD FEARED JOHN. Once again the verb is in the imperfect tense and indicates a continuing state of fear. He knew that John was a just man who represented God.

OBSERVED HIM. The verb is *suntereo*. It actually means *"to preserve something from perishing or being lost; to guard one; that is, to keep him safe."* The King James translation does not give the true feeling of the situation. Actually, Herod was holding John in safekeeping to protect him from the evil plots of Herodias — who wanted desperately to have him killed. Once more, the verb indicates a *continuing* process of keeping him safe, as Herod maintained his watch over John.

HE HEARD HIM GLADLY. The expression in the Greek implies that Herod frequently visited John in the prison of Machaerus. No doubt Herod was moved with conviction. The Spirit of God was dealing with this king.

He was perhaps much like King Agrippa who told Paul in Acts 26:28, *"Almost thou persuadest me to be a Christian."*

When John preached, he pulled no punches. This is, of course, what got him into trouble. John's preached had caused Herod to come under conviction. His conscience was uneasy and his wife's insistent demands caused Herod perplexity and much distress. The Greek states, he was *"in perplexity about many things."* Despite John's scathing denunciation of his sin, Herod still returned to listen.

Herod was almost persuaded and came close to a commitment. There are many who hear God speaking in their hearts and lives, who sense God moving upon them in a special way, yet they fail to respond — waiting for a more convenient day or time. Satan strives to hold one back, doing everything possible to create procrastination. A postponed decision for Salvation will probably end up *no* decision — with eternal damnation as the final outcome.

(6:21) Herod was celebrating his birthday. Lords, military commanders, and the chief men of Galilee were invited to his supper. Herodias used this gala event as an opportunity to spring her trap and thus force Herod to have John murdered. Satan is out only to ruin, kill, and destroy.

(6:22) Salome, the daughter of Herodias, performed a licentious and immoral dance before Herod and the mighty men assembled. The filth and degradation that were in evidence overcame Herod and those with them. Herod told Salome that she could ask whatever she wished and it would be granted. When Herod told Herodias' daughter to name her desire, he had stepped into the trap prepared by Herodias — and Satan.

(6:23-25) Herod had put himself under oath (*omnuo,*) saying she could have anything she asked — up to half the kingdom. She went to her mother for help in determining her reward. Of course, it was a simple choice for Herodias. Before the king could arrange an escape from his predicament, she asked for the head of John the Baptist on a charger (*pinax — "a dish, plate, or platter"*).

(6:26) THE KING EXCEEDING SORRY. The words used here indicate that the king underwent a severe emotional reaction. He was *"exceeding sorry."* Although he had been drunk moments before, he apparently sobered up rapidly. He was about to become the murderer of the Prophet he both feared and respected. Because he had made an oath — and because this was done in the presence of important personages — he morosely granted Herodias' request.

(6:27-29) EXECUTIONER. The king called for the executioner (*spekoulatora*). This is a Latin word from which we get the word *"spectator,"* which means *"a watcher."* Originally, it had to do with the guards who *"watched"* or spied out matters. With time this came to be used for those who surrounded the emperor carrying spears or lances, and then even to designate those willing to kill for a fee.

Herod would never forget this scene. The order was given to the executioner, who descended to the dungeon. His sword was raised and flashed downward. John's head was severed from his body and a short time later brought into the king's presence on a silver platter and presented to Salome — who triumphantly transferred her prize to her mother.

What a gruesome picture — and how unnecessary. It was all due to the actions of an evil and vindictive woman, Herodias. She had been obsessed with the desire to have John the Baptist killed. A guilty conscience never ceases its torment. Herod would never forget, and his massive guilt would plague him throughout his lifetime.

Following all this, John's disciples came and took his corpse and laid it in a tomb. His earthly life had ended and he had been removed from the scene. Yet his words kept ringing in the hearts and minds of those who had heard them . . . and they still ring today. Repent! Repent and be saved!

JESUS WITH THE TWELVE AND THE FEEDING OF THE FIVE THOUSAND

"And the Apostles gathered themselves together unto Jesus, and told Him all things, both what they had done, and what they had taught. And He said unto them, Come ye yourselves apart into a desert place, and rest a while: for there were many coming and going, and they had no leisure so much as to eat. And they departed into a desert place by ship privately.

"And the people saw them departing, and many knew Him, and ran afoot thither out of all cities, and outwent them, and came together unto Him. And Jesus, when He came out, saw much people, and was moved with compassion toward them, because they were as sheep not having a shepherd: and He began to teach them many things.

"And when the day was now far spent, His Disciples came unto Him, and said, This is a desert place, and now the time is far passed: Send them away, that they may go into the country round about, and into the villages, and buy themselves bread: for they have nothing to eat. He answered and said unto them, Give ye them to eat. And they say unto Him, Shall we go and buy two hundred pennyworth of bread, and give them to eat? He said unto them, How many loaves have you? Go and see.

"And when they knew, they say, Five, and two fishes. And He commanded them to make all sit down by companies upon the green grass. And they sat down in ranks, by hundreds, and by fifties. And

when He had taken the five loaves and the two fishes, He looked up to Heaven, and blessed, and broke the loaves, and gave them to His Disciples to set before them; and the two fishes divided He among them all.

"And they did all eat, and were filled. And they took up twelve baskets full of the fragments, and of the fishes. And they who did eat of the loaves were about five thousand men" (Mk. 6:30-44).

(6:30) The Disciples returned and gathered themselves unto Jesus. They had preached, healed, and cast out devils. Great things had been done in the Name of the Lord Jesus Christ, and they were excited. They shared everything with Him that had occurred during their short ministry.

(6:31) Jesus told the Disciples, COME YE YOURSELVES APART INTO A DESERT PLACE, AND REST A WHILE. Jesus was, in effect, telling them that they had been involved in great activity and that they now needed rest. They had obeyed Him and performed a great work. Now He was telling them to momentarily pause until their weary bodies were replenished. They accompanied Him to a deserted place *(eremos)* for their sojourn. This was a solitary, lonely, and uninhabited place. It wasn't a desert in the sense of being arid and without vegetation, but a deserted or uninhabited section where they could presumably be removed from the crowds to renew themselves physically, mentally, and spiritually.

Jesus is ever conscious of the need for rest and recuperation for those who serve Him. It is always important for the servant of God to take care of his body. There can be an intense drain of energy, with subsequent exhaustion, as a consequence of ministering.

They were to REST A WHILE. The word for rest is *anapauo,* which means to cease from labor in order to recover and collect strength. It means to give one's self rest. They had been so active and without leisure that they barely had time for eating.

Work is noble, and certainly sloth is totally without virtue. Yet the Master recognized the necessity for rest, relaxation, refreshment, and retreat.

(6:32-33) AND THEY DEPARTED INTO A DESERT PLACE BY SHIP PRIVATELY. They went by the *ploion* — that is, the large fishing boat kept ready to remove Jesus from the danger of the crushing crowd. So they went by ship to a private and uninhabited region.

MANY KNEW HIM. The throngs that constantly followed Jesus saw that the Lord and His Disciples were going away. Some of them recognized and understood *(epiginosko)* their need for rest.

RAN AFOOT THITHER OUT OF ALL CITIES. However, some of the people began to run after Jesus' party along the way. This resulted in a steadily growing stream of individuals who wanted to see and hear the Master. The word for *"ran"* is from *suntrecho.* This means *"to run along with others, to rush with."* They were *"hurrying with one another"* and coming from all the towns along the way.

The people were frantic to get to Jesus. They were hungry for a moving of the Spirit. They were disenchanted with the powerless teaching and bankrupt traditions that had starved their souls.

There were times when the Lord had a problem getting people to pay attention to Him — but not this day. They came in large numbers. Although He was seeking rest, He gave of Himself to the great crowd that gathered. They numbered five thousand men, plus women and children, so the total number would have been much larger.

(6:34) HE BEGAN TO TEACH. Literally, *"Jesus taught them and kept on teaching."* Both Matthew and Luke indicate that He also healed some. There were perhaps only a few sick people in the crowd because they had possibly come in such a hurry that only the healthy could keep up. They listened intently, and Jesus was moved with compassion as He looked upon them.

(6:35-36) The day was now well gone and it was approaching sunset and evening. The Disciples pointed out to Jesus that they were in a desert place, so the people should be sent away to the villages to buy bread as they had brought nothing to eat.

(6:37) GIVE YE THEM TO EAT. In the Text the emphasis is *"ye."* Jesus told the *Disciples* to give them to eat. The Disciples then asked whether they should go and buy two hundred pennyworth of bread to give to the people. Some expositors say that this would amount to about $35. Apparently this was about the amount the Disciples had with them.

(6:38-40) Jesus told them to look and see how many loaves they had. They had five loaves and two fishes. There was a little boy there, as John records it, who had the five barley loaves and two fishes (Jn. 6:9). Then they asked in that same account, *"What are they among so many?"* This meant, *"What can it amount to with so many to share?"* Jesus commanded the people to sit, and they were arranged in small companies, or ranks, on the grass. The people did as they were bidden.

(6:41) Jesus took the five loaves and the two fishes in His Hands and the Bible says He blessed them. He thanked God for these provisions, and then He broke the loaves and gave them to His Disciples. He also divided the two fishes among them. The expression used in the Greek states literally, *"He broke and kept on giving."*

(6:42-44) All the people ate and were filled. There were about five thousand men, and Matthew adds that there were additional women and children. This event is recorded by all four of the Gospel writers.

What a marvelous miracle this was! Twelve wicker baskets full of fragments were left. He sent them away full. Praise God! He *always* sends people away full.

SELF-HELP
STUDY NOTES

JESUS WALKS ON THE SEA

"And straightway He constrained His Disciples to get into the ship, and to go to the other side before unto Bethsaida, while He sent away the people. And when he had sent them away, He departed into a mountain to pray. And when evening was come, the ship was in the midst of the sea, and He alone on the land. And He saw them toiling in rowing; for the wind was contrary unto them: and about the fourth watch of the night He cometh unto them, walking upon the sea, and would have passed by them. But when they saw Him walking upon the sea, they supposed it had been a spirit, and cried out: For they all saw Him, and were troubled. And immediately He talked with them, and said unto them, Be of good cheer: it is I; be not afraid. And He went up unto them into the ship; and the wind ceased: and they were sore amazed in themselves beyond measure, and wondered. For they considered not the miracle of the loaves: for their heart was hardened" (Mk. 6:45-52).

(6:45) Immediately Jesus compelled His Disciples to board the boat and proceed to the other side (to Bethsaida), while He dismissed the crowd.

(6:46) AND WHEN HE HAD SENT THEM AWAY. The verb in this statement is *apotasso,* and it means *"to separate one's self, withdraw, to take leave of, to bid farewell to."* Jesus sent the crowd away and went to a mountain to pray. As we have noted, Jesus frequently withdrew to a quiet place to commune with the Father in prayer. The word translated here as *"pray"* is *proseuchomai.* The first part of this word, *pro,* is a preposition which means *"toward or facing."* It gives emphasis to the direct approach of the one praying, in seeking the Face of God. When a person prays, he is actually in the Presence of God, and God hears his prayers directly.

There are significant lessons to be learned from Christ relative to His departing to pray. First of all, prayer was a priority in His Life and He spent much time in prayer. Secondly, it should be noted that sometimes people reach a position of acclaim (as the Lord had now reached) due to the great moving of the Holy Spirit. At this point some become lax in prayer. After great manifestations of God (healing the sick, miracles, raising the dead, and people desiring to crown Him king), it would have been easy for Jesus to become caught up in the excitement and frenzy and to have begun spending more time with the crowds.

In similar situations, men often grow careless in their attention to prayer. Their eyes focus on their own magnetism, their own popularity, and on the power they see manifested. They begin to think they are important. However, Jesus never did this. He went often to a quiet place for prayer and to seek the Face of God. We should all pray regularly. There needs to be much time spent in prayer — believing God according to His Word — and

100

receiving His bountiful, glorious answers.

(6:47) WHEN EVENING WAS COME. It was now about sunset. The boat was in the midst of the sea and Jesus was alone on the seashore.

(6:48) AND HE SAW THEM TOILING IN ROWING. The Disciples were toiling and working hard at their rowing. The wind was blowing against them, and they were making no headway. It was windy, perhaps even stormy. In any event, they were not making progress. Apparently Jesus remained in prayer for some hours, because it was at about the fourth watch of the night (between 3 and 6 a.m.) when He came to them.

WALKING UPON THE SEA. The word translated *"upon"* is *epi*, and in the construction used, it signifies contact. Jesus was walking *on* the surface of the sea. His sandals had contact with the water and He walked on it as we would walk on pavement. He was not floating above it but in firm contact with it. It was truly a miracle.

WOULD HAVE PASSED BY THEM. The word which is translated *"would"* is *thelo*, which means *"I desire."* The word *para* is translated *"by"* and means *"beside."* The word for *"passed"* is *erchomai*, and it means *"to go."* Some translations leave the impression our Lord *desired* to pass by, while in fact He went out on the turbulent sea to aid them. They were having difficulties, and the preposition *para* (as used here) means He went near or beside them. It was His intention right from the beginning to go to them.

(6:49) When the Disciples saw Jesus walking upon the sea, THEY SUPPOSED IT WAS A SPIRIT. The word translated *"spirit"* here is not *pneuma* — which is also translated spirit and refers to a disembodied individual who has died. The word here is *phantasma*, and it means *"an apparition or a specter."* This word is used more in the area of magic. After His Resurrection, when Jesus appeared to the Disciples, the word used is *pneuma* and not *phantasma* as used here. We might say they thought they had seen a ghost.

AND THEY CRIED OUT. Here the verb is *anakrazo*, and it means to cry out with a shriek of terror; scream. They actually screamed in terror.

(6:50) THEY ALL SAW HIM, AND WERE TROUBLED. The word is *tarasso*, and it means to be agitated; troubled; to have inward commotion. It is sometimes translated afraid. They were obviously agitated and troubled by what they saw.

HE TALKED WITH THEM. Mark's expression indicates that Jesus spoke in a reassuring and encouraging manner to them. The Lord seldom speaks harshly. The Holy Spirit always moves sweetly and gently. When people are in need, the Lord wants to help and bless them.

The only times Jesus spoke harshly were when the proud religious leaders displayed Pharisaical attitudes. But to the person in need — the adulterer, the sorrowing heart, and individual besieged by the storms of life — our Lord comes to bless, forgive, encourage, save and raise to new heights of victory and glory.

BE OF GOOD CHEER: IT IS I; BE NOT AFRAID. *"Be of good cheer"* is the translation given for the word *tharseo,* and it also means *"to be of good courage."* The Disciples, stricken with terror, needed renewed courage. The next expression, *"It is I,"* has emphasis on the pronoun. Literally, He said, *"It is I and nobody else."*

He also spoke a command to them saying, *"Stop being afraid."* There is never need to be afraid when the Lord is near. The winds may be contrary and circumstances difficult. There may be a multitude of problems and everything may look hopeless in the natural; but we, as Children of God, are encouraged to stand on the promises and believe in the miracles of God.

He says, *"Be not afraid, be of good courage."* This is not easy when problems beset us and the winds are high enough to capsize the boat. Still, we are told to be of good courage and *then* we can shout the victory.

(6:51) THE WIND CEASED. When Jesus entered the ship, the wind *"ceased from its violence and raging."* A rather picturesque word is used to describe this. It is *kopazo,* and it means to grow weary and tired. The noun form refers to beating, toil, weariness. As if exhausted by the beating and toil, the sea simply sank to rest when Jesus came on the scene. The Disciples were amazed beyond measure, and were totally awed by what they had seen.

In Matthew's account of this same event, we are told of Peter's request to Jesus to call him to Him on the water. Peter did walk on the water, but began to sink when fear entered. He then cried out to the Lord to save him.

Jesus immediately stretched forth His Hand to support Peter and rebuked him for lack of Faith. Matthew and John also indicate that when Peter and Jesus entered the boat, the wind ceased. All was quiet as soon as Jesus arrived (See Mat. 14:24-33; Jn. 6:16-21).

THEY CONSIDERED NOT THE MIRACLE OF THE LOAVES FOR THEIR HEARTS WERE HARDENED. This indicates that somehow the Disciples failed to correlate this present miracle with the miracle of the loaves and fishes. They should have realized that if the Lord could — through supernatural power — feed a great multitude by multiplying the loaves and fishes, He could also quiet the wind, still the stormy sea, and walk on the surface of the water.

Somehow their hearts had become dull of understanding. It says their *"hearts were hardened."* The verb is *poroo,* which means *"to grow hard or calloused, to become dull and lose the power of understanding."* People often fail to perceive the full significance of the working of God and also the tremendous possibilities available for those in unpleasant predicaments. God is able. Jesus performed miracles then and still does today.

A BIG RECEPTION AT GENNESARET

"And when they had passed over, they came into the land of Gennesaret, and drew to the shore. And when they were come out of the ship, straightway they knew Him, And ran through that whole region round about, and began to carry about in beds those who were sick, where they heard He was. And whithersoever He entered, into villages, or cities, or country, they laid the sick in the streets, and besought Him that they might touch if it were but the border of His garment: and as many as touched Him were made whole" (Mk. 6:53-56).

(6:53) DREW TO THE SHORE. The verb used here is *prosormizo,* and it literally means *"to bring a ship to moorings"* — that is, to anchor a ship. It was at Gennesaret that they anchored and came ashore.

(6:54-55) THEY KNEW HIM. The people immediately recognized Jesus when He came off the ship. The verb is *epiginosko,* and it means to *"know by experience."* Jesus was becoming so well-known by this time that crowds formed wherever He appeared. Immediately, the people began to pour from the entire region bringing their sick and even those confined to beds. Wherever Jesus was reported to be, they struck out for that place carrying their sick on pallets. Jesus' popularity at this time was phenomenal. There was much excitement as the people poured out to see Jesus and to be healed.

One can imagine the many afflictions that were healed: blinded eyes opened, lepers cleansed, and souls saved. The Lord came to heal, to touch the brokenhearted, and to transform lives. Our Lord is able.

(6:56) Wherever Jesus went within the region, the sick were brought to Him. They laid them on the streets that they might but touch *"the border of His garment."* The word translated *"border"* is *kraspedon* and it means the fringe of a garment — a little appendage which hung down from the edge of the mantle or the cloak.

The Jews used these fringes as reminders of the Law. The word translated *"garment"* is *himtion,* and refers to the *outer* garment — the cloak or mantle. One is reminded of the woman with the issue of blood, who felt she would be healed if she could but touch the hem of His garment.

Masses of people were doing this now. Her story had probably been related to others and large numbers of people came from all over begging to touch His garments. The Scriptures state, *"and as many as touched Him were made whole"* (6:56).

Chapter 7

Jesus Explains What Defiles

SUBJECT   **PAGE**

THE DAUGHTER OF A GREEK WOMAN IS HEALED **112**
JESUS HEALS A DEAF MUTE **113**

CHAPTER 7

JESUS EXPLAINS WHAT DEFILES

"Then came together unto Him the Pharisees, and certain of the Scribes, which came from Jerusalem. And when they saw some of His Disciples eat bread with defiled, that is to say, with unwashed, hands, they found fault. For the Pharisees, and all the Jews, except they wash their hands often, eat not, holding the tradition of the Elders. And when they come from the market, except they wash, they eat not. And many other things there be, which they have received to hold, as the washing of cups, and pots, brasen vessels, and of tables. Then the Pharisees and Scribes asked Him, Why walk not your Disciples according to the tradition of the Elders, but eat bread with unwashed hands? He answered and said unto them, Well has Isaiah prophesied of you hypocrites, as it is written, This people honor Me with their lips, but their heart is far from Me. Howbeit in vain do they worship Me, teaching for doctrines the commandments of men. For laying aside the Commandment of God, you hold the tradition of men, as the washing of pots and cups: and many other such like things you do.

"And He said unto them, Full well you reject the Commandment of God, that you may keep your own tradition. For Moses said, Honor your father and your mother; and, Whoso curses father or mother, let him die the death: But you say, If a man shall say to his father or mother, It is Corban, that is to say, a gift, by whatsoever you might be profited by Me; he shall be free. And you suffer him no more to do ought for his father or his mother; Making the Word of God of none effect through your tradition, which you have delivered; and many such like things do you. And when He had called all the people unto Him, He said unto them, Hearken unto Me every one of you, and understand: There is nothing from without a man, that entereth into him can defile him: but the things which come out of him, those are they that defile the man. If any man have ears to hear let him hear.

"And when He was entered into the house from the people, His Disciples asked Him concerning the Parable. And He said unto them, Are you so without understanding also? Do you not perceive, that whatsoever thing from without enters into the man, it cannot defile him; Because it enters not into his heart, but into the belly, and goes out into the draught, purging all meats? And He said, That which comes out of the man, that defiles the man. For from within, out of the heart of men, proceed evil thoughts, adulteries, fornications,

*murders, Thefts, covetousness, wickedness, deceit, lasciviousness, an
evil eye, blasphemy, pride, foolishness: All these evil things come from
within, and defile the man"* (Mk. 7:1-23).

(7:1) Jesus was tremendously popular at this time, and huge throngs
followed Him wherever He went. And now the religious leaders — the
Scribes and Pharisees — came to Jesus.

In contrast to the great outpouring of warmth from the crowds, these
religious leaders came with a hostile attitude. They did not care about
people being healed. They did not concern themselves with lives being
transformed, the Gospel being preached, or hope being restored in the
hearts of the people. They were concerned only with their traditions and
had come to find fault with the Master.

(7:2) These religious leaders paid very close attention to Jesus and His
Disciples. The Scribes and Pharisees were notoriously attentive to minute
details and legalistic traditions. They noted that the Disciples of Jesus ate
bread with *"defiled"* (unwashed) hands.

The word for *"defiled"* is *koinos.* This refers basically to anything
common to everyone. Later it came to mean something profane, as opposed to that which was sacred. As such, it eventually came to be applied to anything *ceremonially* unclean. The washing of hands was, in
this instance, not for the purpose of cleanliness; it was strictly for Ceremonial Law.

There had been times when the Pharisees said that failure to wash the
hands was a crime worthy of death: an example of how important they
considered their rituals. They were totally bound by them; while Jesus, on
the other hand, paid little attention to their meaningless ceremonies that
had no basis in God's Word. Consequently the Scribes and Pharisees,
seeing their revered traditions ignored and violated, found Jesus and His
many Followers a threat to their positions.

Religious traditions exist in many places in *our* world today and often
put people under grievous bondage. Religion binds people. Pharisaic teaching missed the point and intent of God's Law. All too many religious activities and earthly traditions blot out God's spiritual intent. It has no relationship to true spirituality and is completely unnecessary for anyone wishing a
relationship with God the Father and His Son, the Messiah.

(7:3) These Pharisees washed their hands often, for it was a religious
ritual based on Pharisaic tradition. In a prescribed manner they poured
water high up on their arms and let it run down over their wrists and fingers.
They would not eat until they completed this ceremonial washing.

HOLDING THE TRADITION OF THE ELDERS. The word
paradosis is translated *"tradition."* It refers to something being delivered
by someone for their care and keeping. Here it refers to instructions handed

down from one generation to another. These were religiously observed and *"carefully and faithfully kept"* (*krateo*).

THE ELDERS. The word *"Elder"* comes from *presbuteros*. It was often used with reference to age but here it related more to rank and position. The *"traditions of the Elders"* involved their Ceremonial and Ritual Laws, which had originated within the Jewish leadership and were passed down from generation to generation. They did not come from the Word of God.

The *"traditions of the Elders"* survive today within the ritual of Jewish worship in the Talmud. Several influences crept into God's prescribed worship format and affected the basis for the *"traditions"* which Jesus refused to observe. Jesus observed every nuance of the *Mosaic* Law given to Israel by God through Moses, but He went out of His way to demonstrate His disdain for the pagan corruptions and adulterations which were being practiced by the Pharisees.

It is easy for man to add to what God says. This then can become a tradition, or doctrine, which becomes binding on the people. The real conflict between Jesus and the Scribes and Pharisees arose over this point. Their man-made Ceremonial Laws came into conflict with the Message of Christ declaring God's Word. One can look about today and see much *"religious activity"* that has nothing to do with spirituality. This is, in fact, most often instigated by Satan.

(7:4) THE MARKET. The word is *agora,* and it means the public forum, which every town had, like a courthouse square, where the people gathered. When the Jews mingled in public with others, they became ceremonially defiled.

THEY WASH. They would go through their ceremonial washings to be ritually clean. It was not a washing for the purpose of physical cleanliness, but rather for religious and ceremonial purposes. They also washed their cups and utensils, which may have been more of a conventional washing.

(7:5) The original Text emphasizes the *"continual asking"* by the Scribes and Pharisees. They questioned Jesus endlessly concerning His Disciples and why they did not follow the *"tradition of the Elders."* The conflict in attitudes toward the Ceremonial Law between Jesus and the Pharisees was very apparent and a matter of great contention.

(7:6) Jesus said Isaiah expressed it well. *Kalos* means *"beautifully, finely, excellently, well."* The prediction of Isaiah, that the people would honor God with their lips but not their hearts, was clearly demonstrated by the Pharisees in their deliberate and repeated rejection of God's Word.

Jesus called them hypocrites. The definite article is used for the Pharisees, giving special emphasis to them as *outstanding* hypocrites. The word hypocrites comes from the Greek word *hupocrites*. This is made up of two words: the first, *hupo,* which means *"under"*; and the second, *krino,* which means *"to judge."* The original idea suggests one who judges from under a mask.

Persons acting on the Greek stage wore masks, pretending to be something they weren't. Jesus announced to the world that the Pharisees were religious *"actors,"* pretending to be one thing on the outside while they were something completely different on the inside. He spoke very forthrightly to them. He was stern and direct in His comments on the *"religious"* Pharisees — the hypocrites.

It is also interesting to note that while Jesus was quick to forgive and minimize sins of many types during His Ministry when the people were sincere, He dealt harshly with hypocrisy. We as Christians should be especially cautious in guarding against falling into a posture of sanctimoniousness. This is closely related to hypocrisy — the sin Jesus obviously hated.

THEIR HEART IS FAR FROM ME. The verb *"is"* comes from the word *apecho.* The preposition (*apo*) prefixed to this word (*echo*) literally means *"to hold off from."* It pictures one holding himself a great distance from someone else. The way the verb is used means *"to be away, absent, or distant."* Their hearts were far from God.

(7:7) Their worship was in vain (*maten* — fruitless, without profit). The verb form is *mataioo,* and this means to *"make empty, vain."* Their acts of worship were futile and failed utterly to attain the proposed end and purpose. Worship is from *sebo,* which means *"to revere, to worship."* It has to do with veneration, fear, piety, devotion.

This quotation from Isaiah 29:13 goes on to state that they were *"teaching for doctrines the commandments of men."* They were not teaching the Word of God, but principles and philosophies devised by men. The people were thus required to adhere to the commandments of mere men.

(7:8) LAYING ASIDE. They laid aside the Commandments of God. The verb is *aphiemi,* which means *"to send away, bid to go away, or depart, to let alone, to disregard."* They laid aside and abandoned God's principles for the commandments of men.

YOU HOLD THE TRADITIONS OF MEN. The word for *"hold"* is *krateo,* meaning a person with a powerful grip on something. As it is used in this context, the Pharisees kept a careful and faithful hold in their *"traditions of men."* They were zealous in observing their *own* traditions, the mess of pottage delivered to them by men's perverted minds.

(7:9) Jesus used a fine bit of biting sarcasm when He told them that they had *"full, excellently, finely, well"* rejected the Commandments of God. The word for *"reject"* is *atheteo,* and means *"to thwart the efficacy of anything,"* or *"to nullify, make void, to frustrate."* The Pharisees were making null and void the Word of God by their own pointless traditions.

(7:10) Jesus went on to say that Moses had said that they should honor their parents. The word for honor is *timao*. It means *"to revere, venerate, or honor."* It contained the idea of having proper respect for the value of someone or something. In the case of parents, respect and reverence were to be demonstrated to them because of who and what they were.

CURSES. This is a warning about cursing parents. *Kakologeo* means *"to speak ill of, revile, or abuse."* It is used in the sense that an habitual offender would receive the death penalty. It was a very serious sin within the Commandments of God.

(7:11-13) The Jews had found ways of circumventing the Laws requiring them to honor their parents. They could declare *"Corban,"* which is a Hebrew word carried over into the Greek language of the New Testament, having reference to a gift.

Under Mosaic Law the individual had a responsibility to his parents; and if in need they were to be cared for, whether physically or financially. The Rabbis, however, could authorize retention of money that *should* go toward the support of an individual's parents — if he would declare it to be a gift to God. No doubt a percentage of the monies saved might have found its way into the coffers of the Rabbi.

This was in direct violation of the command of God to honor parents and provide them the necessities when need existed. They made the Word of God of *"none effect"* by their traditions and actions. The word is *akuroo,* which means to *"render void, deprive of force and authority, to make invalid."*

They were rendering void the authority of God's Word — which had been entrusted to them as Israel's spiritual leaders. Instead they observed their own traditions and imposed these on the unsuspecting masses who assumed they were keeping *God's* Laws. Jesus demonstrated very clearly that they were following *their* will instead of God's.

It is easy for people to follow the traditions and practices of respected elders. What constitutes a respected elder? All too often this is anyone clothed in the *authority* of an official church position. By blindly following such leaders it is easy to be led away from the True Message of the Word of God. While not a perfect parallel today, there are innumerable doctrines that seeking Christians have had imposed upon them which involve a great deal of *religious* activity with no true end result in the fact of a dynamic spiritual life. Many get into the rut of ritualism and religiosity while failing to experience the personally dynamic effect of the Gospel in their lives.

(7:14) HE HAD CALLED ALL THE PEOPLE UNTO HIM. It is felt by some expositors that out of deference (perhaps even fear) of the religious leaders from Jerusalem, the people might have retired a little into the background — shrunk back from the confrontation between Jesus and the Scribes and Pharisees. So Jesus called the people *back* into the center of the discussion to *publicly* expose the hypocrisy of the Pharisees.

He wanted to reveal the true character of these *"religious leaders"* to the people being led. The Scribes and Pharisees were concerned only with the technical defilement that came about from disobeying their man-made regulations. Jesus clearly and directly exposed the fallacy of their regulations. He told the people to listen to Him and to understand.

(7:15) He then proceeded to explain what defilement really means. It comes from the word *koinoo,* as used in the Second Verse, referring to that which pertained to everyone in common — and only later came to be a contrast between that which was profane and that which was hallowed or sacred. The word *"profane"* suggests anything secular or nonreligious. There was an element of the *"put-down"* here in that anything pertaining to Pharisaical practice was *"sacred"* — while everything else was *"profane."*

When Jesus talked about the things entering into a person, He was talking about food. He said nothing could make them ceremonially unclean — even though one didn't go through the religious ritual of hand-washing. He pointed out to them that what comes *out* of an individual is what defiles him. He was referring of course to the teachings of the Pharisees which were not Biblical.

These Pharisaic teachings defiled them because they were in direct opposition to God's Word. As such, they were false teachers and not set aside for God. They held false doctrines as all-important even though they were in direct opposition to God's Word.

(7:16) Numerous times in Scripture there are exhortations to take heed and listen to what God is about to deliver. While some expositors feel that these words were not in the Original Manuscripts, we *can* assume that Jesus did use this exhortation as it brings attention to a point needing serious and sincere application in every person's life.

(7:17) ENTERED INTO THE HOUSE. The Original Manuscript states that they entered *a* house, not *the* house, so it may or may not have been Peter's house. In any event, they were separated from the people for the moment, and Jesus was questioned by the Disciples about the Parable. They wanted to better understand the discussion between the Lord and the Scribes and Pharisees.

(7:18-29) ARE YOU SO WITHOUT UNDERSTANDING ALSO? It was a disappointment to Jesus that His chosen Disciples didn't clearly understand the discussion. However, in defense of the Disciples, we should realize that they had lived their lives under the Pharisaical theology, so their minds were not conditioned to an immediate and complete break with tradition. Levitical teachings pertaining to clean and unclean had been deeply ingrained in them. They were, however, seeking to learn and understand more fully, so Jesus went on to explain that those things that come from *without* do not defile a man. He said this was because ingested foods go into the belly (*koilia* — the bowels).

Then He went on to explain that the things of the *heart* are what influence and defile a person. Jesus was not implying that it is proper for a person to take just *anything* into his system. Some have perverted this Scripture to mean that it is proper for a person to indulge in alcoholic beverages, narcotics, or even poisons, with no resulting harm to the body. This is, of course, untrue and not at all what Jesus was saying. we know that the body is the Temple of the Holy Spirit; and as such, it is *not* to be desecrated by the intrusion of harmful substances. Jesus was referring to basic foods, and He made this completely clear. This Scripture is in no way to be twisted and perverted to approve the intake of harmful substances.

The Jews had all kinds of laws relative to the preparation and eating of meats, dairy products, and so forth. Some expositors feel that this Passage is related to Peter's vision in Acts 11:1-10, where substances previously considered unclean were placed in a new light within the New Covenant.

Here Jesus was demonstrating that basic foods will not harm us, nor is there any defilement in not following certain rituals before eating. The foods we take in enter the system and are discharged as a natural part of the digestive process. He continues beyond this, though, and points up the *real* problem.

(7:20-23) Our Lord explained that what habitually comes *out* of a person is what defiles him. Out of our hearts come evil thoughts. The word for evil is *kakos,* and means *"of a bad nature, base, wrong, wicked."* The inference is of something sinful. Then He lists evil practices and refers to *"covetings"* (*pleonexia* — a greedy desire to have more, or avarice). The word *"wickedness"* is from *poneria,* which means depravity or iniquity. It speaks of a definite, active wickedness — and carries with it the idea of something that is dangerous and destructive.

The word *"lasciviousness"* is from *aselgeia.* This is taken by some expositors to mean unrestrained sexual instincts and is also used for lawless insolence and wanton capriciousness. The word translated *"evil eye"* is *opthalmos poneros.* This is defined as a *"malicious or evil-working eye."* There is direct, positive, injurious activity implied.

The word translated *"blasphemy"* comes from *blasphemia,* which does not necessarily refer to blasphemy against God. It refers rather to reviling or evil speaking in general, and malicious misrepresentations — malicious gossip, in other words. *"Pride"* is translated from *huperephania.* This involves two words: *huper,* meaning *"above"* and *phanesthai,* which means *"to show one's self."* It portrays an individual who holds himself high above others. It infers the sin of an uplifted heart, placing one's self above one's fellowman, and even God. This word is related to the Pharisee's practice of *"putting down"* anyone who didn't conform exactly to their rituals and ceremonies.

The word translated *"foolishness"* is *aphrosune,* and has to do with *"a lack of sense, folly."*

Basically, Jesus was saying that all these pernicious faults and short-comings, which have their origins within the heart of man, are the factors which cause man's defilement. Physical elements taken in from outside aren't the problem; man's heart is.

THE DAUGHTER OF A GREEK WOMAN IS HEALED

"And from then He arose, and went into the borders of Tyre and Sidon, and entered into an house, and would have no man know it, but He could not be hid. For a certain woman, whose young daughter had an unclean spirit, heard of Him, and came and fell at His Feet: The woman was a Greek, a Syrophenician by nation; and she besought Him that He would cast forth the devil out of her daughter.

"But Jesus said unto her, Let the children first be filled: for it is not meet to take the children's bread, and to cast it unto the dogs. And she answered and said unto Him, Yes, Lord: yet the dogs under the table eat of the children's crumbs. And He said unto her, For this saying go your way; the devil is gone out of your daughter. And when she was come to her house, she found the devil gone out, and her daughter laid upon the bed" (Mk. 7:24-30).

(7:24) Having apparently been in Capernaum, Jesus now withdrew to the area of Tyre and Sidon. He wanted to be alone; perhaps for some sorely needed rest. He entered into a private home with instructions that no one know His whereabouts; but even with these precautions, it was impossible. News concerning this great Teacher and Healer had spread about the country. This was in Phoenicia — deep in the interior of that country.

(7:25) There was a certain woman who, upon hearing Jesus had come to Phoenicia, *"immediately"* (*euthus*) came to Him. She had a small daughter who needed deliverance from demonic possession. The woman fell at Jesus' Feet.

(7:26) She was a *"Greek"* (*Hellenis*), referring not to race but to religion. She was a Gentile, not a Jew; a Phoenician by race and a Syrian by tongue. This was Phoenicia of Syria as distinguished from Phoenicia of North Africa.

SHE BESOUGHT HIM. She persisted in seeking the Lord's

intervention. The verb is *erotao,* and it means she *"was requesting."* She wanted Jesus to *"cast out"* the demon. This is from the word *ekballo,* which means *"to throw out."* This lady, a Gentile and a Syrophenician by race, persistently beseeched Jesus to expel the demon from her daughter.

As she aggressively continued her plea for help, Jesus answered her in a peculiar fashion. He first said that the children need to be filled. Then He said, *". . . it is not meet to take the children's bread and to cast it unto the dogs."* The Gentiles were looked upon as dogs by the Nation of Israel. It was a term of mild reproach. Essentially, Jesus was saying that His Commission was to Judah first and *after that* to the Gentiles.

This was not a matter of favoritism. His primary Mission *was* to Israel. God's whole Plan for the spreading of the Gospel was predicated on this. Only *after* Jesus' rejection by Jewry would the Gospel be carried further — to the *"nations."* This statement is not quite as curt in the original Greek as it appears in the King James translation. God does not discriminate, nor is He a respecter of persons. He does, however, choose individuals and groups for special purposes according to His Will. Jesus used an illustration wherein the children of the household would be fed first and only then would their *"little dogs"* (pets waiting under the table) receive their food.

(7:28) The woman then pointed out that the dogs *do* get some of the crumbs. She used the words *"little dogs," kunarion;* little children, *paidion;* and little morsels, *psichion.* Little dogs kept as household pets were deeply loved by the children and became almost a part of the family. They were never ignored, but rather would receive leftovers from the children's meal. She referred to Jesus as *"Lord"* (*kurios*), which means: master of a thing, or one who disposes of something.

This woman knew her position as a Gentile. Jesus' retort was not a racial put-down, as such, but merely an explanation of the way God was working. She accepted her position and did not allow it to deter her.

(7:29) FOR THIS SAYING. Literally, *"because of this word"* Jesus granted the woman's request. She maintained a responsible attitude with Faith, sincerity, and earnestness. Jesus responded to her need and ministered to her.

THE DEVIL IS GONE OUT. *"The devil is gone out"* from the daughter is an expression inferring an immediate and permanent cure. When the woman returned to her home, she found the little girl quietly lying on her couch with the demons gone.

JESUS HEALS A DEAF MUTE

"And again, departing from the coasts of Tyre and Sidon, He came

unto the Sea of Galilee, through the midst of the coasts of Decapolis. And they bring unto Him one who was deaf, and had an impediment in his speech; and they beseech Him to put His Hand upon him. And He took him aside from the multitude, and put His Fingers into his ears, and He spit, and touched his tongue; And looking up to Heaven, He sighed, and said unto him, Ephphatha, that is, Be opened. And straightway his ears were opened, and the string of his tongue was loosed, and he spoke plain. And He charged them that they should tell no man: but the more He charged them, so much the more a great deal they published it; And were beyond measure astonished, saying, He has done all things well: He makes both the deaf to hear, and the dumb to speak" (Mk. 7:31-37).

(7:31) Jesus left the region of Tyre. Looking at the map of the area, one sees that Phoenicia is northwest of the Sea of Galilee. Jesus would have traveled southeast, around the eastern shore of the sea, to get to Decapolis. The Greek Text literally reads, *"And again, having gone out of the region of Tyre, He went through Sidon to the Sea of Galilee, in the midst of the regions of Decapolis."*

(7:32) A man with a speech impediment was brought to Jesus. This was translated from the word *mogilalos*. *Mogi* means *"with difficulty,"* and *lalos* means *"to speak."* Although this man was deaf, he wasn't completely dumb (mute). He had *difficulty* in speaking, and subsequent reading indicates that he was *"tongue-tied."* The crowd begged Jesus to place His Hand on this man.

(7:33) HE TOOK HIM ASIDE FROM THE MULTITUDE. The word translated *"aside"* is from *katidian*. (The latter means privacy.) For some reason Jesus took this man aside, or away from the crowd.

AND PUT HIS FINGERS INTO HIS EARS. The verb is *ballo*, which means *"to throw or thrust."* He placed a finger in each ear and then spat and touched the tongue. There is no real amplification of the reasons behind these actions. Neither is there reason given why Jesus chose to perform this healing privately. Indication may be that He didn't want it to turn into a sideshow, and an event of this type could appear to be a deliberate display. Apparently, Jesus put a Finger of His right Hand into one of the man's ears and a Finger of His left Hand into the other. No further explanation is given as to the specifics of the incident.

(7:34) AND LOOKING UP TO HEAVEN HE SIGHED. The word for sigh is *stenazo*, and it means *"to sigh or groan."* He looked up toward Heaven with a sigh or groan, no doubt in sympathy for the man's bondage or affliction. Perhaps He also groaned at the thought of Satan having caused the problem. Jesus had deep sympathy and understanding for individuals as He ministered to them. He looked up as He commanded that the ears be opened.

(7:35) HIS EARS WERE OPENED. The word used here in the Greek is *akoe,* and it means *"hearing, sense of hearing."* It further states that the *"string of his tongue was loosed."* Literally it is *"that which bound his tongue* (*desmos* — a band or bond) *is loosed."* This is a perfect description of a malformed lingual phrenum, which causes tongue-tie. Today children with this problem are surgically cured by cutting the offending cord that attaches the tongue to the floor of the mouth.

HE SPOKE PLAIN. The man was suddenly able to speak plainly. Instead of his tongue being attached to the floor of his mouth, he could now move it normally. Prior to this all his vocal sounds were distorted because of the inability of the tongue to move.

(7:36) Jesus then commanded (*straightly charged*) them not to tell anyone. The command was given for a purpose and no doubt had to do with His Ministry, but no further explanation is given. The more He charged them, however, the *"more abundantly"* they broadcast it.

THEY PUBLISHED IT. The verb used here is *kerusso.* As we have seen previously, this means to make a public pronouncement and is also used for *"preaching."* The more He commanded them to say nothing, the more they proclaimed it publicly. Obviously the people were excited by the healing.

(7:37) AND WERE BEYOND MEASURE ASTONISHED. The people were *"struck with astonishment beyond measure."* This is rendered in the passive form. The verb is *ekplesso,* and in this case means *"to strike one out of self-possession."* The word in the Greek translated *"beyond measure"* is *huperperissos.* This is a very strong word, being a double superlative; with *perissos* meaning *"in superabundance."* *Huper* means *"above"* and is used in the English as hyper. The people therefore were astonished above measure, to the point that they were almost *"beyond self-possession."* To be exact, they were past the point of being superabundantly astonished! From this we can assume that they were very impressed with the healing.

The people acknowledged that Jesus had done all things well. After the preceding superlatives, this is something of an understatement. The people were completely convinced that the Lord had done a marvelous work. He made the deaf to hear and the dumb to speak. This marvelous and miraculous healing was cause for enthusiastic rejoicing.

Chapter 8

Jesus Feeds The Four Thousand

SUBJECT	PAGE
THE PHARISEES AND SADDUCEES TEST JESUS	118
THE LEAVEN OF THE PHARISEES	120
JESUS HEALS A BLIND MAN	121
PETER'S CONFESSION	123
JESUS FORETELLS HIS DEATH	124

CHAPTER 8

JESUS FEEDS THE FOUR THOUSAND

"In those days the multitude being very great and having nothing to eat, Jesus called His Disciples unto Him, and said unto them, I have compassion on the multitude, because they have now been with Me three days, and have nothing to eat: And if I send them away fasting to their own houses, they will faint by the way: for divers of them came from far. And His Disciples answered Him, From whence can a man satisfy these men with bread here in the wilderness?

"And He asked them, How many loaves have you? And they said, Seven. And He commanded the people to sit down on the ground: and He took the seven loaves, and gave thanks, and break, and gave to His Disciples to set before them; and they did set them before the people. And they had a few small fishes: and He blessed, and commanded to set them also before them. So they did eat, and were filled: and they took up of the broken meat that was left seven baskets. And they who had eaten were about four thousand: and He sent them away" (Mk. 8:1-9).

(8:1-3) Once again a great throng of people surrounding Jesus were without food. This is the second time our Lord fed the multitudes. Both Matthew and Mark record these incidents.

HAVE COMPASSION. From *splagchna*, this verb means *"the inward parts."* This has special reference to such organs as the heart, lungs, liver, and kidneys. Over the years this term came to denote the seat of affection, just as our own reference to the heart does today. This word is translated *"bowels"* in some translations and it is used in the sense of tender mercy, affection, and compassion. Today one would say, *"My heart goes out to them."*

Jesus had a sincere compassion for the multitudes and a deep love for the people. They had been with Him for three days now, and He chose not to send them away fasting lest some faint along the way.

Some of the people might have brought light provisions with them but probably never dreamed they would be there for three days. Apparently events were so interesting and exciting that they just stayed there.

Whenever a wonderful meeting takes place, the people are reluctant to leave. When God's Presence is real, the Spirit of God is moving, and lives are being refreshed the deepest needs and desires of the heart are being met. Nothing compares and everything else becomes insignificant. Trivialities are forgotten in the Presence of Almighty God.

(8:4) In the area where the multitudes gathered, no food could be bought. Once again the Disciples asked how they could satisfy the people's needs. They had completely forgotten the miracle of the five loaves and two fishes which had happened only a short time before. They had witnessed the Lord multiplying the loaves and fishes, yet they asked how they could satisfy such a crowd in the wilderness. How quickly we all forget what God can do.

They asked *"from whence"* which derives from *pothen.* This was used in asking the source of supply for the food they needed. One suggested translation of this is: How can it be that we can fill (or *"satisfy"* — *chortazo*) these men?

THE WILDERNESS. They refer to themselves as being in the wilderness. The word used is *eremia,* which means *"a solitary or uninhabited region."*

(8:5-6) Then Jesus *"went to asking them"* how many loaves of bread they had. The Disciples told Him they found seven loaves, but there is no indication of where these came from. He then gave the command for the crowd to rest on the ground. He took the seven loaves and, after giving thanks, broke the bread. It is properly stated, *"He broke and continued giving them to His Disciples, in order that they might continue setting them forth."* The Disciples served the crowd.

(8:7) They also had a few small fishes. Jesus blessed these. The word is *eulogeo,* and means, among other things, *"to ask God's Blessing on a thing,"* and also to bless something for one's use. This is the basis for the Christian practice of giving thanks before a meal and praying God's Blessings on it.

(8:8-9) The bread and fish had been served to the people; they ate and were filled. The Disciples then took up seven baskets of leftovers. The word broken *"meat"* is in italics, which indicates it was not in the original Greek Text. This was inserted by the King James translators to clarify the meaning for the English reader. The word *"meat"* simply meant food of any kind. Today it implies animal flesh. The word for *"broken"* is *klasma,* which means *"a fragment, a broken piece,"* and was used to convey the thought of scraps of food.

How wonderfully and bountifully God supplies. He has provisions for our every need. God works in many ways — even in mysterious ways — to perform wonders in providing for His Children.

THE PHARISEES AND SADDUCEES TEST JESUS

"And straightway He entered into a ship with His Disciples, and came into the parts of Dalmanutha. And the Pharisees came forth,

and began to question with Him, seeking of Him a sign from Heaven, tempting Him. And He sighed deeply in His Spirit, and said, Why does this generation seek after a sign? verily I say unto you, There shall no sign be given unto this generation" (Mk. 8:10-12).

(8:10-11) Jesus and His Disciples entered into a ship and came into *"the parts of Dalmanutha."* This place is unknown today but is possibly somewhere in the region of Decapolis.

THE PHARISEES CAME FORTH. Decapolis was a heathen country and the Pharisees stayed mostly in *"the Holy Land,"* normally shunning this area. Now, however, in their zealous opposition to Jesus, they followed Him to Decapolis in order to further harass and cross-examine Him. The expressions used indicate a dispute, with Jesus defending His position.

SEEKING OF HIM A SIGN FROM HEAVEN. The word *"sign"* is *semeion*. This is one of several words used to designate a miracle. They wanted Him to perform a miracle to *prove* He was the representative of God.

TEMPTING HIM. The verb is *peirazomai,* and means *"to put to the test."* The usual meaning is to demonstrate what good or evil exists within a situation or person. This word is also used in the sense of tempting a person to do evil, but here the Pharisees were *"putting Jesus to the test"* to force Him to *prove* to them whether He was indeed the Messiah.

(8:12) AND HE SIGHED DEEPLY IN HIS SPIRIT. The verb used is *stenazo*. It means *"to groan or to sigh."* Here it has a preposition prefixed, *ana,* which magnifies the meaning, indicating that Jesus sighed from the very *depths* of His Spirit. His Ministry was being questioned, not by the ordinary sinner, but by the corrupt religious hierarchy of Israel.

They were bound by their traditions and rituals and deeply immersed in their ecclesiasticism. Jesus performed countless public miracles, many of them within the sight of the Pharisees. Instead of falling to their knees before their Messiah, they attributed them to Satan. The Scribes, Pharisees, and Sadducees were spiritually blind and given over to reprobate minds. They were totally committed to the demon spirits who guided and influenced their sordid activities. It was these same religious leaders who ultimately arranged our Lord's Crucifixion.

It is not at all uncommon for religious leaders to be controlled by demonic *"religious spirits."* There is enormous *"religious"* activity going on wholly removed from God. The spiritual forces involved are hardly *"Divine."* It is truly important that Christians attend a Church where the true and total Word of God is preached.

THERE SHALL NO SIGN BE GIVEN UNTO THIS GENERATION. In Matthew 12:39 the Lord is quoted a little more fully and it is given as, *"an evil and adulterous generation."* This does not necessarily refer to a *"generation"* as we think of it, as an entire age-group living at a time. Jesus was referring to the Scribes and Pharisees specifically.

This group was *"testing"* Jesus by asking for a miracle, or a sign. Jesus said they would not be given a sign and the expression used is part of a Hebrew idiom and literally states, *"if a sign shall be given."*

Jesus absolutely refused to perform miracles on demand for an unbelieving, apostate group. However, His response in no way indicates a reluctance to reveal or demonstrate the Power of God.

Spiritual matters are *never* to be revealed before those who will desecrate and trample them underfoot. On another occasion (reported in Mat. 7:6) Jesus said, *"Neither cast you your pearls before swine, lest they trample them under their feet."*

Priceless gems of spiritual truth and experience should not be subjected to desecration.

THE LEAVEN OF THE PHARISEES

"And He left them, and entering into the ship again departed to the other side. Now the Disciples had forgotten to take bread, neither had they in the ship with them more than one loaf. And He charged them, saying, Take heed, beware of the leaven of the Pharisees, and of the leaven of Herod. And they reasoned among themselves, saying, It is because we have no bread. And when Jesus knew it, He said unto them, Why reason you, because you have no bread? perceive ye not yet, neither understand? have ye your heart yet hardened?

"Having eyes, see ye not? and having ears, hear ye not? and do you not remember? When I broke the five loaves among five thousand, how many baskets full of fragments took ye up? They say unto Him, Twelve. And when the seven among four thousand, how many baskets full of fragments took ye up? And they said, Seven. And He said unto them, How is it that you do not understand?" (Mk. 8:13-21).

(8:13) Jesus and His Disciples left the crowd and, entering into a ship, went to the other side. The words, *"He left them"* are from the verb *aphiemi,* which means *"send away from one's self"* or to *"bid to go away."* It was used by teachers and speakers in the context of letting go, leaving, or ending a discussion. Jesus abruptly terminated the dispute and left the skeptics.

(8:14) After they were in the boat, the Disciples noticed there wasn't any food. They had just one loaf of bread as they had forgotten to provision the ship. The word *"forgotten"* is from *lanthano,* which means to forget, and it has a preposition prefixed which makes it mean they had *completely* forgotten.

(8:15) HE CHARGED THEM. The verb is in the imperfect tense and so means, *"He repeatedly charged them."*

He warned them to take heed and beware. The expression *"Take heed and beware"* is made up of two verbs. The first one is *harao,* and means *"to see, to become acquainted with be experience."* This implies thinking about a situation and using discrimination. They were to put the teachings of the Pharisees and Herodians to the test — not by actually following them but by observing their ultimate consequences. The verb is in a tense indicating that they were to *continually* do this.

The second verb is *blepo,* and this means *"to perceive by the use of the eyes."* They were to *see* and take heed. They were to remain watchful and consider the ultimate consequences of this leaven of the Pharisees.

LEAVEN. The word used is *zume.* This was used in the Septuagint (the first part of the Old Testament) in referring to beer-making yeast (Ex.12:15). This refers to the process of fermentation and is used as a symbol of corruption. Whenever the word leaven is used in Scripture, it refers to evil in some form. The Disciples were warned to be on the lookout for the leaven (the evil ferment) of the Pharisees and Herodians.

(8:16) AND THEY REASONED AMONG THEMSELVES. The verb is *dialogizomai,* which means to gather different thoughts, to deliberate. Our word *"dialogue"* comes from this. The imperfect tense indicates that they continued reasoning among themselves. The Disciples clearly didn't understand what Jesus was talking about.

(8:17-21) The Lord was disappointed in their failure of perception and discernment. They were His *"Disciples"* (*mathetes* — pupils or students) and He rebuked them for their preoccupation with such temporal matter as bread and their inability to think in more profound terms.

Jesus was not criticizing them for having forgotten bread. He reminded them of the baskets of remaining fragments from the time He had fed the five thousand with five loaves and two fishes and the four thousand with seven loaves. He asked how it was that they didn't understand. This had no reference to bread — He could *create* bread from thin air. He was talking about the leaven of the Pharisees — doctrines which could influence and corrupt men's minds.

JESUS HEALS A BLIND MAN

"And He comes to Bethsaida; and they bring a blind man unto Him, and besought Him to touch Him. And He took the blind man by the hand, and led him out of the town; and when He had spit on his eyes, and put His Hands upon him, He asked him if he saw ought. And

He looked up, and said, I see men as trees, walking. After that He put His Hands again upon his eyes, and made him look up: and he was restored, and saw every man clearly. And He sent him away to his house, saying, Neither go into the town, nor tell it to any in the town" (Mk. 8:22-26).

(8:22-23) When they reached Bethsaida, a blind man was brought to the Lord. They asked Jesus to touch him. He took the blind man by the hand and led him out of the village away from the crowd so He might minister to him without the throng pressing in upon them.

WHEN HE HAD SPIT ON HIS EYES. This seems strange but there is no explanation offered. Some expositors propose that the reason for doing this was that the people considered spittle to have curative powers. We can speculate as to just why Jesus did this, but the Bible simply states that He did it. He also placed His Hands upon him and asked him if he could see.

(8:24-25) The man looked up. The word is *anablepo,* and means simply that he looked up. Some texts use *diablepo,* which means *"He looked through,"* indicating that he stared fixedly. The man saw men as trees walking. Jesus replaced His Hands upon his eyes and made him look up again. Now the man could see clearly. The word translated *"saw"* is *emblepo,* which means *"looking into"* or *"to see distinctly."* The word translated *"clearly"* is *telaugos,* and it is made up of *tele,* which means *"afar"* and *auge,* which means *"radiance."* The compound word thus means *"far-shining"* and has been translated by some as *"at a distance and clearly."*

This is an interesting healing in that it was not completed instantaneously, but in two stages. In other cases blind individuals experienced instantaneous healings. Jesus obviously ministered in different ways to different people.

Individuals like to teach prescribed forms for receiving miracles from God. Unfortunately, things seldom go according to a set format. Just because something happened in a certain way for one person does not imply that it has to happen exactly that way for another.

There are those in our own day who have been healed of major afflictions in marvelous and miraculous ways. Some who *haven't* been healed have been advised to stop taking their medicine and *"make a step of Faith."* This does not mean, however, that everyone should throw away his medicine. In some cases, doing so may jeopardize the safety of the individual and that of others. To do so also comes very close to ignoring Jesus' admonition in Luke 4:12, *"You shall not tempt* (test) *the Lord your God."*

To pray for healing is always in order. To trust God and believe for a

miraculous cure is certainly Scriptural. But if the cure has not been manifested, one should not act presumptuously and disregard practical aids in
keeping the condition under control.

(8:26) After the man was healed, Jesus sent him away to his house,
instructing him not to go into town nor to noise it about. At this particular
time Jesus wanted to avoid the sensation it would cause.

Even when there is much to do, there are times when the laborer must
rest. In any event, Jesus apparently had other priorities at the moment.

PETER'S CONFESSION

*"And Jesus went out, and His Disciples, into the towns of Caesarea
Philippi: and by the way He asked His Disciples, saying unto them,
Whom do men say that I am? And they answered, John the Baptist:
but some say, Elijah; and others, One of the Prophets. And He said
unto them, But whom say you that I am? And Peter answered and
said unto Him, You are the Christ. And He charged them that they
should tell no man of Him"* (Mk. 8:27-30).

(8:27-28) Jesus and His Disciples went into the area of Caesarea
Philippi. Mark uses the term *kome,* which means *"a village"* while Matthew uses the word *mere,* which means *"region."* Some expositors feel
that perhaps Jesus did not go into the city itself but ministered in the general
area. He was avoiding towns at this time for several reasons, one perhaps
being that He desired solitude. Additionally, the Scribes and Pharisees
were, of course, disrupting His meetings with their disputations. His Crucifixion was only a few months away and He was spending more time alone
with His Disciples as He prepared them for the responsibilities of their
future ministries.

Jesus asked the Disciples, *"Whom do men say that I am?"* The
imperfect tense indicates *"He continued to ask."* He was seeking to
draw from His Disciples what they thought of Him. Throughout the area
there was a great deal of speculation in this regard.

The Disciples replied that some thought He was John the Baptist raised
from the dead. Herod held this view and obviously others agreed. Some
said He was Elijah. Others thought He might be one of the old Prophets
who had returned.

(8:29) After they told Jesus who *others* thought He might be, He then
asked them, *"But whom say you that I am?"* In the expression *"He said
unto them,"* the word for *"said"* is *eperotao,* which means *"to ask, to
question."* It is in the imperfect tense and indicates that he *persisted* in
questioning them. There is also emphasis on *"you"* from the word *humeis.*
Literally, He is saying, *"As for **you**, disregarding the opinions of others,*

*who do **you** think I am?"*

YOU ARE THE CHRIST. Here again the specific pronoun is used for emphasis and it would literally mean, *"Speaking of You, You are the Christ."*

The word *Christos* is translated *"Christ"* and means *"the Anointed One."* The word *"Christ"* is simply the English spelling of the word *Christos*.

The Hebrew word for this is translated *"Messiah"* in English. Some expositors feel that Peter was saying, *"You are the Messiah."* Peter, always quick to speak, was stating boldly that he believed Jesus of Nazareth to be the Messiah, *"the Anointed One,"* Who would save Israel and the world.

(8:30) Jesus now told them not to divulge that He was the Messiah. It says He *charged* them not to tell. The word for *"charged"* is *epitimao*, which means *"to admonish or charge sharply."* The term is so strong that some expositors feel He literally *threatened* them should they disobey, as it was not yet the proper time.

There is a time to be silent and to wait. He did not want to be publicly revealed as the Messiah at this time. Jesus' triumphal entry into Jerusalem was to be the significant demonstration and proclamation, but that was to come later. For now it was expedient that He remain quietly with His Disciples.

The Herodians, the Sadducees, the Pharisees, the Scribes, and many others hated and wanted to kill Him. He wanted to fulfill His Commission and lay a solid teaching foundation before they could accomplish His Crucifixion. His Disciples needed more preparation before they would be ready to carry out their mission after the Lord's Death. Publicly proclaiming His Divinity would create a tremendous uproar that would effectively end His Ministry and bring about His premature death.

So He charged them to tell no one what He was about, explaining to them that He must be killed and raised again.

JESUS FORETELLS HIS DEATH

"And He began to teach them, that the Son of Man must suffer many things, and be rejected of the Elders, and of the Chief Priests, and Scribes, and be killed, and after three days rise again. And He spoke that saying openly. And Peter took Him, and began to rebuke Him. But when He had turned about and looked on His Disciples, He rebuked Peter, saying, Get thee behind Me, Satan: for you savor not the things that be of God, but the things that be of men. And when He had called the people unto Him with His Disciples also, He said unto them, Whosoever will come after Me, let him deny himself, and take

up his cross, and follow Me. For whosoever will save his life shall lose it; but whosoever shall lose his life for My sake and the Gospel's, the same shall save it.

"For what shall it profit a man, if he shall gain the whole world, and lose his own soul? Or what shall a man give in exchange for his soul? Whosoever therefore shall be ashamed of Me and of My Words in this adulterous and sinful generation; of him also shall the Son of Man be ashamed, when He comes in the Glory of His Father with the Holy Angels" (Mk. 8:31-38).

(8:31) AND HE BEGAN TO TEACH THEM. During this time Jesus was devoting particular attention to His Disciples. He was training and preparing them for the events that would precede and follow His Death.

THE SON OF MAN MUST SUFFER. The word translated *"must"* is *dei*, and means *"it is necessary in the nature of the case."* Jesus *had* to die on the Cross to satisfy the claims of Holy justice. Man is a sinner and needs to be saved. God, in His love for man, provides the Salvation man is incapable of providing for himself. It was essential that Jesus must suffer and die.

He went on to say that He would *"be rejected of the Elders, the Chief Priests, and the Scribes."* The word for *"rejected"* is *apodokimazo*. This is a compound verb. The prefix *apo* means *"off, away from."* The basic verb means *"to put a person to the test."* This involves approval within the specifications laid down. The broader meaning infers rejection following such a test. Jesus did *not* meet the specifications laid down by the Jewish leaders. He was not the kind of Messiah the Jews were looking for.

They wanted a military leader who would free them from the yoke of Roman bondage. They were not concerned about, nor sympathetic to, a Saviour who would free them from the bondage of sin. Jesus' purpose was spiritual while theirs was strictly temporal. Jesus said that not only would they reject Him, but they would kill Him, and after three days He would rise again.

(8:32) HE SPOKE THAT SAYING OPENLY. Jesus didn't just make a quick, short statement in passing, but repeatedly emphasized this thought to them. The word *"openly"* is from *parresia*, and it means that He spoke plainly and unmistakably. In the Thirty-first Verse it says He *"taught"* them and the word used is *didaskein*. Here He has made a *statement*. Jesus was completely open and without reservation when directly revealing these truths to the Disciples.

PETER TOOK HIM. The word in the Greek is *proslambano*, and it is made up of two words. The simple verb means *"to take."* The prefix, which is the preposition *pros*, means *"facing."* The idea conveyed is that

SELF-HELP
STUDY NOTES

125

of someone taking hold of another, facing him. Peter may have taken hold of the Lord by the arm, perhaps even leading Him aside in order to rebuke Him.

PETER . . . BEGAN TO REBUKE HIM. What Peter said is not revealed, but Jesus had clearly stated what was going to take place and Peter was upset and reacting to it.

(8:33) WHEN HE HAD TURNED ABOUT. The word used is *epistrepho,* which means *"to turn one's self about."* When Jesus heard what Peter said, He turned around and faced the other Disciples. Apparently they too had heard what Peter said to the Lord, so He spoke to all of them.

HE REBUKED PETER. Now Jesus rebuked Peter. Peter did not realize what a dreadful statement he had made but Jesus said, *"Get thee behind Me, Satan."*

He then went on to state that Peter did not understand (have a mind for) the things of God. The cry that Jesus made was an agonized one. It was Satan who was putting these thoughts into Peter's mind. Peter was looking, through Satan's influence, at the worldly aspects of the situation. He and the Disciples appreciated and *needed* Jesus as their leader. Life without Him would be unbearable. Peter therefore was a willing tool for Satan's thoughts and words.

Satan can speak through the best-intentioned of people. The words uttered by Peter were put there by Satan. A person may be committed to Christ and *still* make erroneous statements. A person may be right in his heart yet wrong in his head.

Jesus told Peter, *"you savor not the things that be of God."* The word for *"savor"* is *phroneo,* and means *"to direct one's mind to a thing, to seek or strive for."* Paul used this word in Philippians 2:5, concerning the Mind of Christ, when he said, *"Let this mind be in you."* Peter simply did not *"have a mind for"* the things of God.

There are many men today who love God with all their hearts, who desire to see people saved, but who consistently fight the mighty movings of the Holy Spirit. Peter was sincere and he loved Jesus. But Satan was allowed to speak through him. This also happens today.

While Jesus rebuked Peter, He was also speaking to Satan. Satan was not visible to the Disciples, but he was assuredly there.

(8:34) Following this, Jesus called the people and the Disciples unto Him and instructed them on the costs of discipleship. He said that whosoever *"will"* *(thelo* — to desire) come after Him must make a definite commitment.

LET HIM DENY HIMSELF. The Greek word is *aparneomai,* and the manner in which it is used in this expression means *"to forget one's self"* or *"to lose sight of one's self-interest."* It has the idea of entering into a new state of being.

Then He said, *"take up his cross. . . ."* The cross was an instrument of death and this spoke of a person dying to self, to *find* life in Christ. He said, *"follow me,"* which means, *"to take the same road."*

The person who is committed to Christ must come after Him and take up his cross — following Jesus. These acts are to be a permanent attitude in one's life. It is not a momentary or temporary matter, as the expressions used clearly indicate. This was to be a *habitual "coming after"* and a *continual "taking up of one's cross."* This of course is God's Will for one's life. Once a person's life is given over to Christ, it is no longer his own. He belongs to the Lord and becomes the Lord's *property.* A person choosing to follow Jesus must lose sight of self and personal interests, take up his cross, and *persevere* in the walk with Jesus.

(8:35-37) WHOSOEVER WILL SAVE HIS LIFE. This does not refer to one's physical existence, but rather to the soul — the part of man which thinks, feels, and has willpower, emotions, hopes, and aspirations.

God so created man that he cannot truly find rest and satisfaction until his entire *being* is consumed with the desire to do the Will of God. He is not speaking about Salvation here. Jesus saves us because God loves us. This is through Grace, which involves His *undeserved* love and *unmerited* favor.

Jesus is pointing out one of life's paradoxes; that it is only when a person *gives* of himself that he comes into the full realization of his potential. The person who selfishly wants to *"save"* his life — that is, keep it all for himself — will inevitably *lose* it. If one truly gives himself over to the Lord and fully trusts Him, he will come into the realization — not only of God's Salvation and Grace — but of fulfillment for his life too.

While overcoming self-centeredness does not in itself save a person, the *failure* to overcome self-interest can result in being lost eternally. In trusting Christ, a person commits one's *entire self* to Him. Jesus went on to point out that there would be no profit to a man if he gained the whole world and lost his soul. There is nothing a person could acquire with value equal to his soul. By giving ourselves whole-heartedly to Christ, we become more alive, more aware, and more satisfied. Only by ignoring self can we gain life.

(8:38) WHOSOEVER THEREFORE SHALL BE ASHAMED OF ME. . . . Some expositors feel that this Passage should really have been incorporated into the next Chapter. When Jesus was transfigured, He was glorified, just as He will be in the Millennium. This logically refers to the Millennial Kingdom and His Reign as King of kings and Lord of lords.

Anyone denying His Kingship *prior* to the inception of His earthly Reign can expect that Jesus will similarly deny *his* credentials for inclusion in His kingdom. *Today* is the time when Faith counts. Once Jesus is reigning in Power and Glory, *everyone* will accept His Divinity. It is today — when the world rejects Him, persecuting and scoffing at the Believer — that *"Faith will be imputed (considered or credited) as Righteousness"* by God, as it was to Abraham (James 2:23).

Notes

Chapter 9

The Transfiguration Of Jesus

SUBJECT   PAGE

A BOY IS DELIVERED OF A DEMON 135
JESUS FORETELLS HIS DEATH AND RESURRECTION 140
GOD'S PEOPLE MUST BE CHILDLIKE 141
DON'T STOP OTHERS FROM DOING GOOD 142
TEMPTATIONS TO SIN 143

CHAPTER 9

THE TRANSFIGURATION OF JESUS

"And He said unto them, Verily, I say unto you, That there be some of them who stand here, which shall not taste of death, till they have seen the Kingdom of God come with power. And after six days Jesus took with Him Peter, and James, and John, and leadeth them up into an high mountain apart by themselves: and He was transfigured before them. And His raiment became shining, exceeding white as snow; so as no fuller on earth can white them. And there appeared unto them Elijah (Elias) with Moses: and they were talking with Jesus.

"And Peter answered and said to Jesus, Master, it is good for us to be here: and let us make three Tabernacles; one for You, and one for Moses, and one for Elijah (Elias). For he wist not what to say; for they were sore afraid. And there was a cloud that overshadowed them: and a Voice came out of the cloud, saying, This is my Beloved Son: hear Him.

"And suddenly, when they had looked round about, they saw no man any more, save Jesus only with themselves. And as they came down from the mountain, He charged them that they should tell no man what things they had seen, till the Son of Man were risen from the dead. And they kept that saying with themselves, questioning one with another what the rising from the dead should mean. And they asked Him, saying, Why say the Scribes that Elijah (Elias) must first come? And He answered and told them, Elijah (Elias) verily cometh first, and restoreth all things; and how it is written of the Son of Man, that He must suffer many things, and be set at nought. But I say unto you, That Elijah (Elias) is indeed come, and they have done unto him whatsoever they listed, as it is written of Him" (Mk. 9:1-13).

(9:1) The proximity of this Verse — to the subsequent account of the transfiguration of Christ — indicates that the Transfiguration was to be understood by the Disciples as having a significant relationship to the phrase *"...the Kingdom of God come with power."* All three synoptic Gospels include this in close proximity to the Transfiguration.

"He was transfigured" is a translation of the Greek word *metemorphothe*. It literally means *"to change a pattern."* Moses and Elijah appeared and were changed. This occurrence was a *preview* of that which will be more completely and permanently fulfilled at some time in the near future. It was an anticipatory disclosure of the Millennial condition. The Lord Jesus Christ is the Messiah. He was transfigured then and will be

again throughout the Millennium.

Peter, James, and John are dead now, and they were told *they would not die* (Mk. 9:1) until they saw the Kingdom come with power. They saw that in the preview, at the Transfiguration. They saw Moses who serves as the type for *all* the Saints who lived from Adam's time to the Rapture — those who died as Believers.

Elijah is the type of those who are *alive* on the Earth at the time of the Rapture — who will be glorified and translated *without* dying — because Elijah didn't die, he was translated.

In this same Chapter there is a great multitude referred to in the Fourteenth Verse which will need the Ministry of the Messiah. These are the type of Gentile nations which will receive the Ministry of Israel during the Millennium. The Disciples were shown the Millennium from afar. Just a small part was revealed to them when they saw the glorified Lord Jesus in the condition He will assume throughout the Millennium.

Israel, having rejected Jesus Christ for thousands of years, will accept Him at the close of the Tribulation period and at the beginning of the great Millennial Reign. Peter, James, and John represent Israel. Israel will be cleansed and restored in the Second Advent — which is the Second Coming of the Lord Jesus Christ. Peter, James, and John were the type for restored Israel. Of course, at the time they didn't truly understand what was happening.

The Transfiguration was a preview, in microcosm, of the Millennial Kingdom. The Disciples were told they would see the Kingdom coming in power before they died, and this is precisely what they saw on the Mount of Transfiguration.

(9:2-3) HE WAS TRANSFIGURED BEFORE THEM. The simple verb translated *"transfigured"* here refers to the act of giving outward expression to one's inner character. This outward expression is the *true* representation of the inner character. The preposition prefixed to the verb signifies a change. Jesus *appeared* (to the general mass of the people) as a Galilean peasant. He was *"the man of sorrows"* and *"acquainted with grief."* But in His innermost being He was the very Son of God and that glory glowed constantly *within* Him.

Jesus took Peter, James, and John with Him. These three accompanied Him as an *"inner circle."* There are no specific reasons or explanations given for their selection, but Jesus knew their hearts and He knew the purpose He had for their lives. He chose them as a *"special elect"* within the main body of the Disciples.

LEADETH THEM UP INTO AN HIGH MOUNTAIN. Traditionally, Mount Tabor has been identified as the site of the Transfiguration. What happened there was significant from several points of view.

First, Jesus is clearly the *fulfillment* of *"the Law and the Prophets."* The Law was represented by Moses (who delivered it) and the Prophets were represented by Elijah — perhaps the premiere Prophet in all of history.

Secondly, Jesus was seen in the glorious splendor that will be His when He returns. It is, however, doubtful that the full *magnitude* of this glory was displayed here, because Scripture reveals that on His Return He will light up the heavens (Mat. 24:27). Obviously, this was *not* evident to that degree here, because only Peter, James, and John were aware of it, while the crowds below saw no manifestation of what occurred on the mountain.

Thirdly, *both* classes of Believers affected by the return are represented. Moses died and was buried (Deut. 34:5-6), so he represents those who have died in the Lord and who will be resurrected and glorified at Christ's coming in glory. Elijah was *translated*. He did not pass through the experience of death (II Ki. 2:11). He thus represents those who will be *alive at the* Lord's return, and who will be caught up in the air to be with the Lord (See I Thess. 4:13-17). The entire incident displays, in miniature, the coming of the glorious Millennial Kingdom of Christ.

(9:4) ELIJAH (ELIAS). The spelling here is Elias because the Greek alphabet does not have the letter *"J."* However, it actually refers to Elijah.

THEY WERE TALKING WITH JESUS. The emphasis of the word is that it was a *protracted* conversation. The dialogue went on for some time.

(9:5-6) PETER ANSWERED. Peter was impetuous and unpredictable. Time and again he blundered into embarrassing situations by blurting out words which might better have been left unsaid.

The word for *"answered"* is *apokrinomai*. It is a compound word meaning *"to give off judgment from one's self."* Peter *intruded* into the conversation and interjected his judgment or assessment of the situation. The form of the expression infers some deliberation, but it is hard to picture Peter as having given *anything* much thought. There is no indication that Peter's opinion was sought; he simply intrudes, offering his judgment as to what ought to be done. To interrupt any conversation to interject irrelevant comment is always in poor taste, but how much more so for Peter to interrupt the Lord Jesus Christ, the God of Glory, and two of the greatest personalities who ever lived, Moses and Elijah. Also, how *typical* of Peter.

MASTER. Three titles were used for Jewish teachers. *"Rab"* was used to identify any teacher. *"Rabbi"* was used to denote skillful or noted teachers. The word *"Rabboni"* was reserved for a special, *master* teacher. On this occasion Peter uses the word *"Rabbi,"* which is here translated *"Master."* This word in Hebrew means, *"much, great."* It was a term of respect and honor. It might well be translated *"my great one"* or *"my honorable sir."*

IT IS GOOD FOR US TO BE HERE. In the Greek language there are two special words used for *"good."* One is *agathos*, which has to do with intrinsic goodness. The other word is *kalos,* and this refers to goodness as it is *perceived.* It also projects the idea of *"beautiful,"* and the Greeks used it for anything especially noteworthy within the idea of excellence, goodness, usefulness — or anything particularly pleasing. It could be applied to something handsome, useful, suitable, or commendable. This is the word used here.

LET US MAKE THREE TABERNACLES. The expression *"let us"* as used here does not simply state *"allow us."* It is rather an exhortation for others to join and participate in a project. The word translated *"tabernacles"* is *skene,* which means *"tent."* It comes from the Greek word which means *"to cover."*

Peter's problem was that he didn't really know what to say. The wise course would have been for him to remain silent, but he was so frightened that he blurted out his comments. The words *"sore afraid"* are translated from *ekphobos.* This means *"to throw into a violent fright."*

Peter expresses his opinion and calls Jesus *"Rabbi."* He suggests that it would be well for them to make three tents — one for Jesus, one for Moses, and one for Elijah.

(9:7) A cloud suddenly appeared. The expression indicates suddenness and the fact that this is a remarkable event. The cloud overshadowing them was not a meteorological cloud; it was the Shekinah glory cloud. This was the cloud that led Israel out of Egypt, and which existed above the Mercy Seat beneath the Golden Cherubim in the Holy of Holies. This cloud enveloped Peter, James, and John, together with Moses, Elijah, and the Lord Jesus. What a precious experience it must have been!

God spoke to them out of the cloud. He said, *"This is my Son, the Beloved One."* The word translated *"beloved"* is *agapetos.* This expresses a love drawn from one's heart by something very precious within the person who is loved.

The Disciples were commanded to *"hear Him."* The literal meaning of the verb is *"to constantly hear Him."* The verb translated *"hear"* is *akouo,* and in the context used does not refer merely to the act of hearing — in the sense of listening — but rather to the act of *obeying* what is heard. They were to constantly *hear* Him and to always *obey* Him.

God was not seen by the Disciples. He was revealing to them that Moses and Elijah were not to be compared with His Beloved Son. The emphasis was on listening to His *Son,* the Lord Jesus Christ. This is infinitely more important than listening to a Prophet, who is merely mortal.

Jesus was the Son of God. Of course, in Peter's defense, he was *accustomed* to seeing Jesus (although not in the glorified, transfigured state), while he was *not* used to seeing Moses and Elijah.

(9:8) Suddenly there was a change. They looked around and there was no more cloud, and Moses and Elijah were gone. Only Jesus was now with them.

(9:9) When they came down from the mountain, Jesus charged them not to *"narrate the things which they saw"* until the Son of Man should arise from the dead.

(9:10) AND THEY KEPT THAT SAYING WITH THEMSELVES. The word for *"kept"* is *krateo*, and it means *"to keep carefully and faithfully."* This is a strong word that means to hold something strongly. It also refers to complete mastery of something.

Next, it says they were questioning among themselves. This is from the word *sunzeteo*. The verb *zeteo* means *"to seek."* The first part of the word is a preposition meaning *"with."* The phrase might be more correctly translated *"they were disputing among themselves."* It was a discussion wherein they were searching for a solution. The specific concept puzzling them was the matter of arising from the dead.

(9:11) They asked Him. The imperfect tense of the verb implies a continuous questioning. Apparently they then went on to question Him about the necessity of Elijah coming first.

(9:12-13) ELIJAH (ELIAS) VERILY COMETH FIRST. The word translated *"verily"* is *men*, which means *"it is true."* It was true that Elijah must come first and restore all things. Restore is from the Greek, *apokathistanei*, which means *"to restore order"* or to *"restore health."* This was what the Scribes taught, and Jesus simply said that this was correct.

Elijah will come later, during the closing days, in the midst of the Great Tribulation period. He will come with Enoch and will testify for a number of months to Israel and Jerusalem (Rev. 11:3-12). John the Baptist *had* come, but he was not Elijah. Rather, he came in the *spirit and power* of Elijah. John the Baptist fulfilled the prophecy concerning the preparation of the hearts of Israel for the *First* Advent of the Messiah. Elijah will return and prepare Israel for His Second Advent.

A BOY IS DELIVERED OF A DEMON

"And when He came to His Disciples, He saw a great multitude about them, and the Scribes questioning with them. And straightway all the people, when they beheld Him, were greatly amazed, and running to Him saluted Him. And He asked the Scribes, What question ye with them? And one of the multitude answered and said, Master, I

have brought unto You my son, which has a dumb spirit; And wheresoever he takes him, he tears him: and he foams, and gnasheth with his teeth, and pines away: and I spoke to Your Disciples that they should cast him out; and they could not. He answered him, and said, O faithless generation, how long shall I be with you? how long shall I suffer you? bring him unto Me.

"And they brought him unto Him: and when he saw Him straightway the spirit tore him; and he fell on the ground, and wallowed foaming. And He asked his father, How long is it ago since this came unto him? And he said, Of a child. And ofttimes it has cast him into the fire, and into the waters, to destroy him: but if You can do any thing, have compassion on us, and help us. Jesus said unto him, If you can believe, all things are possible to him who believes. And straightway the father of the child cried out, and said with tears, Lord, I believe, help Thou mine unbelief. When Jesus saw that the people came running together, He rebuked the foul spirit, saying unto him, You dumb and deaf spirit, I charge you, come out of him, and enter no more into him. And the spirit cried, and rent him sore, and came out of him: and he was as one dead; insomuch that many said, he is dead. But Jesus took him by the hand, and lifted him up; and he arose. And when he was come into the house, His Disciples asked Him privately, Why could not we cast him out? And He said unto them, This kind can come forth by nothing but by prayer and fasting" (Mk. 9:14-29).

(9:14) When the Master, together with Peter, James, and John, came down from the mountain after the Transfiguration, they saw a great multitude around the Disciples. The Scribes were questioning (disputing) with the nine Disciples. A man had brought his demon-possessed son, and the Disciples had tried to deliver the boy but failed.

The Scribes, who hated the Lord Jesus Christ, were delighted with the failure of the Disciples and were taunting them. A large crowd watched. This was the scene that Peter, James, John, and Jesus encountered when they suddenly returned. The watching crowd was no doubt sympathetic to the nine remaining Disciples, but the boy was still bound by the spirit.

(9:15) WERE GREATLY AMAZED. When Jesus walked into their midst, the people were *"utterly amazed."* They were surprised because they had no idea that Jesus was about to appear.

The Scribes were undoubtedly taking the Name of the Master in vain. The people were in sympathy with the Disciples, having become accustomed to seeing healings take place. As the Master appeared, they greeted Him with mixed emotions. They were ashamed, yet delighted, to see Him. They saluted Him. The word translated *"saluted"* is *aspazomai*. It means to greet one, bid him welcome, or wish him well.

(9:16) HE ASKED THE SCRIBES. Jesus asked what was going on. He said in essence, *"What are you questioning them about?"*

(9:17-18) The crowd was silent. The man spoke saying he had brought his son who had a dumb spirit. The boy was unable to talk. The demon had bound the boy's tongue and vocal cords. The man addressed Jesus with the word *didaskalos,* which means *"teacher,"* but it is here rendered *"Master."* He had not known that Jesus was absent when he brought his son to the Disciples. When he discovered that Jesus wasn't there, he sought the aid of the Disciples in casting out the demon. They were unsuccessful.

HE TAKES HIM. The man explained that the demon spirit would take control of the boy and throw him into convulsions. The word *katakambano* is used and means *"to lay hold of so as to make one's own, to seize upon, to take possession of."* Then it says the demon *"tear"* him. The word used means *"to distort, convulse."* He would grit or gnash his teeth as he experienced these frightening seizures.

He said the boy *"pines away."* The verb is *xeraino,* meaning *"to dry up, to wither."* It means *"to waste away."*

He wanted the Disciples to cast out this demon spirit, but they did not have the power to do so. The effects of the demon spirit were indeed terrible. Seizures or convulsions wracked the boy's body and threatened his life. The parents were frantic and the Disciples were powerless, but Jesus assured the father that his Faith (declared in Verse 24) would be rewarded.

(9:19) O FAITHLESS GENERATION. Jesus was perhaps talking mainly to His Disciples here, but assuredly He included the Scribes. The crowd may have been included. The Greek word is *apistos,* which means *"without faith, unbelieving."* The Disciples were the ones who should have possessed Faith sufficient to cast out the demon. Perhaps the presence of the faithless Scribes and Pharisees helped to prevent positive results. Jesus asked how long He would have to be with them. In effect He was asking how long He would have to put up with such manifestations of disbelief.

HOW LONG SHALL I SUFFER YOU? The verb used is *anecho.* It means to hold one's self erect and firm against a person or thing. It projects the idea *"to bear"* or *"to endure."* Then He asked that the boy, who was off a short distance for safekeeping, be brought to Him.

(9:20) As he was brought to Jesus, the demon — knowing his control of the boy would soon be ended — *"tare"* the boy in one last, spiteful attack. The verb for tare is *sunsparasoo.* It means *"to convulse completely."* The boy was thrown into severe convulsions and began to *"wallow"* on the ground. The word for *"wallow"* is *kulio,* which means *"to be rolled."* The boy rolled on the ground while foaming at the mouth.

(9:21-22) Jesus then asked the father how long this situation had been going on. The father said the demonic troubles had been evidenced since the time the boy was small. He also said that the boy had been *"cast into"* the fire and the waters. The word used is *ballo,* which means *"to throw."* The boy didn't *accidentally* fall into the fire or water during an attack; it was the actual power of the demon causing this. The demon was trying to destroy the boy. It was inducing a type of suicidal mania, trying to drive him to self-destruction. Why should some demons promote the death of the bodies in which they reside? No one knows, but this is not uncommon among the demon-possessed.

The father's Faith shaken by the failure of the Disciples, he asked Jesus if He would help him. The question included the word *dunami,* which means *"power"* in the sense of overcoming resistance. He asked Jesus if He could, and would He have compassion on them? He knew the Lord *had* compassion, so he wasn't questioning this but rather the possibility of the boy being delivered.

The expression used for compassion is an appeal for immediate help. The expression *"have compassion on us and help us,"* is literally *"help us at once, having **had** compassion on us."* He knew Jesus *cared;* he only questioned the *ability* of Jesus to cope with his desperate situation after the Disciples had failed.

(9:23) IF YOU CANST BELIEVE. There is some difficulty in translating this expression. It seems that the emphasis is on the negative because *"canst"* sounds much like our *"can't."* Actually the import is that if he *could* believe, *"all things are possible."* If you can *believe,* it can *be.* It doesn't really matter how *difficult* a problem, if a person can truly believe, it can *be.* The Lord said that *all* things are possible for him who believeth.

(9:24) The father of the boy gave forth an *"inarticulate"* cry or groan which was followed by the words, *"Lord, I believe."* He gave a fear-stricken, piercing cry, and then declared that he believed.

Next he said, *"Help Thou my unbelief."* The word for *"help"* is *boetheo.* It means *"to run to one who is in danger and crying out, to succor, to bring aid, to help."* He was asking for instant and permanent help for his unbelief. The father recognized that he needed *help* to believe. The father recognized that the boy couldn't believe for himself, so it was essential that he believe for him. He knew he had to believe, so he cried out asking for help. He had already witnessed failure in this matter so his Faith was weak. He knew he needed Jesus' support.

(9:25) The Lord was with the father and the boy a short distance from the crowd. Their cries brought the crowd running, making it impossible for them to remain isolated. The picture presented by Mark is of the crowd rapidly gathering about Jesus and the demon-possessed boy.

HE REBUKED THE FOUL SPIRIT. The word for *"rebuke"* is *epitimao*. It actually refers to a rebuke that is ineffectual and does not bring a person to recognize his sin, or to confess it. Demon spirits cannot be corrected or changed. When the word is used in the sense of a change in attitude, *elegcho* is used. It means to rebuke a person in a sense of his understanding, coming under conviction, and even making confession. The other word (*epitimao*) is used since demons will *not* repent or confess and cannot be changed.

The word for *"foul"* is *akathartos*. It comes from the word *katharos,* which means *"clean, pure, free from evil things that soil."* In an ethical sense it speaks of being *"free from corrupt desires, sin, and guilt."* When the Greek letter alpha is prefixed to the word, it gives it the opposite meaning, so the word *"foul"* is a good translation and a perfect description of the demon.

I CHARGE YOU. The verb translated *"charge"* is *epitasso*. The basic word is a military term and means to *"arrange soldiers in ranks."* So it came to mean *"to order or to charge."* The command given by our Lord to the demon was sharp and firm. He ordered the demon not only to come out of the boy, but also to *stay* out of him. Jesus told the demon to never come back.

(9:26-27) THE SPIRIT CRIED, AND RENT HIM SORE. As the spirit was ordered out, there was a fresh seizure. The demon spirit wreaked its revenge on the victim. It was a last vicious attempt to harass the poor boy before the demon spirit was expelled forever. The convulsions were violent and prolonged. When they finally ceased, the young man was so exhausted that he appeared to be dead. In fact, many thought he *had* died. The word translated *"rent"* is *sparasso,* and it means *"to convulse."*
As the young man lay as dead, Jesus *"having taken a strong grip of his hand, went to raising him up."* He arose. The man's Faith had been encouraged and the Lord accomplished a miracle. It was a wonderful event and a glorious victory.

It is interesting to note that there were three notable *"failures"* at performing miracles in the Gospel of Mark: in the land of the Gadarenes where Jesus healed no one — after sending the demons into the swine; in His own home city of Nazareth where *"He could do no mighty work";* and here where the Disciples had been unable to cast out the demon possessing the young boy. It is interesting that in each case there was much doubt, skepticism, and unbelief permeating the atmosphere of the three environments, (the apostate people at Decapolis; Jesus' skeptical neighbors; and the Scribes and Pharisees who disputed with the Disciples as they tried to cast out the demon).

Once the boy's father (with Jesus' help) developed sufficient Faith, the demon departed. Obviously, an atmosphere of Faith is *conducive* to the manifestation of God's Power, while an atmosphere of skepticism can *dampen* the likelihood of God's miracles.

(9:28-29) The Lord Jesus went inside the house where the party was lodging to escape the enthusiasm and excitement of the crowd. There was so much elation after the boy's healing and deliverance that it wasn't possible for Jesus to continue teaching. It was a time for them to rejoice, for they were deliriously happy over the expulsion of the demonic spirit.

Once in private, the Disciples asked why they could not dispel the demon's hold. They had previously been successful when the Lord had empowered them especially for their mission. But this time they were confronted with a situation for which they were not spiritually prepared, and Satan knew this. The demon spirit was unyielding in its defiance of their orders.

The demonic spirit was not *forced* to obey in this case because of certain factors. There are times when demonic forces will taunt the individual, trying to take authority over them, because of insufficient spiritual power within that person. But they instantly recognize it when someone is prepared and equipped to truly take authority over them. Apparently, lack of prayer and spiritual preparation were factors in this unusual case.

To remove this demon required the power and support that comes from time spent in prayer and fasting. Once again the Disciples were learning a valuable lesson under the Master.

JESUS FORETELLS HIS DEATH AND RESURRECTION

"And they departed thence, and passed through Galilee; and He would not that any man should know it. For He taught His Disciples, and said unto them, The Son of Man is delivered into the hands of men, and they shall kill Him; and after that He is killed, He shall rise the third day. But they understood not that saying, and were afraid to ask Him" (Mk. 9:30-32).

(9:30) The Lord and His Disciples had been resting at the foot of Mount Hermon, but now they traveled southward through Galilee. At this point Jesus was concentrating largely on the training of His Disciples. He didn't want word to spread of His whereabouts, so He could uninterruptedly spend time teaching and expanding the understanding of the Disciples.

(9:31-32) THE SON OF MAN IS DELIVERED. The verb used is *paradidomai*. This means *"to give,"* and it has a preposition (*para*) prefixed which means *"alongside."* This compound word means *"to give alongside."* Today we would say *"sell down the river."* It suggests the handing over of a person to someone else in an act of betrayal.

Jesus was revealing that the Son of Man would be delivered (betrayed) into the hands of men. He further added that they would kill Him and — having been put to death — that He would rise after three days. The Disciples failed to understand this. Even though He had already told them several times that He would die and be raised again, they couldn't grasp this concept and were frightened to ask Him for an explanation.

GOD'S PEOPLE MUST BE CHILDLIKE

"And He came to Capernaum; and being in the house He asked them, What was it that you disputed among yourselves by the way? But they held their peace: for by the way they had disputed among themselves, who should be the greatest. And He sat down, and called the Twelve, and said unto them, If any man desire to be first, the same shall be last of all, and servant of all. And He took a child, and set him in the midst of them: and when He had taken him in His Arms, He said unto them, Whosoever shall receive one of such children in My Name, receives Me: and whosoever shall receive Me, receives not Me, but Him Who sent Me" (Mk 9:33-37).

(9:33) Jesus and His Disciples returned again to Peter's home in Capernaum, their usual base in that city. The Disciples had been disputing along the way as to how they would be ranked in the Kingdom after the Messiah set up His Rule. They didn't discuss the imminent Death of Christ, although Jesus had informed them of His forthcoming betrayal and death. They were more concerned with their personal situations.

Some expositors feel that Jesus did not always walk closely with His Disciples. It appears that many times He walked by Himself, in deep thought and communion with the Father. Apparently during these times, the thoughts of the Disciples were selfish. When they arrived at the house, Jesus asked what they had been disputing about.

(9:34) The expression used is translated, *"but they kept on being quiet."* Our Lord knew He faced a cruel death, but His Disciples could only think about their own selfish ambitions. It's no wonder they were reluctant to reveal their conversation. They were ashamed and preferred not to answer the Lord on this matter.

(9:35) Jesus always taught and demonstrated humility. His words on this occasion provide a significant lesson. Having sat down, He called the Twelve and told them that if anyone desired to be first, *"let him be last of all — and a servant of all."*

The word *"servant"* is *diakonos,* and it refers to one who ministers to others. It is the word from which we get *"deacon,"* and it means to minister and be a servant. The way to exaltation is humility. The last shall be first and the first last.

(9:36-37) Jesus then took a child and put him in the midst of them. He told them that the secret of greatness is in the character of the child. The one who is the most childlike, the most trusting, the least self-conscious, and the least self-sufficient is the one who will be the greatest in the Kingdom.

DON'T STOP OTHERS FROM DOING GOOD

"And John answered Him, saying, Master, we saw one casting out devils in Your Name, and he followeth not us: and we forbad him, because he followeth not us. But Jesus said, Forbid him not: for there is no man which shall do a miracle in My Name, that can lightly speak evil of Me. For he who is not against us is on our part. For whosoever shall give you a cup of water to drink in My Name, because you belong to Christ, verily I say unto you, he shall not lose his reward" (Mk. 9:38-41).

(9:38) This is the only remark specifically attributed to John to be found in the synoptic Gospels (Matthew, Mark, and Luke). John was very sincere and conscientious. In the light of the teaching Jesus had just given, He brings up an event that had apparently happened in their recent journey through northern Galilee.

John addressed Jesus as Teacher, telling Him that they saw an individual casting out demons in Jesus' Name. He indicated that this individual was not one of their group. There is a hint of jealousy in this remark. John said they forbade the individual's exorcising of the demons because he was not a formal member of their group. This, of course, was contrary to the Lord's wishes.

(9:39-40) John was speaking sincerely so Jesus did not censure him, but He did correct the error. They were not to forbid the using of the Name of Jesus when somebody was working for a moral purpose. Nor were they necessarily to seek inclusion of such a person into their group. Perhaps his motives might not be all they should be.

Jesus encouraged the Disciples to at least remain *neutral* in their evaluation of such a one until they could form a more definite opinion of the situation. This doesn't suggest that *everyone* claiming a commitment to Christ should be wholeheartedly welcomed into fellowship, but Jesus specifically instructed the Disciples that they were not to hinder or discourage someone who was at least *outwardly* seeking to do things in the Name of Christ.

In regard to John's remark about the man not belonging to their group, it is natural for individuals to come to feel that only they or their small circle are going to Heaven. There is a great danger in this feeling of exclusiveness. But *in*clusiveness can also be unwise and dangerous.

(9:41) Some expositors feel this is a resumption of the subject Jesus had been discussing when John broke in with his question. It seems to be allied to the previous matter of who would be greatest, and the resulting revelation that a childlike attitude and acceptance of the position of a servant results in eternal blessings. Then it is pointed out that the simple gift of anything needed, such as a glass of cold water, is worthy of an eternal reward. He further stated that somebody doing this for another *"will not lose"* his reward. Jesus clearly declared here that whoever would as much as give a drink of cold water to someone belonging to Him would definitely be rewarded.

TEMPTATIONS TO SIN

"And whosoever shall offend one of these little ones who believe in Me, it is better for him that a millstone were hanged about his neck, and he were cast into the sea. And if your hand offend you, cut it off: it is better for you to enter into life maimed, than having two hands to go into Hell, into the fire that never shall be quenched: Where their worm dies not, and the fire is not quenched.

"And if your foot offend you, cut it off: it is better for you to enter halt into life, than having two feet to be cast into Hell, into the fire that never shall be quenched: Where their worm dies not, and the fire is not quenched. And if your eye offend you, pluck it out: it is better for you to enter into the Kingdom of God with one eye, than having two eyes to be cast into Hell fire: Where their worm dies not, and the fire is not quenched.

"For every one shall be salted with fire, and every sacrifice shall be salted with salt. Salt is good: but if the salt have lost his saltness, wherewith will you season it? Have salt in yourselves, and have peace one with another" (Mk. 9:42-50).

(9:42) Just as a person is rewarded for doing good to those serving the Lord, the reverse is also true. If a Disciple is *wronged*, this is considered to be most serious and will bring evil upon the perpetrator. It is possible for a person to cause another to stumble. Putting stumbling blocks in someone's path, thus excluding them from the Kingdom of God, is an abominable act.

The word translated *"offend"* is *skandalizo*. This means setting up a stumbling block or an impediment upon which someone may trip or fall. The noun form is *skandalon,* which refers to something like the trigger of a trap (that is — a snare), or to *any* impediment causing one to stumble or fall.

Jesus said it would be better for one who caused someone to stumble to have a millstone hanged about his neck and to be cast into the sea. A millstone is a flat, round, *heavy* rock used for grinding in a mill.

There are many who put stumbling blocks in the way of others in this day and age. Many are kept from the Kingdom because of this. One should do all one can to help people *into* the Kingdom, rather than hindering their spiritual development, and thus excluding them.

(9:43) Jesus states that it one's hand offend, he should *"cut it off."* He was not actually recommending mutilation of the physical body. But Jesus did imply (in the strongest possible terms) that where evil exists it must be rooted out. The basic principle is that the results of eternal damnation are so horrendous that it should be totally unthinkable. *Anything* would therefore be preferable to the eternal loss of one's soul. Certainly, maiming of the physical body would not direct one to greater spiritual insights, but Jesus used this powerful analogy to point out the *crucial* importance of Repentance, Reform, and Salvation.

The word translated *"maimed"* is *kullon.* This word is used in classical Greek for one with a crushed or crippled limb. The word *zoe* is translated *"life"* and refers to the *higher* life which is to be sought. This does not refer to Eternal Life as such.

The words *"never shall be quenched"* come from *to asbeston.* This is from the Greek word *sbennumi,* which means *"to quench."* The alpha prefixed makes it mean the opposite — *"unquenchable."* We get our word *"asbestos"* from this.

(9:44-48) Jesus said, if some failing or shortcoming produces a stumbling block, literally *"tear it out and cast it away."* Taking drastic measures is certainly preferable to losing one's whole being. There is either self-discipline or a *"refining by fire"* in the life of every Christian.

WHERE THE WORM DIES NOT. The worm is pictured as preying upon the inhabitants of this *"dead"* realm. The fire is undying and so is the worm.

(9:49-50) There has been emphasis on fire and quenching, and now the emphasis shifts to *"salting"* — one must be salted with either the unquenchable fire of Gehenna (Hell), or with a severe fire of *self*-discipline. The one who is wise will discipline himself.

There are many Scriptural references to salt. The Christian is referred to as *"the salt of the Earth"* in Matthew 5:13. Christians are warned against losing their saltiness; that is, the *quality* that makes them a preservative in a society careening into complete corruption.

Every individual, Saint or sinner, will undergo periods of difficulty in life. These times are like a refining fire — they burn off the impurities. If these didn't occur, the unquenchable fire of Hell would await — as it does for those who *refuse* to be changed and who refuse to accept the transforming and redeeming Grace of Jesus Christ. The more *self*-discipline exerted, the *fewer* the times the Lord will be compelled to *"chastise"* with *external* difficulties.

Chapter 10

Jesus' Teaching On Divorce

SUBJECT   PAGE

JESUS BLESSES THE CHILDREN 151
THE PERILS OF RICHES 152
JESUS SPEAKS AGAIN OF HIS DEATH 157
THE REQUEST OF JAMES AND JOHN 159
BLIND BARTIMAEUS AND HIS COMPANION HEALED 162

CHAPTER 10

JESUS' TEACHING ON DIVORCE

"And He arose from thence, and cometh into the coasts of Judaea by the farther side of Jordan: and the people resort unto Him again; and, as He was wont, He taught them again. And the Pharisees came to Him, and asked Him, Is it lawful for a man to put away his wife? tempting Him.

"And He answered and said unto them, What did Moses command you? And they said, Moses suffered to write a bill of divorcement, and to put her away. And Jesus answered and said unto them, For the hardness of your heart he wrote you this precept. But from the beginning of the Creation God made them male and female. For this cause shall a man leave his father and mother, and cleave to his wife; And they twain shall be one flesh: so then they are no more twain, but one flesh. What therefore God has joined together, let not man put asunder.

"And in the house His Disciples asked him again of the same matter. And He said unto them, Whosoever shall put away his wife, and marry another, commits adultery against her. And if a woman shall put away her husband, and be married to another, she commits adultery" (Mk. 10:1-12).

(10:1) AND HE AROSE FROM THENCE, AND COMETH. This phrase indicates the commencement of a considerable journey. Jesus was leaving Galilee and Capernaum and *"His face is turned toward toward Jerusalem."* He was going to the *"coasts"* (*horion* — a bound or a limit). He was going to the boundaries of the region — that is, of the land of Judea.

The Bible says *"the people resort unto Him."* The verb is *sunporeuomai*, which means *"to take one's self, to go to some place."* The prefix for the main verb means *"with"* and conveys the thought of going *with* someone on a journey. The people often traveled in caravans; many people were Followers of the Lord Jesus, while an even *larger* number felt kindly disposed toward Him. All these apparently joined the Lord and His Disciples and journeyed together. As was His custom, Jesus again taught as they journeyed down the road.

(10:2) As soon as Jesus renewed His public teaching, the Pharisees returned and reestablished their attack.

TEMPTING HIM. The verb that is used here is *peirazomai*. As we have seen, this means to put a person to a test. Because this was usually done to disclose evil, it came to mean *"to tempt"* in the sense of encouraging a person to do evil.

The Scribes and Pharisees didn't hope to get Jesus to do *wrong,* but they were trying to put Him to a test. They wanted Him to publicly repudiate the Law of Moses in order to accomplish their evil purposes. They tried to trap Him in His words, so they could condemn Him before the people.

They planned to demonstrate that He was opposed to the Mosaic Law. They were frustrated, however, because Jesus *wasn't* against the Law of Moses, He was against the Pharisaical *adulterations* of the God-given Mosaic Law. They continued their campaign because they felt the people would turn against Him if they could demonstrate that He was a *"blasphemer"* by showing discrepancy between their philosophy and His.

They asked Him if it was legal for a man to put away his wife. The word translated *"to put away"* is from *apoluo,* which means literally *"to release."* When this was used in connection with divorce, it meant *"to repudiate."* So they were asking if it were lawful for a man to *repudiate* his wife.

(10:3) Jesus asked them what Moses commanded. They thought He was referring to Deuteronomy 24:1 — which indicates that some allowance can be made. But Jesus was referring to Genesis 2:24 when He said, *"What God has joined together, let not man put asunder"* (Mk. 10:9). The Lord answered them from God's Perfect Will and Mind rather than from the *allowances* caused by man's hardness of heart.

(10:4) The Pharisees quoted the reference from Deuteronomy, which states that Moses allowed a husband to write a bill of divorcement to put his wife away.

(10:5-9) Jesus told them that the writing of the bill of divorcement (which was *allowed* under the Mosaic law) was due to the hardness of men's hearts. Divorce *had been permitted.* The Commandment — for the writing of a bill of divorcement — amounted to a *restriction* on the excesses *already* occurring. It was not *approval* of divorce; it was a refinement and a restriction of a process already in existence because of the hardness of men's hearts.

The Greek word *sklerokardia* is translated *"hardness of heart."* The word *skleros* means *"hard, stiff, rough, harsh."* The people of Israel had hardened their hearts (*kardia*), resulting in a decadent nature and apostasy. As in so many Jewish practices, there was much *verbal* claiming of Righteousness but little spiritual manifestations of it. Jesus said that *"from the beginning"* (better, *"**in** the beginning"*), things were different. He was referring back to the Creation of man and woman as recounted in Genesis 2:24.

He quotes the Genesis Passage directly when He says that a man should *"leave his father and mother, and cleave to his wife."* The word *kataleipo* is a strong word meaning leave. As used here, with the prefix *kata* appended, the normal thought of leaving is magnified. The compound word means that one is to *"leave behind, to depart from, to forsake"* one's parents and *"cleave"* (*proskollao*) — which means *"to be glued to, to join one's self to, to cleave closely, to stick to"* — one's wife. They were to become one flesh, and what God had joined together no man should put asunder.

The word *suzeugnumi* is translated *"join together,"* and it means *"to fasten one's yoke with another."* Marriage is a tying together. The prefix *suz* means *"with"* and the idea is sometimes translated *"yokefellow."* *"Put asunder"* is from *chorizo,* and means *"to separate, divide, part."*

Two joined together are *not* to be separated or divided. Two people joined in marriage are to be *"glued together"* and inseparable. They are to live together until *"death do them part."* Due to conditions, divorce *had* been allowed (and there *are* times when there is no alternative), but God's *basic* desire and plan is here presented by Jesus.

(10:10-12) Much can be said about divorce and remarriage. We know that God hates divorce; the Word of God indicates such. Jesus said that those joined together should not be *"put asunder"* — that is, separated. There are many divorces in this day and age, and this is a tragedy. The matter of divorce is a difficult subject which raises many questions and invites many opinions.

For the Christian husband and wife, there should be *no* grounds for divorce. If they love the Lord Jesus Christ, and have been separated unto God, they should not be guilty of any of the evil or unfortunate actions that *cause* divorce. Christians should be able to resolve their differences and live in harmony.

There are times, however, when a marriage partner becomes unfaithful and involved in perversion and filth. Even when this occurs, forgiveness should be extended to the guilty but repentant party and the matter resolved in love and forgiveness. By God's Grace and help they should attempt to work out the situation and guard against future failures.

If a person *was* married and divorced, and then remarried before becoming a Christian — there is a question as to the responsibility of that person *after* becoming a Christian. We should remember, however, that what happened *before* a person is saved is washed away by the Blood of Christ. There are many sins that can mar a person's past — lying, cheating, stealing, cursing, profanity, adultery, fornication, and even murder. When a person is changed by the Blood of Christ, he is a new creature and old things are passed away. He is now completely new in the Lord. A past divorce can *also* be washed out under the Blood.

There are some who teach that upon becoming a Christian — if they were formerly divorced — that the present marriage should be broken and the first one restored. This is neither rational nor scriptural. Many things in life can be neither undone nor reestablished. Whatever happened in the past has been washed by the Blood of the Lamb. (There are, of course, situations where restitution can and should be made.) But to undo a *happy* home, in trying to reestablish an unhappy one that was broken before a person became a Christian, is unthinkable.

The spouse one lives with at the time of Salvation is recognized as such by God. Satan would like to intrude guilt and condemnation. There should be no condemnation for those who are in Christ Jesus.

In Matthew 5:32 and 19:9 an exception was given by Jesus for permitting divorce. *We* believe He said that the unsaved partner of a Christian, in committing fornication, frees the Christian partner to divorce. Some would disagree and say that the Christian partner has grounds for divorce but not for *remarriage*. Of course there is a basis for much discussion here, but we believe they have the right to remarry.

Based on Mark 10:11-12, Christian couples have no real grounds for divorce. They are not to commit adultery, fornication, or indulge in the sins of the unbeliever. A Christian is to be a true imitator of the Lord Jesus Christ in life, conduct, and works.

Speaking more generally, Jesus did indicate that fornication is justification for divorce and remarriage. Some hold to the idea that fornication applies only to sexual sins committed *before* marriage, but the word has several meanings as used in Scripture.

First, it means sexual deviation or perversion — running the gamut from mild abnormalities to incest, homosexuality, and lesbianism. Secondly, it means *repeated* adultery. Thirdly, it is used symbolically in a number of Scriptures to refer to idol worship. Finally, it means, by definition, consorting with prostitutes.

The second definition above — repeated adultery — refers to persons who are compulsive predators of the opposite sex. They go from one partner to another, starting their search anew as soon as they have accomplished their latest conquest. These are dedicated and habitual fornicators. To illustrate, the Bible states that David was an adulterer, while Esau was a fornicator. There was obviously a considerable difference between the two. David, more or less by chance, fell into a licentious affair with Bathsheba. It was sordid, dirty, tragic, and stupid. It had long-lasting and appalling consequences. But even though he was an adulterer, David was not basically a *fornicator.*

To the Christian wife, discovery that her husband has had an adulterous affair would be demoralizing and shocking — and he would be guilty of defiling his marriage and sinning against God. His actions would *not*, however, be grounds for divorce. Every effort would have to be made to reconcile the problem and restore the marriage — whether the offender were a Christian or not. Christians in particular are not only to refrain from sin but also *to forgive*. So there are no real grounds for divorce for true Christians.

However, other kinds of situations can exist. Paul gave special instructions in I Corinthians 7:1-16 regarding the institution of marriage. He spoke particularly of cases where a Christian and a non-Christian are unequally yoked. Sometimes *one* of the marriage partners becomes saved. The husband may be saved and the wife unsaved, or vice versa. When this happens, very real problems can result.

Consider the unsaved husband and the Christian wife. He refuses to have anything to do with spiritual matters and has little concept of proper living. He wants his wild living, and ends up deserting her. Under these or similar conditions we feel that the Apostle Paul is saying that the Christian spouse is not to be under bondage. We believe this wife has a right to divorce and remarry, and that the sins of the ungodly are not to keep her from having a life of fulfillment and blessing.

It might be reemphasized that, for the Christian, there is no legitimate reason or justification for divorce and remarriage. There should be forgiveness and the working out of difficulties. There *are* cases, however, where one individual in the partnership is living an evil and ungodly life, making it impossible for the relationship to continue. These are the cases where divorce and remarriage are justified.

The subject of divorce and remarriage is a broad one, and we have other publications dealing more extensively with this matter.

JESUS BLESSES THE CHILDREN

"And they brought young children to Him, that He should touch them: and His Disciples rebuked those who brought them. But when Jesus saw it, He was much displeased, and said unto them, Suffer the little children to come unto Me, and forbid them not: for of such is the Kingdom of God. Verily I say unto you, Whosoever shall not receive the Kingdom of God as a little child, he shall not enter therein. And He took them up in His Arms, put His Hands upon them, and blessed them" (Mk. 10:13-16).

(10:13) It is altogether fitting that this delightful incident involving Jesus blessing the children should follow immediately after His dissertation on marriage and divorce. Our Lord placed great significance on the sanctity of marriage, children being products of marriage.

The people brought their children to the Lord Jesus so He might touch and bless them. Some of these may have been infants in their mother's arms, while others might have been from five to ten years old. We believe they were young children, as they were brought *by their parents* to the Lord.

The custom of laying hands on children with a prayer of benediction can be seen as far back as Genesis 48:14-15. Luke 2:22-38 recounts the events accompanying Jesus' own presentation at the Temple. This was commonly done in the Synagogue, with the Ruler of the Synagogue praying a blessing on the child. And here was One greater than the Synagogue Ruler, so the parents wanted His blessing for their children.

They continued to bring their children to Him and the Disciples rebuked them for burdening the Lord. They perhaps thought it was beneath the dignity of the Master, or they might have considered it *"a waste of His time."* But the people loved the Lord, worshipped Him, respected Him, and held Him in extremely high esteem.

(10:14) When Jesus saw what was happening, He was moved with indignation and was deeply displeased. The verb used is *aganakteo,* which means *"to feel pain."* Obviously He experienced a deep emotion, as this could well be translated *"He was moved with indignation."* The Disciples had misunderstood the nature of the Kingdom.

Jesus told the Disciples, *"Suffer (aphiemi* — permit, allow) *the little children to come to me."* He said, *"Do not forbid (koluo* — forbid, hinder, prevent) *them."* The literal rendering of the wording used is *"stop hindering."* Jesus told the Disciples to *cease preventing* the little ones from coming to Him because *"of such is the Kingdom made."*

(10:15) The Lord held up a small child as a model to His Disciples and to all those nearby. He told them that they were going to have to become as children. The small child is trusting and obedient, and lives a life of complete simplicity. A child is quick to forgive. Jesus told them that if they could not enter in a *childlike* manner, they would not be *able* to enter the Kingdom of God.

(10:16) Jesus had called the children to Himself so now they came, one after another, to be taken into His Arms and blessed. The word *"blessed"* has an intensive force, meaning *"to bless fervently."* It also indicates that *"He kept on blessing them."* Jesus took each child in His Arms and, one by one, blessed them and continued blessing them until every one present had received His personal benediction.

THE PERILS OF RICHES

"And when He was gone forth into the way, there came one running, and kneeled to Him, and asked Him, Good Master, what shall I

*do that I may inherit Eternal Life? And Jesus said unto him, Why do
you call Me good? There is none good but one, Who is, God. You
know the Commandments, Do not commit adultery, Do not kill, Do
not steal, Do not bear false witness, Defraud not, Honour your father
and mother. And he answered and said unto Him, Master, all these
have I observed from my youth. Then Jesus beholding him loved him,
and said unto him, One thing you lack: go your way, sell whatsoever
you have, and give to the poor, and you shall have treasure in Heaven:
and come, take up the Cross, and follow Me.*

"*And he was sad at that saying, and went away grieved: for he
had great possessions. And Jesus looked round about, and said unto
His Disciples, How hardly shall they who have riches enter into the
Kingdom of God! And the Disciples were astonished at His words.
But Jesus answered again, and said unto them, Children, how hard is
it for them who trust in riches to enter into the Kingdom of God! It is
easier for a camel to go through the eye of a needle, than for a rich
man to enter into the Kingdom of God. And they were astonished out
of measure, saying among themselves, Who then can be saved? And
Jesus looking upon them said, With men it is impossible, but not with
God: for with God all things are possible.*

"*Then Peter began to say unto Him, Lo, we have left all, and have
followed You. And Jesus answered and said, Verily I say unto you,
There is no man who has left house, or brethren, or sisters, or father,
or mother, or wife, or children, or lands, for My sake, and the Gospel's,
But he shall receive an hundredfold now in this time, houses, and brethren, and sisters, and mothers, and children, and lands, with persecutions; and in the world to come Eternal Life. But many who are first
shall be last; and the last first*" (Mk. 10:17-31).

(10:17) The "*one*" who came running to Jesus was undoubtedly a
person of great prominence. In the parallel account of this incident in
Luke, it refers to him as an *archon*. This literally means "*a first one.*"
Matthew calls him a *neaniskos,* which means "*a person of preeminence.*"
This expression was used at times for the Chief of a Synagogue or of a
Chief Pharisee. It was sometimes used of members of the Sanhedrin (the
ruling council). It could even imply a prince. This man was undoubtedly a
man of position and wealth.

GOOD MASTER. The literal order of the words in the Greek Text
are "*teacher, good one.*" He calls Jesus "*teacher*" — which was a
popular designation for Him. The man then gave Jesus a sincere compli-
ment in calling Him "*good.*"

This was undoubtedly a man of action and much zeal. He had somehow acquired riches and position, and was now showing the same type of

153

zeal in trying to receive a spiritual benefit from the Master. He not only came running to Jesus but also knelt before Him and, after addressing Him, asked what he might do to inherit Eternal Life.

(10:18) Jesus gently corrected the inquirer for his comment that He was good. Certainly Jesus *was* good. But He wanted people to measure goodness by God and by no other standard. The Jews had a massive problem in that their leaders (the Pharisees and Sadducees) measured goodness only by the keeping of the Law and their man-made rules. Their whole focus was on legalisms and ceremonial displays. Jesus was demonstrating that the ultimate example is God.

The Master was paying tribute to the Father. Jesus was God manifested in the flesh, but He always paid tribute to the Father. Jesus said that He did nothing of Himself, but that which the Father told Him to do. He also instructed His Disciples to pray *to* the Father in *His* Name after He had gone to Glory. He was trying to instill within this man the truth that real goodness comes only from God. Certainly Jesus *was* good, for His goodness came from God.

(10:19) Then Jesus reviewed some of the Commandments regarding man's relationships and duties toward his fellow man. This man knew well the Divine precepts as the Lord listed them. They involved basic principles and commandments.

(10:20) This man might well have been considered an outstanding person in religious circles. He was successful and wealthy, and kept the Commandments. He further stated that he had observed and followed the Commandments from his youth. The word for *"observed"* is *phulasso*. This means *"to take care not to violate."* In classical Greek this word was a military term meaning *"to guard, to watch."* It was used in reference to sentinels standing guard. The man was saying that he had kept all these things *carefully* from his childhood.

(10:21) JESUS BEHOLDING HIM. The word used is *emblepo,* and it means to look at an individual with a searching gaze. As Jesus *"fixed"* His Eyes on the man, it says He *"loved him."* The Greek word is *agapao*. This is a deep, God-given, heartfelt love. Jesus saw many virtues in the man, but He told him there was something that he yet lacked. He said to sell what he had, give the proceeds to the poor (so he could have treasures in Heaven), and then to come and follow Him.

This is not to imply that the Lord was establishing an inflexible, general doctrine. He was not commanding *every* person with material goods to dispose of them, distribute the proceeds, and then follow Him without resources. It was simply that wealth occupied too great a place in this particular man's life. Whatever is of primary importance in a person's life becomes, for all practical purposes, his god.

Jesus put His Finger on the heart of this individual's problem. The First Commandment deals with putting God first. And it isn't just money that can stand between us and God; it can be anything. For some it may be position, pride, clothes, entertainment, or almost any worldly lure. God must come *first!* Jesus invited the man to come and follow Him, but worldly considerations caused him to walk away.

(10:22) The words translated *"he was sad"* are from the Greek verb *stugnazo.* This word is used only one other time in the New Testament, in Matthew 16:3. The verb literally means *"to be shocked, appalled"* or *"to be gloomy, dark; to be sad or sorrowful."* He was overcome with sadness and went away grieving. His possessions occupied the preeminent place in his heart. It states that "he had great possessions" so he went away grieving — at the same time failing to respond to the invitation and demands of the Master.

(10:23) Jesus did not beg the man to stay. After he had left, Jesus *"looked roundabout"* the circle of His Disciples and drew a lesson for them from this incident.

The phrase translated *"how hardly"* is from *pos duskolos.* The first word means *"how."* The second word, *duskolos,* means *"with difficulty."* It might better have been translated *"How difficult it is."*

Jesus said it is difficult for a wealthy person to be saved. Certainly He didn't say it was impossible. Other Scriptures confirm that God has chosen the poor of *this* world, rich in Faith, as heirs of the Kingdom of God. Because it is so easy for a person to trust in riches, it is difficult for the wealthy to enter into the Kingdom of God.

(10:24) This startled the Disciples, for it was contrary to the common thinking of the day. The Jews equated wealth with Godliness. They had considered wealth as an obvious evidence of God's favor. The Disciples were *"astonished"* and undoubtedly puzzled over what manner of Kingdom this was where men should become as little children, and where people of great substance and wealth could scarcely enter at all. Jesus had said earlier (10:15) that a person had to receive the Kingdom of God as a little child. Now He was talking about the difficulty, for those who trusted in wealth, to enter into the Kingdom.

(10:25) Jesus used an illustration to point up the difficulty. He said that it would be easier for a camel to go through the eye of a needle than for a rich man to enter the Kingdom of God. Some feel the *"needle's eye"* here refers to a gate in the wall of Jerusalem where it was difficult for a camel to enter. These gates were called *"needle's eyes."* The Greek term used here, however, favors a sewing needle. This was a term used in Jewish writings — the Talmud presenting the impossibility of an elephant going through the eye of a needle.

This illustration is called a *hyperbole*. It is a gross exaggeration. Jesus was not saying that riches are repugnant to God, but rather that man's tendency to *trust* in them with total devotion makes a rich man's entry into heaven difficult indeed.

(10:26-27) They were *"astonished out of measure,"* and asked, *"Who then can be saved?"*

The word translated *"astonished"* is *ekplesso,* and means *"to strike out, to expel a blow, to strike out of self-possession."* It suggests *"a slap in the face."*

WITH MEN IT IS IMPOSSIBLE, BUT NOT WITH GOD: FOR WITH GOD ALL THINGS ARE POSSIBLE. The thought conveyed by the original language is this: If you accept *men's* evaluation of riches it will be impossible to be saved, because men will trust in riches. But, if you accept God's perspective on this matter, that which seems impossible becomes possible. Simply put, almost *everyone* wants to be rich. Instead, we should strive for the *greater* awareness and not *desire* money or the things of this world. It is not evil to have material things, but they must be kept in perspective. One's primary affection must *not* be focused on material pleasures.

(10:28) LO, WE HAVE LEFT ALL, AND HAVE FOLLOWED YOU. The word translated *"lo"* is *idou,* and means *"to behold, see, lo."* It is a call for the hearer's attention. Peter said that they had left all to follow Jesus. The word translated *"left"* is *aphieme,* which means *"to send or bid go away, yield up."*

Literally, Peter said they had abandoned everything. The expression in the original Greek indicates a once-and-for-all act. They didn't do it on a trial basis, but left *everything* to follow Jesus Christ. Peter and John were fishermen who left a prosperous business. Matthew, the tax collector, had a *lucrative* source of income. They left all to follow Jesus — the itinerant preacher of the Gospel.

Jesus said that the foxes had holes in which to reside and the birds had their nests, but the Son of Man did not have a place to lay His Head. Of course, God provided what He needed in this world, but the Lord *owned* nothing. He had no interest in things of this world. Surely, *"the things of this world **will** grow strangely dim"* for any Christian exposed to the Light of God's Glory and Grace.

(10:29-31) Jesus continued by saying that those who sacrifice will be rewarded. Sacrifices can come in any number of ways: leaving home, relatives, and material possessions. It may result in persecution in addition to the sacrifice of leaving worldly comforts behind. But the price will be worth the reward. Compensation will be made in this age — and in the world to come.

Our Lord is not suggesting that poverty imparts some special blessing. Poverty comes from the Devil, and God will prosper those who live for Him. The point is, one must get his eyes *off* material things and onto the Lord Jesus Christ. It is Scriptural and proper for one to use his Faith to believe God for a better lifestyle for his family, a better automobile (when needed), for decent clothes to wear, and for other needs to be met. But these should not become priorities in one's life or the basis for a smug attitude.

It is certainly good for a businessman to ask God to bless his business — but he then becomes responsible for using that money wisely. He should be a good steward, supporting the dissemination of the Gospel. Giving out of gratitude to the Lord for His bountiful Blessings can be one of life's great satisfactions.

Some, of course, try to reap personal rewards by promoting the thought that God's Plan for the world works basically like a trading stamp Redemption center. They promise that when you donate money or goods to His Work — He *automatically* returns your offering to you, *with interest.* Under this theory, offerings to God aren't really offerings at all, they're down payments on the goods and materials you *want* from God. Want a new car, a bigger house, or fatter paycheck? Throw something in the basket and God will *immediately* multiply this and return it to you. God, of course, *doesn't* work this way.

God will give back in many ways. There are many blessings provided to the Believer who shares with other Believers. Establishing spiritual priorities will result in *adequate* provision and God's bountiful Blessings. But one's primary interest and concern must *not* lie in material rewards.

The Kingdom of God is to be our priority. Jesus said that the first would be last and the last first. Those who proudly elevate *themselves* to a place of prominence will be debased, because Jesus *clearly* taught that those who *humble* themselves will be exalted. The very act of *seeking* spiritual recognition will ensure humiliation.

Those who would seek a position of eternal spiritual honor can gain it in only one way — and that is by emulating the Master. Demonstrate humility at all times. Be servant to all and master to none. Seek the material *needs* and not the wants. In this way we can *know* our eventual condition, because Jesus Himself said that the first shall be last and the last first.

JESUS SPEAKS AGAIN OF HIS DEATH

"And they were in the way going up to Jerusalem; and Jesus went before them: and they were amazed; and as they followed, they were afraid. And He took again the Twelve, and began to tell them what things should happen unto Him, Saying, Behold, we go up to Jerusalem;

157

and the Son of Man shall be delivered unto the Chief Priests, and unto the Scribes; and they shall condemn Him to death, and shall deliver Him to the Gentiles: And they shall mock Him, and shall scourge Him, and shall spit upon Him, and shall kill Him: and the third day He shall rise again" (Mk. 10:32-34).

(10:32) At this point in Mark's narrative, the Lord's active Ministry is rapidly drawing to a close. Jesus and the Disciples are already on the road to Jerusalem; in fact, the Lord's Crucifixion. The Disciples don't realize this, but Jesus is all too well aware of the humiliation and agony He must shortly undergo.

JESUS WENT BEFORE THEM. The scene portrayed is one of Jesus walking a short distance before His Disciples. He apparently did this fairly often, discussing with them certain matters as they walked.

Jesus' Ministry, as revealed in the four Gospels, demonstrates a constant undercurrent of seriousness, approaching solemnity. No mention is ever made of His entering into any lighthearted banter or frivolous sideplay. The burdens and concerns of His Work obviously weighed upon Him continuously. This is not to say that people should habitually walk about with long faces and solemn airs. But on this occasion Jesus was *unusually* somber and they could sense, by His whole Spirit and attitude, the aura of dark foreboding that had come over Him.

His preoccupation was finally beginning to penetrate the minds of the Disciples. They were just now beginning to realize that dire events loomed just over the horizon. He had repeatedly tried to prepare them, but now the first insights of what lay ahead began to penetrate their minds and spirits. There were crowds following Jesus who also sensed the ominous, solemn atmosphere oppressing the Master and the Twelve.

There are times when the Child of God has reason to be deeply serious and quiet. There are times when he is under a great burden because of events *about* to transpire or needs that exist. One should be happy *despite* difficulties and problems, of course, but at the same time the Christian *does* have burdens and concerns. We see the plights of souls headed for Hell. Satan is dedicated to harming, hurting, and hindering. We are, with the world situation today, in a constant spiritual battle.

But, the Christian has a deep, calm peace in his soul — even when the storms rage about. And even people of great Faith, consecration, and dedication labor sometimes under deep oppression. The Lord Jesus Christ was carrying such a burden at this moment. He was going to the Cross, and it was a tremendous weight upon Him.

HE TOOK AGAIN THE TWELVE. The Disciples were uneasy, and the crowds were afraid. Jesus took the Twelve apart to tell them more specifically what was to transpire. There was a palpable tension that could have easily erupted into panic if the crowds were included in this discussion. Jesus told the Disciples what was about to happen. Literally it translates, as *"the things that were about to be converging upon Him."*

(10:33-34) Jesus explained the events that were about to unfold. They were going to Jerusalem, and He would be delivered unto the Chief Priests and the Scribes and condemned to death. He told the Disciples that His enemies would mock and scourge Him, spit on Him, and kill Him. Of course, this was the basis for Jesus' solemn demeanor, which had caused the Disciples and the crowds to be amazed and fearful.

Jesus was determined to fulfill His Mission and, as the Prophet Isaiah revealed (50:7) of the Messiah, *"I set my face like a flint."* Jesus also declared to them that He would rise on the third day. The Disciples were still unable to fully comprehend what this implied.

THE REQUEST OF JAMES AND JOHN

"And James and John, the sons of Zebedee, come unto Him, saying, Master, we would that You should do for us whatsoever we shall desire. And He said unto them, What would you that I should do for you? They said unto Him, Grant unto us that we may sit, one on Your Right Hand, and the other on Your Left Hand, in Your glory. But Jesus said unto them, You know not what you ask: can you drink of the cup that I drink of? and be baptized with the baptism that I am baptized with?

"And they said unto Him, We can. And Jesus said unto them, You shall indeed drink of the cup that I drink of; and with the baptism that I am baptized withal shall you be baptized: But to sit on My Right Hand and on My Left Hand is not Mine to give; but it shall be given to them for whom it is prepared.

"And when the ten heard it, they began to be much displeased with James and John.

"But Jesus called them to Him, and said unto them, You know that they which are accounted to rule over the Gentiles exercise lordship over them: and their great ones exercise authority upon them. But so shall it not be among you: but whosoever will be great among you, shall be your minister: And whosoever of you will be the chiefest, shall be servant of all. For even the Son of Man came not to be ministered unto, but to minister, and to give His life a ransom for many" (Mk. 10:35-45).

(10:35-37) Jesus was facing the imminent reality of the tremendous price He was to pay for the sins of mankind. He was faced with the most horrible agony and death imaginable — and His Disciples were thinking only about personal stature and gain. How easy it is for people to be diverted by money and position, stature and gain.

It was but a short time before Jesus would suffer ultimate torture and death, yet James and John come to Him with a ridiculous request. The contrast between their self-interest and His Self-Sacrifice stands out vividly. While He was steeling Himself to go to the Cross, they thought only of their self-interest. One of the first things Christ will do in a person's life — if one allows it — is to put *self*-will behind.

(10:38-40) YOU KNOW NOT WHAT YOU ASK. Utterly selfish in their motives, their self-seeking brought a quick reprimand. Jesus did not lose patience with them, but only asked instead, *"Are you able to drink of the cup I am drinking?"*

The cup He refers to is a special one. It is clarified in His Gethsemane Prayer (Mat. 26:39). He is referring to the sufferings He will experience on the Cross, which will overwhelm His Soul and break His Heart. Of course the didn't understand what He was asking, nor did they really answer. They gave a lighthearted reply, saying they *could* drink of the cup and go through whatever He was talking about.

While they didn't comprehend at that time, the Disciples *did* go through great suffering and die difficult deaths much later. They *were* to drink of it, but they didn't know it at this time. Jesus said they would indeed drink from the cup He was about to drink and be baptized with the Baptism with which He was to be baptized.

The whole picture presented is one of His suffering, agony, and Death. Christianity is unfortunately being presented by some today as nothing more than a glorified material grab bag where the idea is to look to God and He will give you riches, fame, and popularity.

But God is not a glorified Santa Claus, nor is Jesus a deified bellhop who will provide anything and everything — the minute we speak the word. That is *not* a true and accurate picture. Many of the greatest individuals of Faith have paid a huge price. There is nothing wrong in preaching Faith and believing God for one's needs — but the true import of the Gospel is *not* some type of magic slot machine to shower us with jackpots.

It is popular (and profitable) to appeal today to selfish motivation. But Jesus foresaw His Disciples going through a baptism of *suffering*. Paul told Timothy that those who would live Godly in Christ Jesus *would* suffer persecution. Suffering does not mean physical sickness — which some are quick to equate with suffering. The Lord Jesus did indeed come to heal, to bless, and to save those who are lost. But as He invited people to follow Him, He said they would have to take up their crosses *daily,* and follow Him.

Living for God is, despite the price, the greatest blessing known to mankind. It provides joy, peace, security, hope — and God's Blessings in every area and dimension of life. God does heal, provide, and bless. But the *True* Blessings — the honor, prestige, and position that the Christian has — do not come *from* this world, nor are they recognized *by* the world. These come from God and they are in your heart.

There is suffering that one has to endure for the Lord Jesus Christ. There are *"pleasures"* one must give up. Jesus told James and John that they would *indeed* go through much of what He was about to endure. As for the opportunity to sit on His Right Hand and on His Left Hand, though — that was not His to give.

Rewards will be distributed in accordance with the Father's dispositions. Once again, the emphasis was back to the Father, and Jesus again showed His complete submission *to* the Father.

(10:41) If the other (Ten Disciples were not present when James and John made their request, they soon heard of it, and an atmosphere of jealousy was precipitated. It threatened the harmony and spiritual life of the Twelve. The immediate correction of this was necessary. Satan *always* tries to disrupt the fellowship of Believers and tries to cause bitterness, dissension, envy, jealousy, and negative attitudes.

It says the Ten were *"much displeased with James and John."* The verb *"displeased"* is from *aganakteo*. It comes from two words meaning *"to feel pain, to grieve,"* and it means *"to be indignant."* The Ten Disciples grew *extremely* indignant and, according to the literal expression, they *"kept it up."*

(10:42-45) Our Lord had to deal with this situation immediately. Satan saw in this an opportunity to create obstacles, and he immediately tried to exploit this opening. Our Lord met this crisis by showing the Disciples the difference between what is esteemed worthy of honor within the *worldly* system and the true standard within the *spiritual* Kingdom He was to institute.

In the world a person is respected for a position of authority, power, and privilege. In contrast, Jesus pointed out that greatness in the Kingdom of God comes from taking a lowly position and being servant of all. The word translated *"minister"* is *diakonos,* and it refers to a servant, as he is occupied with serving. The word translated *"servant"* is *doulos,* and was the term used for a slave. In the Kingdom of God, true honor and respect come when an individual humbles himself and becomes a servant. The Lord Jesus Christ was very God, *of* very God. He became incarnate (clothed in human flesh) so He could live as a servant to all mankind. He explained that this was what they were also to do because *"whoever would be the chiefest shall be servant of all."*

Jesus explained that the Son of Man didn't come to be ministered to, but to minister and to give His Life a ransom for many. Here He is speaking of the substitutionary aspect of His Atonement. He died *in the place of* lost sinners. He shed His precious Blood as the Lamb without blemish so others — through His Redemptive Sacrifice — could be saved. His Followers are *also* to give their lives in service, helping others to find Redemption in Christ.

BLIND BARTIMAEUS AND HIS COMPANION HEALED

"And they came to Jericho: and as He went out of Jericho with His Disciples and a great number of people, blind Bartimaeus, the son of Timaeus, sat by the highway side begging. And when he heard that it was Jesus of Nazareth, he began to cry out, and say, Jesus, Thou Son of David, have mercy on me. And many charged him that he should hold his peace: but he cried the more a great deal, Thou Son of David, have mercy on me. And Jesus stood still, and commanded him to be called. And they call the blind man, saying unto him, Be of good comfort, rise; He calls you. And he, casting away his garment, rose, and came to Jesus. And Jesus answered and said unto him, What will you that I should do unto you? The blind man said unto Him, Lord, that I might receive my sight. And Jesus said unto him, Go your way; your Faith has made you whole. And immediately he received his sight, and followed Jesus in the way" (Mk. 10:46-52).

(10:46) Jesus was on His way to Jerusalem and the Cross. He entered Jericho accompanied by crowds going to the Passover. In this vast crowd was a blind man named Bartimaeus. Blind beggars were a common sight in those days.

(10:47) Bartimaeus knew that something unusual was happening as he heard the crowd passing. He asked what was going on and was told that Jesus of Nazareth was passing by. He decided he must seize this opportunity. The Greek verb indicates that Bartimaeus *continued* crying out to Jesus. He wanted Jesus to have mercy on Him and heal him at once. He called out, *"Thou Son of David,"* and then *kept on* shouting.

(10:48) The people *"charged him"* that he should hold his peace. The word *"charged"* is translated *epitimao,* which means *"to rebuke, to censure severely."* The word *siopao* is translated *"hold his peace."* The people rebuked him for demanding the time of the great Prophet, Jesus. Why should the Master bother with him? They censured him severely, but the more they admonished him, the more he cried out.

(10:49-50) Jesus stopped and commanded that Bartimaeus be called. The crowd then changed quickly from their attitude of censure to one of benign approval. They *"called"* Bartimaeus to Jesus. The word translated *"call"* is *phoneo,* and is a word for calling aloud in a voice that can be heard at a distance. They told him to be of good courage and to rise up;

Jesus wanted to see him.

The blind beggar threw off his garment in elation and rose to meet Jesus. The word *"rose"* is from *anapedao,* and it means *"to leap up, to spring up."* The garment he threw off was the *himation,* the bulky outer garment a man would sleep in. the attitude of the crowd had changed quickly from one of reproval to approval, and they told him to have courage and rise because *"He calls for you!"*

(10:51) Jesus asked what he wanted. The blind man said he wanted to receive his sight. He used the term *"Lord."* In the Greek it is *Rabbounei,* which means *"my Master,"* and was a term of reverence. The words *"receive my sight"* are translated from the word *anablepo,* which means *"to **recover** sight."* The blind man had been able to see at one time and said, *"Lord, I want to see again."*

(10:52) Jesus told the man he could go his way because his Faith had made him whole. The word translated *"made whole"* is from *sozo,* which means *"to save."* It had reference to either physical healing or spiritual Salvation. Jesus told him that he had been healed perfectly, and Bartimaeus immediately received his sight. The perfect tense used in the Greek indicates a permanent cure.

FOLLOWED JESUS. Picture the joyful and happy Bartimaeus, having received a permanent cure and seeing perfectly, joining the crowd to follow Jesus as He heads for Jerusalem.

Chapter 11

Jesus' Triumphal Entry Into Jerusalem

SUBJECT	PAGE
JESUS CURSES A FIG TREE	167
JESUS CLEANSES THE TEMPLE	168
THE BARREN FIG TREE FOUND WITHERED	170
THE RULERS QUESTION JESUS' AUTHORITY	173

CHAPTER 11

JESUS' TRIUMPHAL ENTRY INTO JERUSALEM

"And when they came near to Jerusalem, unto Bethphage and Bethany, at the Mount of Olives, He sent forth two of His Disciples, And said unto them, Go your way into the village over against you: and as soon as you be entered into it, you shall find a colt tied, whereon never man sat; loose him, and bring him. And if any man say unto you, Why do you this? say you that the Lord has need of him; and straightway he will send him hither. And they went their way, and found the colt tied by the door without in a place where two ways met; and they loose him. And certain of them that stood there said unto them, What are you doing, loosing the colt?

"And they said unto them even as Jesus had commanded: and they let them go. And they brought the colt to Jesus, and cast their garments on Him; and He sat upon him. And many spread their garments in the way: and others cut down branches off the trees, and strawed them in the way. And they who went before, and they who followed, cried, saying, Hosanna; Blessed is He Who comes in the Name of the Lord: Blessed be the Kingdom of our father David, that comes in the Name of the Lord: Hosanna in the Highest. And Jesus entered into Jerusalem, and into the Temple: and when He had looked round about upon all things, and now the eventide was come, He went out unto Bethany with the Twelve" (Mk. 11:1-11).

(11:1) Jesus, along with His Disciples, came to Bethphage and Bethany. These were then suburbs but are now a part of greater Jerusalem as the city has grown to include them.

HE SENT FORTH. The verb used is from *apostello,* which means *"to send on a commission."* Two of the Disciples were sent on a special task.

(11:2) The Disciples were told to go to the village before them where they would find a colt. They were to bring this colt to Him. It is interesting to observe that this foal was unbroken and had never been ridden. The animal had never before been used for any work but was now going to serve a sacred purpose. There are many unique *"coincidences"* in the Life of Christ. He was born of a maiden who had never known a man and was buried in a tomb where no one else had ever been lain. He also chose a colt that had never before been ridden.

(11:3) Jesus told the Disciples what to say if anyone questioned them concerning their impressment of the colt. He reassured them that the colt would be returned.

(11:4) The Disciples found the colt as Jesus had told them. The colt was *"tied by the door"* of the house. In those days the better houses had an open court and there was a passageway under the house leading to the street. The Bible says this was where *"two ways met."* We would say it was *"on the corner."* Having found the colt, they *"loose him."*

(11:5-6) The owner was standing by with some neighbors and acquaintances and asked the Disciples why they were loosening the colt. They explained just as Jesus had directed them. The Lord was now well-known, and the owner of the colt had no question about His honesty. He was, no doubt, delighted to think that Jesus would use *his* colt.

(11:7) They brought the colt to Jesus. The colt had not been broken and there was no saddle on it. They put some of their outer clothing on the colt, and Jesus sat on these.

(11:8) AND MANY SPREAD THEIR GARMENTS IN THE WAY. The word translated *"way"* is *hodos,* which means *"a road."* The people threw their garments onto the road and spread them about. They also took branches from the trees and spread these before Jesus.

This was Jesus' formal presentation of Himself as the Messiah. The crowds knew it. They entered into the spirit of the occasion. However, they expected the Lord to set up a rule in opposition to Rome, which would deliver Israel from Roman bondage.

The confusion in Israel stemmed from the fact that Old Testament prophecies cover *both* aspects of Jesus' incarnation: First, as the humble carpenter of Nazareth teaching humility and brotherly love, and *also* as the mighty King of kings and Lord of lords, who will rule the world at His Second Coming. Unfortunately, the powers-that-be in Jerusalem were so preoccupied with the military and political power of the Messiah's *second* appearance that they rejected Him in His *First* Advent. They assumed, being the political and social leaders of Jerusalem, that they would continue on in these positions during the Messiah's Reign. Jesus, of course, with His Doctrines of the meek inheriting the Earth and the first being last — was completely unacceptable to them. To demonstrate His True Mission at this time, Jesus rejected the white steed the Jews *preferred* for their Messiah, and rode instead a humble donkey to *document His humility.*

(11:9-10) Tremendous crowds were present. People were going before Him, while others followed behind. They cried *"Hosanna; Blessed is He who comes in the Name of the Lord."*

The word for blessed is *eulogeo,* which means *"to speak well of, to praise, to eulogize."* It means that the Believer is to receive good things from God. There is another word translated blessed in the New Testament, *makarios,* which means to be spiritually prosperous. The word used in this context means *"to speak well of, and to praise."* They were praising Him, saying, *"Praise be the Kingdom of our father David. Hosanna in the Highest."*

(11:11) Jesus went to the Temple. The part He entered was the area of the porches, courts, and outbuildings. The word used is *hieron,* and has reference to this area. The word *naos* represents the *inner* part of the structure, involving the Holy Place and the Holy of Holies. Jesus went only as far as the outer court this time.

Jesus looked around carefully (*periblepo*). It was as if He was inspecting a house as the *master* of the house would do. He took *note* of what was going on, but did nothing at this time. His actions were to be postponed until just a little later.

Jesus and His Disciples went to Bethany, the home of Lazarus. Jesus often stayed here with Mary, Martha, and Lazarus and found wonderful fellowship with them. However, it may be that He spent these nights on the Mount of Olives as a haven of solitude. It was a place of prayer and meditation. Knowing that He was about to face a trying series of events, culminating in the agony of the Cross, it is logical to assume that He would seek out the Mount of Olives rather than the house of Lazarus.

JESUS CURSES A FIG TREE

"And on the morrow, when they were come from Bethany, He was hungry: And seeing a fig tree afar off having leaves, He came, if haply He might find any thing thereon: and when He came to it, He found nothing but leaves; for the time of figs was not yet. And Jesus answered and said unto it, No man eat fruit of thee hereafter forever. And His Disciples heard it" (Mk. 11:12-14).

(11:12-14) ON THE MORROW. Jesus had made His triumphal entry into Jerusalem on the first day of the week, which was Sunday, our Lord's Day. It was now early Monday morning. According to the expression used by Matthew, it was during the fourth watch — which would be before 6 a.m. They were coming from Bethany and Jesus was hungry. It was not yet the season for figs, but, seeing the leaves on the tree, they hoped they might find fruit also. It appears that the fig trees of Palestine produce figs and *then* leaves, in that sequence.

The Lord condemned the tree. It *appeared* that it should have had fruit when it didn't. This incident illustrates the actual *spiritual* situation in Judah. The Temple and the religious structure of Judah had become so adulterated and polluted by the Pharisaical *"traditions"* that it only *appeared* to be bearing fruit while no *true* fruit was to be found on it.

A parallel lesson can be drawn from this, for undoubtedly the Lord is displeased with Christians who never bear fruit. A person might have all the *trappings* of Christianity — including church attendance, Salvation through the Blood of Christ, and even the infilling of the Holy Spirit — yet bear no fruit. This is certainly displeasing to the Lord and the action He took in condemning the fig tree might be considered a warning to non-productive Christians.

JESUS CLEANSES THE TEMPLE

"And they come to Jerusalem: and Jesus went into the Temple, and began to cast out them who sold and bought in the Temple, and overthrew the tables of the moneychangers, and the seats of them who sold doves; And would not suffer that any man should carry any vessel through the Temple. And He taught, saying unto them, Is it not written, My House shall be called of all nations the House of Prayer? but you have made it a den of thieves. And the Scribes and Chief Priests heard it, and sought how they might destroy Him: for they feared Him, because all the people was astonished at His Doctrine. And when evening was come, He went out of the city" (Mk. 11:15-19).

(11:15-16) This was to be the day our Lord would demonstrate Righteous indignation. He had already cursed the fig tree, and now He was entering the Temple. The scene He had surveyed the previous day had weighed heavily upon His Mind and Spirit. The moneychangers changed the coins of Greece or Rome into Jewish half-shekels. Some of the people came for the Passover from other countries and changed their money into Jewish half-shekels to pay the Temple tax. The moneychangers made a handsome profit from these transactions.

Also, people were unable to bring sacrifices from long distances, so there were merchants selling animals for sacrifice. One of the problems was their tendency to sell flawed or imperfect animals and birds at high prices — even though God's Laws forbade the sacrifice of any but the most perfect of animals.

The problems involved in these transactions went far beyond the normal practices of *"business."* The exorbitant prices for the inferior animals precluded the poor from making their sacrifices, or impoverished them. The moneychangers routinely falsified the rate of exchange to make enormous profits. Jesus expressed His Righteous indignation by overturning the tables and upsetting the money containers. This would have been a serious blow to their business, for it was at the very time when the trade was at its peak during the Passover.

The picture many people have of Jesus is one of constant meekness

168

and humility. He *was* the lowly Lamb of God, but He was also the crowned Prince of Glory. He is revealed here as growing angry and driving the moneychangers and the merchants from the Temple. No doubt He had been brooding about this situation much of the night and was indignant at the iniquity existing in the Temple, and the blatant rejection of Almighty God — whom they were disobeying rather than serving.

Jesus took a firm stand against evil. It is a challenge for spiritual leaders to be firm and strong in the face of evil. Spiritual matters can become perverted in the very midst of religious activity. The Jews of that day had twisted the Law of Moses until it was barely recognizable. It had been perverted to benefit *them,* while working a hardship on the people.

The Priests often found fault with the sacrificial animals brought by the people, thus requiring them to purchase another (perhaps inferior) from a merchant allied with the Priest. The price charged for these animals might be as much as three times the *normal* price for such animals. Is it any wonder that Jesus was distressed? The place of worship and prayer had in fact been converted into a house of merchandise with thieves and robbers acting as the merchants. Jesus drove these men from the Temple.

He also stopped the traffic *through* the Temple. People were carrying their loads of goods and implements through the Temple — using it as a shortcut between the city and the Mount of Olives. This had been forbidden by Jewish authorities but never enforced. The word translated *"vessel"* is *skeuos,* and refers to a household implement or some type of domestic utensil.

(11:17) A crowd gathered as the Lord cleared the Temple, and Jesus used the opportunity to talk to them. He declared that God's House was to be a House of Prayer. It is normal to worship God and to be in prayer when in His Presence. The Temple had held special significance for the Israelites for centuries. It was the place where the Ark of the Covenant had been kept and where the Shekinah Glory dwelt. Our *"churches"* today are *not* a parallel to the Temple at Jerusalem.

Some interpret Jesus' actions here as an example for today, but in the New Covenant our *bodies* are the Temple of the Holy Spirit (I Cor. 6:19). The Holy Spirit did not dwell within individuals in the same manner before Pentecost. Also, individuals were not baptized with the Holy Spirit during the Old Covenant. After Jesus paid the price at Calvary, and was raised from the dead (for our Redemption and cleansing), God made individuals His habitation. Now, through Jesus Christ, the world's Redeemer, the Holy Spirit can come in and take abode.

God no longer dwells in *any* Temple made with hands (I Cor. 3:16). Churches today are not truly Houses of God. Rather, a church is a place where people, led by the Spirit of God and His Presence, come together for worship, prayer, *and* fellowship. Notice what we said here. It is important that Christians gather not only for worship and prayer but also for *fellowship*. Once we perceive the difference between the Temple at Jerusalem and our local churches, it becomes obvious that it is not wrong for a church to include facilities that promote fellowship — such conveniences as kitchens and dining areas.

Various facilities can be provided to enhance the convenience of the congregation in *both* worship and fellowship. There is nothing wrong in having a beautiful church building — but to invest millions of dollars in an opulent cathedral just to impress outsiders with the structure, is to miss the true meaning and *purpose* of the building. The church building is *not* the House of God. Basically, the church building is a place where people may congregate out of the weather.

A proper spirit and attitude must, of course, pervade all activities carried on within the church, but these are not as limited as some might suggest. There is certainly nothing wrong in making available records, books, and other aids which help in a Christian walk. This is in no way comparable to what caused Jesus' indignation when He cleansed the Temple.

The problem Jesus faced was one of blatant graft and corruption. Jesus called them thieves (*leistes* — literally, robbers). They were, in effect, a band of thieves. Jesus also declared that this house of prayer was for all nations.

(11:18) The way the Lord dealt with the Temple market incensed the Chief Priests and Scribes. They met and joined in an attempt to do away with Jesus. The crowds at the Passover were favorable to Him, since so many of them came from Galilee and the areas where He had ministered. They strongly supported Jesus.

The Chief Priests and Scribes *"went to seeking"* how they might destroy the Lord. The people were *"astonished."* This is from the Greek word *ekplesso,* which is a very strong word. The entire multitude was *struck with astonishment* at the teachings Jesus gave.

(11:19) When evening came, Jesus went out of the city. He made it a habit, during this final visit to Jerusalem, to spend the nights *away* from the city. According to the expression used, it appears that Jesus was *glad* to get out of Jerusalem for the night.

THE BARREN FIG TREE FOUND WITHERED

"And in the morning, as they passed by, they saw the fig tree dried up from the roots. And Peter calling to remembrance said unto Him, Master, behold, the fig tree which You cursed is withered away. And Jesus answering said unto them, Have Faith in God. For verily I say unto

you, That whosoever shall say unto this mountain, Be thou removed, and be thou cast into the sea; and shall not doubt in his heart, but shall believe that those things which he says shall come to pass; he shall have whatsoever he says. Therefore I say unto you, What things soever you desire, when you pray, believe that you receive them, and you shall have them. And when you stand praying, forgive, if you have ought against any: that your Father also which is in Heaven may forgive you your trespasses. But if you do not forgive, neither will your Father which is in Heaven forgive your trespasses" (Mk. 11:20-26).

(11:20) Jesus and His Disciples passed by the fig tree in the morning. The word used emphasizes that it was light. They *saw* the tree Jesus had cursed, and it had dried up from the roots. The word translated *"dried up"* is *xeraino,* which means *"to dry up or wither."* The perfect tense is used, indicating that the tree was completely withered away and dead. This was rather remarkable, since the tree had been crowned with green leaves only one day previous. Logically, it is impossible to expect this to happen during a twenty-four-hour period.

(11:21) It was Peter who mentioned the tree, reminding them all that Jesus had cursed it. Undoubtedly this was much on Peter's mind at the moment.

(11:22) Jesus ignored Peter's statement, or at least His words were not related to Peter's. Jesus went on instead to deal with a matter of greater importance to the Twelve and a lesson to be learned on having Faith. He told them to *"have Faith in God."*

(11:23) Jesus and His Disciples were crossing the Mount of Olives, and they could see the mountains of Judaea and Moab on the other side of the Dead Sea. He told them that if they had sufficient Faith, whatever they declared would come to pass. They were in view of a large valley between the mountains, and Jesus pointed out that even this huge basin could be filled in. the mountains could fill even the Dead Sea, if moved by *Faith.*

Faith must be regarded as a *continuous* attitude of the heart and not some passing emotion or an isolated act. To be truly effective, Faith has to cooperate with God. If it is out of harmony with the Will and Purpose of God, Faith might cause all sorts of troubles.

Most of the time, prayers contrary to the Will and Purpose of God will not be answered, because they can cause difficulty and problems. A Child of God should be very careful as to what he asks in prayer. Great responsibility is involved in what we ask of the Heavenly Father, and there are many reasons why various prayers *cannot* be answered. Great things can be accomplished, however — when there is True Faith.

Jesus said that if a person would say to the mountain, be thou removed — and would not doubt in his heart — that what he ordered would come to pass. The word for *"doubt"* is *diakrino.* This means *"to judge between the two,"* indicating a divided judgment, or a wavering between two opinions — which constitutes doubt.

There is great power in words. However, individuals don't always get what they ask for, because of either a lack of Faith or other extraneous factors, which *can* be involved in what seems on the surface to be an uncomplicated request.

(11:24) Jesus declared that *whatever* a person desired could be expected. This does not mean, however, that immature self-indulgence will be honored. The *mature* Christian, truly walking in Faith, trusting in the Lord — and asking according to God's Will — can *expect* to receive answers to his prayers. Great things happen as a result of asking in Faith. There have been miracles of healing and glorious provision made (physically, materially, *and* spiritually) as True Faith has been demonstrated and exercised through requests made in prayer.

When a person prays he must believe it will come to pass. There is, however, a *time* element involved, so patience is necessary. The Bible says that the trying of our Faith works patience — so a person must go *on* believing and trusting God for the answer in order for it to eventually come to pass.

Sometimes discouragement causes Christians to cease praying *before* the answer comes. One should continue believing and trusting God. Even if certain answers aren't forthcoming, there is no need to blame God or one's self. There may be unknown factors preventing the accomplishment of what we want. We should continue to trust God. Sometimes greater insight into God's fuller Purposes may be granted, or the answer may be on the way but a little further down the road. Jesus' statement is a very strong one, and the consequences are very far-reaching. It is a tremendous promise.

(11:25-26) Jesus had just given this great dissertation on Faith. Following His statement on mountain-moving Faith, He launches into a statement on forgiveness.

The word *"when"* is *hotan,* which literally means *"whenever."* The word *"standing"* is used, but this doesn't refer to posture. The general custom of the Jews was perhaps to pray standing — but kneeling seems the accepted prayer posture for many people. This emphasis has nothing to do with whether one is kneeling or standing, however emphasis of these two Passages being on the word *"forgive."*

A great number of problems occur in people's lives because of unforgiveness. Unforgiveness can often *prelude* God's Blessings. One cannot truly be blessed and forgiven — without first *forgiving.* One must not harbor unforgiveness in one's heart against anyone. Scripture exhorts us to be kind, loving, and tenderhearted toward one another, *forgiving one another.*

There are many occasions when others are spiteful toward us. If we allow this to fester in our hearts and to cause us to become bitter, we will certainly forfeit many of God's potential Blessings. A person must be willing to forgive those who have wronged him. There are times when one may not feel like doing it, and it then becomes necessary to *force* a conscious act of the will. We say that we *want* to forgive that person, or that we *choose* to forgive him, despite what we may *feel inside*. When you say you *do* forgive someone and then ask God to give you the strength and grace to *stand* on your statement, you can suddenly find forgiveness flooding your soul.

This is a matter of great importance, and it is a serious problem among God's People. We must learn to forgive others. We cannot harbor resentment and hatred in our hearts. Jesus said if others have ought against us and we don't forgive them — our Heavenly Father can't forgive *us*.

It should be added that when unforgiveness exists, God's Blessings cannot truly and fully abide with that individual. Many have found that when they were unable to make a conscious move to forgive, the gates of God's Blessings remained *closed* in their lives. Once they *did* forgive, they suddenly found they had joy and victory again.

THE RULERS QUESTION JESUS' AUTHORITY

"And they come again to Jerusalem: and He was walking in the Temple, there come to Him the Chief Priests, and the Scribes, and the Elders, And say unto Him, By what authority do You do these things? and who gave You this authority to do these things? And Jesus answered and said unto them, I will also ask of you one question, and answer Me, and I will tell you by what authority I do these things. The baptism of John, was it from Heaven, or of men? answer Me. And they reasoned with themselves, saying, If we shall say, From Heaven; He will say, Why then did you not believe him? But if we shall say, Of men; they feared the people: for all men counted John, that he was a Prophet indeed. And they answered and said unto Jesus, We cannot tell. And Jesus answering said unto them, Neither do I tell you by what authority I do these things" (Mk. 11:27-33).

(11:27-28) Jesus came again to Jerusalem and to the Temple. He had gone outside the city each night, staying either in the Mount of Olives or at the home of Mary, Martha, and Lazarus. This is the third consecutive day the Lord was to visit the Temple.

The first day He observed the moneychangers and the illicit merchants cheating the people. The second day He drove them out, infuriating the High Priests (as well as the moneychangers and the merchants).

And now it is the *third* day. While His return might seem foolish to some due to the animosity generated on the previous day, Jesus had His reasons. He had taken a Righteous stand, and no one could doubt where He stood.

The Chief Priests, the Scribes, and the Elders approached Him. They had now thrown aside old differences in order to present a united front against the Lord. These men considered themselves to be the custodians of Israel's spiritual standards and also of the Temple. Jesus, by His actions, had demonstrated a superior jurisdiction. They now demanded to know His authority — how Jesus felt He had the *right* to take charge of *"their"* Temple.

(11:29-30) The Lord Jesus responded to their question with another question. Because the Master was very popular, undoubtedly a large crowd had gathered. They waited with bated breath for the outcome of the debate. The High Priests, Scribes, and Elders had hoped to entrap Him with a single question. But He asked another question which exposed the crux of the issue.

Jesus was not trying to be clever or crafty. He simply asked them, concerning the baptism of John — whether it was of Heaven or of men. John the Baptist had proclaimed the Divinity of Jesus, placing them in an untenable position. If they acknowledge the Divine basis of John's ministry, they would have to accept what he said. Because John had proclaimed that Jesus was the Lamb of God, they would also have to admit the Divinity of Jesus Christ.

(11:31-32) The religious leaders *"reasoned with themselves."* They were placed between *"a rock and a hard place."* Whichever side they took, their bargaining position would evaporate. If they accepted the Divinity of John's mission, they would have to accept Jesus' Divinity — and the propriety of what He had done. On the other hand, if they *rejected* the baptism and the work of John, they would infuriate the crowd which had loved John — and invite stoning by the crowd. The throngs believed John to be a great Prophet, so the Scribes and Pharisees equivocated by saying that they could not tell. They *could* have, but their answer would not have been acceptable.

(11:33) Because of their dilemma, the Jewish leaders refused to answer Jesus. Jesus replied that He would not then tell *them* by what authority He did these things. They should have recognized that He *had* authority, for the people were amazed as they listened to Jesus *"because He spoke as one who had authority."* The *people* recognized the authority of the Master, but the religious leaders, bound by their traditions and personal interests, failed to see it. They arbitrarily rejected Him.

Notes

Chapter 12

The Parable Of The Wicked Husbandmen

SUBJECT   **PAGE**

THE QUESTION OF TRIBUTE TO CAESAR 179
THE SADDUCEES POSE A QUESTION ABOUT THE RESURRECTION 181
THE GREAT COMMANDMENT 183
THE QUESTION OF DAVID'S SON 185
JESUS DENOUNCED THE SCRIBES 186
JESUS COMMENDS THE POOR WIDOW FOR HER GIFT 186

CHAPTER 12

THE PARABLE OF THE WICKED HUSBANDMEN

"And He began to speak unto them by Parables. A certain man planted a vineyard, and set an hedge about it, and digged a place for the winefat, and built a tower, and let it out to husbandmen, and went into a far country. And at the season he sent to the husbandmen a servant, that he might receive from the husbandmen of the fruit of the vineyard. And they caught him, and beat him, and sent him away empty. And again he sent unto them another servant; and at him they cast stones, and wounded him in the head, and sent him away shamefully handled. And again he sent another; and him they killed, and many others; beating some, and killing some. Having yet therefore one son, his wellbeloved, he sent him also last unto them, saying, They will reverence my son.

"But those husbandmen said among themselves, This is the heir; come, let us kill him, and the inheritance shall be ours. And they took him, and killed him, and cast him out of the vineyard. What shall therefore the lord of the vineyard do? He will come and destroy the husbandmen, and will give the vineyard unto others. And have you not read this Scripture; The Stone which the builders rejected is become the Head of the Corner: This was the Lord's doing, and it is marvellous in our eyes? And they sought to lay hold on Him, but feared the people: for they knew that He had spoken the Parable against them: and they left Him, and went their way" (Mk. 12:1-12).

(12:1) This time our Lord delivered a Parable. He had been speaking the unvarnished truth, but, with the coldhearted religious leaders arrayed against Him, He now spoke in a manner that revealed while it also concealed. This allowed Him to deliver His thoughts so they would *understand* them, while at the time discussing their shortcomings without specifically confronting them.

Jesus was compassionate, tender, kind, merciful, and longsuffering when He spoke to the lost. When He spoke to the religious leaders of the community, however, He pulled no punches. To whom much is given, much is required. In dealing with the religious leaders, Jesus spoke forcefully and often in undisguised disapproval. On this occasion, He was revealing them as the future murderers of the Messiah.

In this Parable, the one who planted the vineyard is God. The husbandmen represent Jewry and the servants are the Prophets. The Son is, of course, Jesus. They knew, when He spoke of the vineyard and the husbandmen, that He was speaking about them. The vineyard symbolized Israel in Scripture, and the members of the Sanhedrin knew Scripture well and understood the symbolism. They realized that it was God who had planted the vineyard, and they knew that the leaders of Judah were the husbandmen. The Jews had a responsibility to God and to Israel. Reference is made to a hedge that was set about the vineyard, which speaks of God's protection over the land of Judah and the blessings He had reserved for His Chosen People.

(12:2-5) These Verses picture servants being sent to receive the fruits of the vineyard. The word for *"servants"* is *doulos,* which means a bondslave. The servants were sent at the time of harvest — and represent Old Testament Prophets sent to the Hebrews at various times. The first servant sent was beaten. The word for *"beaten"* is *dero,* which means to *"beat severely, to scourge."*

The Prophets had preached and pleaded with the Israelites to repent and change their ways, but there was total rejection by Israel. The husbandmen beat the Master's servant and sent him away.

The second bondservant (Verse 4) met with a fate worse than the first. They cast stones at him and wounded him on the head. After being shamefully handled, *he* was sent away. Following this, another servant was sent and was killed. Others were also beaten and killed. This is a picture of the Prophets who were also viciously treated and many were killed.

(12:6) After the Prophets there was yet one remaining who God could send, and this was the Messiah. The reasoning of God, in the words of the Master, was that the Jewish Nation would not dare harm the Son. Jesus was the *"Beloved Son"* of God and He said, *"They will reverence My Son."*

(12:7) Instead of accepting the Son, the husbandmen plotted to kill Him and usurp the inheritance for themselves. It is hard to picture the depths to which man can sink and how utterly depraved he can become. The owner of the vineyard (God) might have expected reverence from the husbandmen, but they were utterly immoral. The leaders of the Sanhedrin knew full well that Jesus was the Son of God — the Messiah of Israel. He had been recognized and accepted by the people. But the spiritual leaders were jealous and, in their desperate desire to recover their waning power over the people, determined to kill Jesus.

(12:8) The husbandmen took the Son, killed Him, and cast Him out of the vineyard. The *"casting out"* deals with the Pharisaical leaders excommunicating our Lord. Jesus was taken outside the walls of Jerusalem. He was turned over to the Romans for punishment, excluded from the community of Israel, and crucified outside the walls.

(12:9) In this Parable Jesus goes on to prophesy the destruction of Jerusalem. This was to happen in 70 A.D. and, as a result, the Jews would be dispersed. The Israelites *have* been dispersed for centuries, until Israel is to be regathered for the Second Advent when it will be restored to fellowship and usefulness with God. The work of the Kingdom was given to the Gentiles as Jesus declared here that *"God would give the vineyard unto others."* After many years Israel is to be reestablished in God's favor, but they have suffered much through the centuries.

(12:10-11) The stone which the builders rejected is our Lord Jesus, the Messiah. The spiritual leaders of Israel rejected Him. The word *"rejected"* is *apodokimazo*. The basic word means to put to a test for the purpose of approving, and the prefix (*apo*) means *"off, away from."* They rejected Jesus after having put Him to the test, but He was to become the head of the corner. Jesus claimed to be the Messiah Israel was looking for, but the spiritual leaders rejected Him because He did not meet their worldly specifications. He did not come primarily to deliver Israel from Rome but to deliver them from sin. He will come again as the Messiah, and be the King of kings and Lord of lords, when He will rule the Millennial Kingdom forever as *"the Head of the Corner."* What a marvelous time that will be!

(12:12) Once again, the Sanhedrin representatives wanted to arrest Jesus in the Temple, but they feared the people. Once again they were defeated and returned to their council chambers to pursue their conspiracy. The Scribes and Pharisees, men of the Sanhedrin, knew He had spoken the Parable against them. As they went their way they vowed not to forget their humiliation.

THE QUESTION OF TRIBUTE TO CAESAR

"And they send unto Him certain of the Pharisees and of the Herodians, to catch Him in His words. And when they were come, they say unto Him, Master, we know that You are true, and care for no man: for You regard not the person of men, but teach the Way of God in truth: Is it lawful to give tribute to Caesar, or not? Shall we give, or shall we not give? But He, knowing their hypocrisy, said unto them, Why tempt you Me? Bring me a penny, that I may see it. And they brought it. And He said unto them, Whose is this image and superscription? And they said unto Him, Caesar's. And Jesus answering said unto them, Render to Caesar the things that are Caesar's, and to God the things that are God's. And they marvelled at Him" (Mk. 12:13-17).

(12:13) The members of the Sanhedrin had just been defeated by Jesus in a discussion. They were so furious they wanted Him arrested and killed, but they still feared the people. They separated into several groups to devise a plot to catch Him. The Pharisees moved first and sent some of their finest debaters and most astute scholars of Jewish Law in an attempt to catch Him in some statement. The word *"catch"* is *agreuo*. It means, *"to catch wild animals."* Their plan was to snare or trap Jesus, as they would a small animal, but in Jesus' case they planned to use His own words as the snare.

(12:14) As these men began to talk to Jesus, they sounded gracious in their compliments as they sought to allay any suspicion of their true purpose. The Pharisees called Him Master, and they said they knew He was true. The word translated *"know"* is *oida,* and refers to positive knowledge. They were totally assured and convinced of this fact. The word *"true"* is *alethes,* and it means true in the sense that He could not lie. They knew He was the Messiah, but they were so utterly devoid of conscience that they tried to lay a trap for Him. It was a terrible, blasphemous activity. As they talked, they assured Him that they knew He couldn't lie, but they were actually revealing barely suppressed sarcasm.

The question they posed involved the payment of tribute to Caesar. The word *"tribute"* is *kenson.* This refers to a poll tax paid by the Jews to the Roman emperor. This was very humiliating for them, because they saw it as a sign of subjection to a foreign power, and, additionally, the coin used for payment displayed the emperor's picture. According to Roman Law, they were to think of the emperor as god.

They were not discussing the legality of paying a poll tax to Caesar, but rather if it was *proper* within the Jewish perspective of their special relationship to God. They pressed Him for an answer. This was, of course, a *"loaded question"* of the *"have you stopped beating your wife?"* persuasion. Whatever answer Jesus gave, it appeared He would be in trouble.

If Jesus answered *"no,"* the religious leaders could report Him to the Roman authorities as one promoting rebellion against Rome. Jesus, of course, had never done this. On the other hand, the Scribes and Pharisees felt that if Jesus said it *was* proper to pay tribute to Rome, He would lose the support of the crowd — perhaps even to the point where they would rise up and slay Him. They smugly awaited His answer, secure in their conviction that they had Him trapped.

(12:15) Jesus knew *"their hypocrisy."* Matthew says Jesus *"perceived their wickedness"* (22:18). In Luke it is stated that He *"perceived their craftiness"* (20:23). These men had an evil motive and were completely unscrupulous in their attempts to trap Jesus. But Jesus, knowing their hypocrisy, asked, *"Why tempt you me?"* The word is *peirazo,* and, as we have seen previously, means, *"to put to the test."*

Next, Jesus asked for a Roman coin in order that He might see it. They were in the area of the Temple, and this type of coin was not used there, so it might have taken a little time for them to locate one.

(12:16) When the coin was brought, He inquired about the image on it. The word *"image"* is *eikon*, and means *"a derived likeness."* The word translated *"superscription"* is *epigraphe*, and literally means *"a writing upon."* The coin had a likeness of Caesar on it, with his name inscribed upon it. The Pharisees answered that Caesar's image was on the coin.

(12:17) As Jesus paused, the air was charged with tension. The Pharisees had set a clever trap. He held the coin so they could see it and then gave an answer remarkable in its simplicity. According to the Greek Text He said, *"The things belonging to Caesar, pay off to Caesar."* The Jewish leaders had used the word *didomi*, which means, *"to give."* Jesus used the word *apodidomi*, which refers to paying something as a debt. In essence, He stated that there are debts payable to man, and debts payable to God. *Both* must be discharged. It was impossible for the chagrined churchmen to refute His reasoning.

THEY MARVELLED AT HIM. The verb used is *thaumazo*, and it is in the imperfect tense, which speaks of continuous action. The people stood amazed, *"marveling at Him."*

THE SADDUCEES POSE A QUESTION
ABOUT THE RESURRECTION

"Then come unto Him the Sadducees, which say there is no Resurrection; and they asked Him, saying, Master, Moses wrote unto us, If a man's brother die, and leave his wife behind him, and leave no children, that his brother should take his wife, and raise up seed unto his brother. Now there were seven Brethren: and the first took a wife, and dying left no seed. And the second took her, and died, neither left he any seed: and the third likewise. And the seven had her, and left no seed: last of all the woman died also. In the Resurrection therefore, when they shall rise, whose wife shall she be of them? for the seven had her to wife.

"And Jesus answering said unto them, Do you not therefore err, because you know not the Scriptures, neither the Power of God? For when they shall rise from the dead, they neither marry, nor are given in marriage; but are as the Angels which are in Heaven. And as touching the dead, that they rise: have you not read in the Book of Moses, how in the bush God spoke unto him saying, I am the God of Abraham, and the God of Isaac, and the God of Jacob? He is not the God of the

dead, but the God of the Living: you therefore do greatly err" (Mk. 12:18-27).

(12:18-23) There are a number of Jewish sects referred to regularly in the New Testament. The Pharisees were strict observers of the Law, deeply committed to religious rituals, and involved in their religious traditions. The Herodians were primarily a political party of Jews allied with the Romans. The Sadducees were a rationalistic group and were more wealthy and aristocratic. They were few in number compared to the Pharisees. The Pharisees and Sadducees were continually at odds, because the Pharisees believed in the Resurrection while the Sadducees did not believe in Angels, spirits — or in a Resurrection.

The question the Sadducees presented to Jesus wasn't really designed to elicit information. It was the *"clever"* type of question they enjoyed, designed to entrap Jesus by forcing Him to make a definite statement that would irritate one group or the other. They presented the case of a man who died after marrying a woman but before she produced an offspring.

Under Mosaic Law there was a provision designed to prevent the family inheritance from being dissipated. It was the responsibility of a brother to take the barren wife so an heir would be produced to receive the deceased's portion. In this case, there was a succession of seven brothers who took her as their wife, but each died leaving her no seed. They asked, therefore, whose wife would she be in the Resurrection?

The point of contention was, if there was a Resurrection (as the Pharisees said), whose wife would this woman be in Eternity? The Sadducees were, of course, contending that there was no Resurrection. They wanted to know the position of the Lord Jesus Christ on this question, which was an issue between them and the Pharisees. Actually, their attitude was one of hostility, and when they addressed our Lord as *"teacher"* it was a formality. They had not really come to learn, but only to *"prove"* their own position because they felt their question was so difficult that no one would be able to answer it.

(12:24-27) Jesus told them that: (1) They did not know the Scriptures, or (2) the Power of God, and (3) they did err. He then continued by saying there is no marriage in Heaven, for no procreation is necessary there. After the Resurrection, the Saints of God will not marry other Saints. There will be no offspring from the Saints of God. He said we would be as the Angels which are in Heaven.

Angels were originally *created.* They do not die, nor do they procreate. They do not start out as *"baby angels"* and grow over the years. When human beings are resurrected they will not *be* Angels as such, but they will be *like* the Angels in this regard. Life after the Resurrection will be quite different from normal *mortal* life here on Earth.

Jesus went on to speak of life after death. He quoted the words of Moses where God stated that He *is* the God of Abraham, Isaac, and Jacob. He did not say He *was* the God of Abraham, Isaac, and Jacob, implying that they *had* existed but were not dead. He said, *"I am the God of Abraham, Isaac, and Jacob,"* certifying — at the moment He was speaking to Moses — that Abraham, Isaac, and Jacob were *alive*.

Our Father is not the God of the dead but the God of the living. The point is, the Patriarchs and other Saints are alive; they have not ceased to exist, and God is their God. The souls of the Saints are with God in Heaven at this moment. When a person dies, his soul does not sleep in the grave as does the body. The soul and spirit of the saved go immediately to be with the Lord in Heaven. The lost are in Hell. Those who die in the Lord go to be with God in Heaven, so He truly *is* the God of the living.

The term *"death"* can be confusing. God told Adam and Eve that if they partook of the fruit of the Tree of Knowledge they would surely die. They ate, but did not physically die at that moment. They died *spiritually* — because of disobedience — and eventually they did die physically. *Physical* death refers to the body — not to the soul and spirit. *Spiritual* death implies separation from God. The soul and spirit are immortal. Jesus was, in essence, saying that Abraham *is* alive, Isaac *is* alive, and Jacob *is* alive. God is the God of the living, and these Patriarchs *are* alive and with God. Not knowing or understanding this, the Sadducees did greatly err.

THE GREAT COMMANDMENT

"And one of the Scribes came, and having heard them reasoning together, and perceiving that He had answered them well, asked Him, Which is the First Commandment of all? And Jesus answered Him, The First of all the Commandments is, Hear, O Israel; The Lord our God is one Lord: and you shall love the Lord your God with all your heart, and with all your soul, and with all your mind, and with all your strength: this is the First Commandment. And the Second is like, namely this, You shall love your neighbour as yourself. There is none other Commandment greater than these.

"And the Scribe said unto Him, Well, Master, You have said the truth: for there is one God; and there is none other but He: And to love Him with all the heart, and with all the understanding, and with all the soul, and with all the strength, and to love his neighbor as himself, is more than all whole Burnt Offerings and Sacrifices. And when Jesus saw that he answered discreetly, He said unto him, You are not far from the Kingdom of God. And no man after that does ask Him any question" (Mk. 12:28-34).

(12:28) After Jesus answered the Pharisees and Sadducees regarding the marital condition after Resurrection, one of the Scribes asked Jesus another question.

WHICH IS THE FIRST COMMANDMENT? The word *"which"* is *poia* and means *"of what sort?"* The questioner appears to be searching for a distinction between the *ritual* laws and observances of the Pharisees, and the ethical ones — the ones that are positive and moral. It was the tendency of the Jews to place great emphasis on such matters as circumcision, Sabbath-keeping, and the technicalities of ritual observance. He does not seem to be asking Jesus to select *one* of the Ten Commandments, but rather to specify a *class* of Commandments of a higher priority.

(12:29-31) Jesus quoted from Deuteronomy 6:4-5 in answering the question. This Scripture was quoted daily by every Jew. They kept it on a parchment rolled in a miniature roll in a small pouch on their arm, or even suspended on their forehead — another ostentatious manifestation of their *"holiness."*

These words were considered more or less *"sacred"* by the Jews. The mention of the heart, the soul, the mind, and the strength speaks of total and complete devotion to God. The word used for love is *agapao,* which infers love which is generated in the heart of a yielded Saint by the Holy Spirit. It is Divine love, a God-given love. He did not use some different word form for love, such as *phileo,* which implies brotherly love. This First Commandment involves absolute commitment to God.

The Second Commandment is similar and has to do with a person loving his neighbor as himself. Selfishness is the root of many problems. If a person loves his neighbor as himself, he is not *capable* of hurting or treating him in an unkindly manner.

These two Commandments summarize the absolute essence of man's relationship to God — which further involves man's relationship to man.

(12:32-33) The Scribe said to Jesus, *"Well, Master, You have said the truth."* The word *"well"* is not an interjection as we might use it. It is the Greek word *kalos,* which means *"good"* and this *could* have been translated, *"You said it well, Master."*

YOU HAVE SAID THE TRUTH. This is a further expression of approval, and he declares, *"You have spoken truthfully, right, well."* The Scribe then added, with reference to God, *"He is the One and there is not another except Him."* He went on to say that loving God and one's neighbor with all one's heart, mind, soul, and strength, is certainly more than Burnt Offerings and Sacrifices.

(12:34) Jesus saw that the man answered *"discreetly."* The word in the Greek is *nounechos.* It means that He answered intelligently, as a result of His own thinking, and in a disarmingly, direct manner, especially within the context of the prevailing mood of the times. He was apparently a sincere individual. Jesus told him that he was not far from the Kingdom.

As a result of Jesus' incisive answers to the questions posed, the Scripture says no man dared ask Him any further questions.

THE QUESTION OF DAVID'S SON

"And Jesus answered and said, while He taught in the Temple, How say the Scribes that Christ is the Son of David? For David himself said by the Holy Spirit, The LORD said to my Lord, Sit thou on My Right Hand, till I make Your enemies Your footstool. David therefore himself calls Him Lord; and whence is He then his son? And the common people heard Him gladly" (Mk. 12:35-37).

(12:35-37) The Scribes, Pharisees, Sadducees, Elders, and Priests had tried to trap Jesus in His own speech. They despised Him. The previous question was asked by a Scribe who was more open to the truth than the others. Now that their direct attack ceased, Jesus asked *them* a question.

They didn't understand the question, or even what He was talking about. The Pharisees and Scribes believed that the Jewish Messiah would come from the royal line of David, and being from the line of David, He would be called the Son of David.

The word Messiah had special meaning for the Jews — namely that the future King of Israel would some day reign on the Throne of David. They believed that the Messiah would come from the royal line of David, and, David being human, they thought the Messiah would also be human. Now the Lord reminds His listeners that David called the Messiah *his* Lord — which you would not call one of your human descendants (Ps. 110:1).

The Messiah was to be recognized as Deity — the Jehovah of the Old Testament. The difficulty Jesus presented to His listeners was: If the Messiah is Jehovah — which is Deity — how can He be human, too? The point that Jesus was directing their attention to was the Incarnation.

The Scribes and Pharisees were angry because Jesus called God His father in a unique sense, thus in effect elevating Himself to a level equal to that of God. (Read Jn. 5:18.) In the Incarnation God became man. He took upon Himself the veil of human flesh and dwelt among men. The Jewish leaders rejected this teaching of the Incarnation and Jesus' claim to Deity. Jesus was referring to Psalm, Chapter 110 and quoting David (who spoke under the Anointing of the Holy Spirit) as saying, *"The LORD said unto my Lord."*

This actually had reference to two persons of the Trinity, God the Father and God the Son. The statement was inspired by the Holy Spirit, so it is a confirmation of the fact of the Trinity. As Jesus presented this concept, the common people listened joyfully to Him.

JESUS DENOUNCED THE SCRIBES

"And He said unto them in His Doctrine, Beware of the Scribes, which love to go in long clothing, and love salutations in the market-places, And the chief seats in the Synagogues, and the uppermost rooms at feasts: Which devour widows' houses, and for a pretence make long prayers: these shall receive greater damnation" (Mk. 12:38-40).

(12:38-40) In these Verses Jesus openly denounced the conduct of the Scribes and Pharisees. He said they loved certain things related to vanity and the praises of men. The word for love is *phileo,* and it means to be fond of or to like. The Lord was not afraid of offending people if they were wrong. If He were preaching publicly today, He would certainly utter strong words of warning against many current religious leaders and politicians.

Jesus had demonstrated such wonders as healing the sick and casting out devils. But the religious leaders hated Him and wanted to kill Him. He exposed their immoral attitudes, their hypocrisy, their pride — and their desire for pretentious positions. The Scribes desired to have special salutations in the marketplace and the chief seats in the Synagogue.

Jesus accused the Scribes of *"devouring widows' houses."* Sometimes their whole fortunes were left to the Temple, and a good part of this money found its way to the Scribes and Pharisees. In order to do this, they would go to the widow's houses and offer long prayers for them. Jesus called their prayers a pretense. Their motives were not pure, and, as a result, their damnation would be great.

The Scribes and Pharisees managed to derive profit from much of the wealth donated to the Temple by the people. Today it would be characterized as a *"rip-off."* It was gross dishonesty, and Jesus unmasked them as the robbers they were. These were immoral men who saw an opportunity to prey on widows and orphans by making pretense of being genuinely pious. Jesus always denounced hypocrisy, and here He promises that their damnation would be great.

Giving for the support of the Ministry and the work of the Gospel is very important, but the money should go where it is used *properly.* That is, of course, to deliver the Gospel Message to the ends of the Earth.

JESUS COMMENDS THE POOR WIDOW FOR HER GIFT

"And Jesus sat over against the treasury, and beheld how the people

cast money into the treasury: and many who were rich cast in much. And there came a certain poor widow, and she threw in two mites, which make a farthing. And He called unto Him His Disciples, and said unto them, Verily I say unto you, That this poor widow has cast more in, than all they which have cast into the treasury: For all they did cast in of their abundance; but she of her want did cast in all that she had, even all her living" (Mk. 12:41-44).

(12:41) Jesus had been in the Court of the Gentiles, and He now passed within the low marble wall fencing off the inner confines of the Temple from the Gentiles. He sat *"over against the treasury"* and observed the people as they made their contributions. There were, of course, rich people who gave much. No doubt Jesus received a Word of Knowledge and had the Discernment of Spirits flowing through Him as He watched what took place.

(12:42) There came a poor widow. The word *"poor"* is *ptochos* and refers to a person who is a pauper, rather than someone merely of the lower economic levels. The poor widow threw in two mites. A mite was the smallest copper coin in circulation and was the eightieth part of a denarius. This was about one-fourth of a penny. She deposited her money in one of the thirteen chests placed at various intervals about the walls. Each was marked with a specific purpose for which the offering was intended. Money could be given for the upkeep of the Temple, support of the Priests, or any number of other religious activities. This poor, poverty-stricken widow placed all she had into one of the repositories.

(12:43-44) As far as God was concerned, this widow cast in more than all the wealthy, although the actual amount was a mere pittance. It isn't the dollars given that count with God — it's what's *left*. How much one holds for one's *self* is the matter of concern to God. Basically, God wants our hearts and lives first and foremost, and we must realize that we are *stewards* of all we have. God wants us to give liberally to Him and is pleased when our motivation is right. He judges us on our giving, and we have a great stewardship responsibility.

Jesus didn't stop this poor widow from casting in all she had, *"even all her living."* He let her do it and was pleased by it. He made her an example of Righteousness. She did not know He was observing her as her giving was not something to be seen and commended. It was her sincere, *total* giving that received the commendation of the Lord.

Chapter 13

The Signs Of The End

SUBJECT   **PAGE**

THE COMING OF THE SON OF MAN **194**

CHAPTER 13

THE SIGNS OF THE END

"And as He went out of the Temple, one of His Disciples said unto Him, Master, see what manner of stones and what buildings are here! And Jesus answering said unto him, Seest thou these great buildings? there shall not be left one stone upon another, that shall not be thrown down. And as He sat upon the Mount of Olives over against the Temple, Peter and James and John and Andrew asked Him privately, Tell us, when shall these things be? and what shall be the sign when all these things shall be fulfilled?

"And Jesus answering them began to say, Take heed lest any man deceive you: For many shall come in My Name, saying, I am Christ; and shall deceive many. And when you shall hear of wars and rumours of wars, be ye not troubled: for such things must needs be; but the end shall not be yet. For nation shall rise against nation, and kingdom against kingdom: and there shall be earthquakes in divers places, and there shall be famines and troubles: these are the beginnings of sorrows.

"But take heed to yourselves: for they shall deliver you up to councils; and in the Synagogues you shall be beaten: and you shall be brought before rulers and kings for My sake, for a testimony against them. And the Gospel must first be published among all nations. But when they shall lead you, and deliver you up, take no thought beforehand what you shall speak, neither do you premeditate: but whatsoever shall be given you in that hour, you speak that: for it is not you who speaks, but the Holy Spirit.

"Now the brother shall betray the brother to death, and the father the son; and children shall rise up against their parents, and shall cause them to be put to death. And you shall be hated of all men for My Name's sake: but he who shall endure unto the end, the same shall be saved. But when you shall see the abomination of desolation, spoken of by Daniel the Prophet, standing where it ought not, (let him that reads understand,) then let them who be in Judaea flee to the mountains: And let him who is on the housetop not go down into the house, neither enter therein, to take any thing out of his house: And let him who is in the field not turn back again for to take up his garment. But woe to them who are with child, and to them who give suck in those days!

"And pray you that your flight be not in winter. For in those days

shall be affliction, such as was not from the beginning of the Creation which God created unto this time, neither shall be. And except that the Lord had shortened those days, no flesh should be saved: but for the elect's sake, whom He has chosen, He hath shortened the days. And then if any man shall say to you, Lo, here is Christ; or, lo, He is there; believe him not: For false Christs and false prophets shall rise, and shall show signs and wonders, to seduce, if it were possible, even the elect. But take ye heed: behold, I have foretold you all things" (Mk. 13:1-23).

(13:1) HE WENT OUT OF THE TEMPLE. Matthew makes the statement, *"Your house is left unto you desolate"* (Mat. 23:38). As Jesus left the Temple, He not only left it physically, He also left it to Judgment. The people had forsaken Jesus, and they had forsaken God.

Forsaking God, and His Plan and Purpose, leaves no recourse but Judgment. They had rejected God. It wasn't, however, that God was angry and determined to impose catastrophe upon them. The sad fact is that without God as your shield, you are abandoned to the Devil, and *he* comes but to steal, kill, and destroy.

So much of the tragedy and difficulties taking place today are not *God's* doing, but the result of Satan's activity in the lives of people who have abandoned God. God is grieved. Terrible things will befall, and Judgment will come. Sadly, it is almost exclusively due to Satan who steals, kills, and destroys (Jn. 10:10).

The Disciples were impressed by the beauty, the architectural design, and the sheer mass of the Temple. They began talking of its magnificence and one of them, speaking for the others, directed their attention to the glory of the buildings. This was the Temple Herod had built for the Jews. Some of the stones referred to were huge — weighing over one hundred tons. The Disciples were completely awed by its opulence and majesty.

(13:2) Jesus directed their attention to the great buildings and told them there would not be one stone left upon another. The great and magnificent Temple would be utterly razed. The words *"thrown down"* are from *kataluo,* which literally means "to loose down." The demolition of the Temple was to take place after the Romans, under Titus, captured Jerusalem in 70 A.D., and, as Jesus prophesied, not one stone would be left upon another. Thousands of Jews would die in the siege, and many would become slaves.

(13:3-4) Jesus had crossed the brook Kedron and ascended the steep road to the Mount of Olives which is *"over against the Temple."* As they sat viewing the Temple, four of His Disciples (Peter, James, John, and Andrew) asked Him privately when all this would take place and what the signs of the fulfillment would be.

The Thirteenth Chapter of Mark is sometimes called *"the Little Apocalypse."* It parallels Passages in Matthew 24-25 and Luke 21:5-36. There are problems in interpretation, because some of it deals with the destruction of Jerusalem in 70 A.D. and some of it deals with the Great Tribulation.

(13:5-6) First, Jesus told them to take heed that no man should deceive them. Individuals would come saying they were the Christ and deceive many. They were to be deceived neither by false christs, nor by wars, nor by troublesome times.

We are living in a day of great deception. There are leaders deceiving the people and individuals claiming Divine status and special position who are also misleading many. Not everything done in the Name of Jesus is truly of God.

We have *"spiritual"* leaders leading large numbers of followers to their deaths while others have ordained homosexuals to preach the Gospel. Abominable things are being perpetrated in the Name of Jesus. There are countless demonic and evil acts occurring in this day and age. Some even declare they are the Messiah — the Christ. Jesus said, *don't be deceived.* The powers of darkness will blind men's eyes so they can't see what's happening.

(13:7-8) The Lord warned His Disciples to not allow political troubles and difficulties to distract them from their evangelistic efforts. Evil exists in this world, but the work of the Kingdom must go on. There will be wars and rumors of wars, all kinds of troubles, yet the end will not be. But Jesus said we should not allow all this to impede our *primary objective* of preaching the Gospel and taking His Message to the world. In recent decades, and especially today, there is a constant backdrop of war — overt or guerrilla — going on throughout the world.

The Lord said His Followers are not to be *"troubled."* This word is from *throeo,* and it means *"to be disturbed, disquieted, or terrified."* The Disciples at that time were already troubled, and Jesus was telling them *not* to be disturbed. He said, these things will be, but you must *continue to proclaim the Gospel Message.* Even in our own perilous times we must not stop building Churches, expanding, getting out the Message, and telling the people that Jesus Christ is Lord.

There have always been, and will continue to be, wars and rumors of wars. Jesus added that there will also be earthquakes in diverse places, in addition to famines and troubles. All these will be signs of the *beginning* of intolerable anguish.

(13:9) BUT TAKE HEED TO YOURSELVES. Jesus told His Disciples to think also of themselves. The pronoun is added for special emphasis, so He is saying, *"But as for you, do not think only of what is coming on the Jewish nation and on the world, but also on yourselves."*

Jesus explained to His Disciples that it would not be easy to continue to follow Him. They would be delivered to the local courts of discipline (council — *sunedria*). They would be beaten and brought before the rulers and kings for the Lord's sake, and for a testimony against them.

Many have suffered through the years for the cause of Christ. Countless Christians were slaughtered in the Coliseum of Rome. They died by the thousands — torn to pieces by wild beasts in the arena. Others were burned at the stake, while some were placed in houses which were then barricaded and set aflame.

The Roman mobs took pleasure in seeing Christians thrown to wild beasts. But all the persecution only resulted in *more* being added to the Kingdom. Many were killed — martyred for the sake of the Gospel.

(13:10) The Gospel of the Kingdom is to be proclaimed to all nations. Jesus is here speaking, in part, of the conditions of the first century, but many of these same conditions will again arise at the close of the Age of Grace — as the Great Tribulation approaches.

(13:11) In the time of our Lord, Christians were often brought before the Roman proconsul or imperator. After Jesus' Death, this was a common practice, and His Followers would be brought before these rulers. Jesus promised them the assistance of the Holy Spirit as guidance in what they were to say.

(13:12-13) Jesus also warned of treacherous relatives. This had some fulfillment in the lives of the First Century Jewish Christians but will be more markedly fulfilled during the Great Tribulation when the Church will be in Glory and the Jews will be forced to choose between Jesus and the Antichrist.

AND YOU SHALL BE HATED OF ALL MEN. This has a more specific Jewish application. The Jewish nation is the *only* one that has ever been the object of global hatred. There has been an almost universal hatred of the Jews, just as Jesus foretold.

There is double meaning and application in this Verse. There will be suffering for those making a commitment to Christ *during the Great Tribulation Period.* Enduring will be critical to Salvation and entry into the Millennial Kingdom. There will be real horror, sorrow, catastrophe, and judgment coming upon the nation of Israel. The Antichrist will endeavor to eliminate the Jewish race from the face of the Earth. Only those who make an enduring commitment will be saved.

(13:14-16) It is apparent that Jesus is now speaking about the period of the Great Tribulation and the fury of the Antichrist. The reference to the *"Abomination of Desolation"* recalls Daniel 11:31. Ancient Israel experienced the desecration of the Temple under Antiochus Epiphanes when he offered a sow upon the Altar of the Temple in the year 168 B.C. That abomination and desecration was the foretype of the Antichrist.

The Antichrist will make a treaty of friendship with Israel at the very beginning of the Great Tribulation. There are millions of people who hate, and would destroy, the Jews. When the Antichrist makes his debut on the world scene, he will be a powerful man offering peace to Israel. He will promise to solve their problems, and they will thus herald to the world that the Messiah has come. This is what is called the Seventieth Week of Daniel. It is actually a period of seven years, and during this time the Antichrist will actually move his headquarters from Babylon to Jerusalem.

Also, in the middle of the Great Tribulation period, the Antichrist will enter the Temple and begin to perform the duties of the Priests, to the utter shock, horror, and amazement of the Jews. He will then desecrate the Temple even as Antiochus Epiphanes did. He will enter the Holy of Holies, ending Temple worship and desecrating the Name of God Almighty. He will violate the covenant completely and reveal himself to be an enemy of the Jews. The people of Judaea will flee to the mountains for safety and protection — to escape the wrath of the Antichrist who desires to destroy the Jews.

(13:17-18) There is a *"woe"* for those who have young children at this time. The word is *ouai,* and refers to grief. It will be much more difficult to flee hastily with little children. He also admonishes them to pray that the flight may not be in winter, when it would be even more difficult. It is going to be a disastrous time, and this catastrophic situation will unfold suddenly. The Antichrist will have made his plans, and his soldiers, by the thousands, will fall upon the inhabitants of Israel to slaughter them.

(13:19-20) There will be great tribulation during this time. The Judgments of God will fall upon unbelieving Israel and also upon the Gentile nations. It will be an unprecedented Judgment, unlike any in history. There has never been *anything* like the days of the Tribulation — which is soon coming.

In the Book of Revelation, the Tribulation period — which follows the Rapture of the Church — is described in painful detail. There is reference to the opening of seals, the blowing of trumpets, and the vials of wrath being poured out upon the Earth. The horror of it defies description, and Israel will be in the midst of it. This is the time of Jacob's trouble and, while it will be of *special* significance to Israel, it will involve and influence the whole world with emphasis on the areas around the Mediterranean. This is what will be required to bring Israel back to God and unless the time is shortened there will be no one left alive in Israel. Judgment will be poured out as the Antichrist attempts to eliminate her from the face of the Earth — but he will not succeed.

In Revelation 7:4-8, reference is made to the 144,000 of Israel. They will be preaching during *part* of the Tribulation — and then raptured into Glory about the middle of the period. These 144,000 are seen in Heaven in Revelation 14.

The period of Divine Judgment will be shortened in order that some might be spared. They will turn to Jesus and accept Him as King of kings and Lord of lords. This shortening of the period of the Tribulation will be for the sake of the elect. The word *"elect"* in the Greek is *eklego,* and it means those chosen out from a number. For those who have accepted Christ and proclaimed His Name, the days *will* be shortened.

(13:21-23) There will be individuals saying they are Christ. The word *"Christ"* is from the Greek word *Christos* which means *"the Anointed One."* Our English word is a simple transliteration of the Greek word. The Greek word is a translation of the Hebrew word meaning *"the Anointed One."* Our word *"Messiah"* is the phonetic English spelling of the Hebrew word.

There is special connotation connected with the Hebrew word *"Messiah"* and it concerns the promised coming of the King of Israel — of the dynasty of David — Who will rule over Israel and the Messianic Kingdom. Jesus said false messiahs would come. False individuals will declare themselves to be the Anointed One. These false messiahs and prophets will deceive many by showing signs and wonders. The Antichrist will also show great signs and wonders so that the beholders will be amazed. Our Lord warns Israel about this. Claims of anyone declaring himself the Messiah on the basis of his ability to perform miracles and wonders must not be accepted. The character of the person and his message must be taken into consideration.

Satan is able to do many things, and there will be great deception with many being deceived. The Antichrist and the false prophet will astound the world with their miracles — inspired by Satan.

Even today there are many charlatans not living what they preach, who disgrace the Ministry and the Work of the Kingdom. Even one of Jesus' chosen Disciples betrayed Him. It is crucial that people avoid gullibility. Just because a thing may *look* remarkable and *seem* to emanate from God, doesn't necessarily prove that it does. Jesus exhorted the Disciples (and us) to be prudent and to remember all He foretold for the latter days.

THE COMING OF THE SON OF MAN

"But in those days, after that tribulation, the sun shall be darkened, and the moon shall not give her light, And the stars of Heaven shall fall, and the powers that are in Heaven shall be shaken. And then shall they see the Son of Man coming in the clouds with great

power and glory. And then shall He send His Angels, and shall gather together His elect from the four winds, from the uttermost part of the Earth to the uttermost part of Heaven.

"Now learn a Parable of the fig tree; When her branch is yet tender, and putteth forth leaves, you know that summer is near: So you in like manner, when you shall see these things come to pass, know that it is near, even at the doors. Verily I say unto you, that this generation shall not pass, till all these things be done. Heaven and Earth shall pass away: but My Words shall not pass away. But of that day and that hour knows no man, no, not the Angels which are in Heaven, neither the Son, but the Father. Take ye heed, watch and pray: for you know not when the time is.

"For the Son of man is as a man taking a far journey, Who left His house, and gave authority to His servants, and to every man His Work, and commanded the porter to watch. Watch ye therefore: for you know not when the Master of the house cometh, at even, or at midnight, or at the cockcrowing, or in the morning: Lest coming suddenly He find you sleeping. And what I say unto you I say unto all, Watch" (Mk. 13:24-37).

(13:24-27) Jesus said there would be functional disturbances in the sun, moon, and stars occurring toward the close of the Great Tribulation. These are to be literal and not symbolic disturbances. They are referred to in the Judgment coming with the sixth seal (Rev. 6:12-14). With the sun and moon affected, it will be an unusual and cataclysmic phenomenon. The whole Earth will be affected because the moon controls the tides and the sun controls our temperature. Disturbances of this nature will logically induce unpredictable, but catastrophic, occurrences. Jesus also explains that the stars will fall and the powers in Heaven will be shaken. It will be a time of unprecedented natural phenomenon.

Jesus then refers to His coming *"in the clouds with great power and glory."* In the original, the word *"clouds"* has no definite article. He is saying that the Son of Man will come *"in clouds."* These are not the ordinary clouds of the heavens which bring rain — these are clouds of glorified Saints and Angels. This is also referred to in Revelation 19:11-16. The word translated clouds is *nephele,* and is used in I Thessalonians 4:17 of a multitude of Angels. Here it states that the Saints will be caught up in clouds. There is no definite article used in that reference in I Thessalonians, or in Mark 13:26. The same thought is expressed in Hebrews 12:1, where the writer visualizes crowds packed in a Greek stadium.

Jesus is talking about His Second Coming in Verse 26. They will see the Son of Man coming in clouds (or with a great multitude) of Saints, with great power and glory. The Rapture will have taken place approximately seven years earlier. At the Rapture no one is going to *see* Jesus coming, for He will come and take His Children away as the Trump of God sounds and the dead in Christ rise. Those who are alive and remain shall be translated with them into Glory.

Here, however, Jesus is speaking of the *Second Advent,* which means the literal Second Coming of Jesus Christ back to this Earth. When He comes at the Second Coming, all the Saints will come *with* Him. At the Rapture He will come *for* the Saints, and at the Second Coming He will come *with* the Saints. So Jesus comes again at the close of the Great Tribulation.

His Second Coming is for many reasons of course, but among the *main* reasons are the defeat of the Antichrist at the Battle of Armageddon and the setting up of the Millennial Reign. The armies of the Antichrist will be destroyed as they endeavor to destroy Jerusalem because of the Antichrist's hatred for the Jews.

The largest portion of the Jews will already have fled Jerusalem at the middle of the Tribulation — when the Antichrist turns on them. They will flee to the mountains and many will find refuge in the rock city of Petra. Then the Antichrist will be away from Jerusalem for a time (fighting other wars), but he will return to destroy Jerusalem and the remnant of the Jews remaining. He will attempt to annihilate the Jews. Satan will be quickly and utterly defeated at the Battle of Armageddon — and the Antichrist will be killed and thrown into the bottomless pit with Satan.

Next, it says He will send His Angels and gather together His elect from the four winds, from the uttermost part of the Earth to the uttermost part of Heaven. There will be a *re*gathering of all Israel at the Second Coming of the Messiah. Some will have fled (as previously indicated) and others will be located in other parts of the world. This gathering (of the chosen of Israel) will be saved by God's Sovereign Grace and restored to fellowship, serving God in the Millennial Kingdom. The long night of darkness, rejection, and rebellion will be over, as John cried out when he closed the Book of Revelation, saying, *"Even so, come, Lord Jesus."* This will be the start of a brand-new day.

(13:28-29) Jesus used the fig tree as an illustration and He simply stated that, when the branch is tender and puts forth leaves, you know summer is near. So, in like manner, when you see all these things begin to come to pass, know it is time for His coming.

Current world events point emphatically to the Endtimes. Troubles are mounting and the signs point to the Rapture, the Tribulation, and the Second Coming. Jesus is referring in this entire section (Mk. 13:30-33) to the appearance of the Antichrist and His own Second Coming. The primary problem with this Text is the word *genea,* translated *"generation,"* but

Jesus was not referring to the generation alive at that moment. He meant the generation alive when these signs begin to come to pass. That generation will not pass until *all* is fulfilled. Much confusion could have been avoided if the King James translators had rendered the line *"**that** genera-tion"* instead of *"**this** generation."*

The generation of men alive when our Lord walked the Earth has long since died. They could not continue to exist until this future time. The word must be understood in the light of its context. The word rendered *"gen-eration"* was also used at times in the sense of *"race or lineage."* It was used to denote a family, and it was used for such expressions as *"the fourth generation."* Two things stand out regarding this: First, it refers to the generation of men living *when the signs start to come to pass*. Secondly, there is a special relationship to *race* here — and that is the Jewish race.

Jesus finally said that His Words will not pass away, and that the exact day or hour will be known by no one but the Father. Jesus, while on the Earth, in the limitations of His human body, did not know when He would come again. Jesus knows now, but He didn't know then. Man does not know, so speculation and predicted dates are worthless. Some will have greater insights through a word of knowledge, the discerning of spirits, or special revelations, but it is never wise to predict specific dates. Jesus said we are to take heed, to keep on watching and praying, because we will *not* know the exact time until it happens.

(13:34-37) Jesus pictures a man gone into a far country. The Son of Man has left *"His house"* and the work has been delegated to Pastors, Teachers, Evangelists, and other Ministries. Each has his particular job to do, and is to stay vigilant and watchful until the Master comes.

He implores, *"Don't go to sleep on the job. Watch, because you can't know when the Master of the house cometh."*

No one will know for sure, but once the signs begin to come to pass, we must be *particularly* alert. Surely, of all the times of history, *this* is the time to be in the Will of God and working toward His ends. Never before in history have all the forces of the world been demonstrating so emphati-cally that, indeed, the time *is* near!

Chapter 14

The Chief Priests Plot Against Jesus

SUBJECT	PAGE
MARY ANOINTS JESUS	199
JUDAS BARGAINS TO BETRAY JESUS	202
PREPARING THE PASCHAL MEAL	202
JESUS PARTAKES OF THE PASCHAL MEAL WITH HIS DISCIPLES	203
THE LORD'S SUPPER IS INSTITUTED	205
GOING TO GETHSEMANE	207
JESUS PREDICTS THE DISCIPLES WILL BE OFFENDED	207
JESUS SUFFERS GREAT AGONY IN GETHSEMANE	208
JESUS IS BETRAYED, ARRESTED, AND FORSAKEN	211
JESUS IS CONDEMNED BY CAIAPHAS AND THE SANHEDRIN	213
PETER DENIES JESUS	217

CHAPTER 14

THE CHIEF PRIESTS PLOT AGAINST JESUS

"After two days was the Feast of the Passover, and of Unleavened Bread and the Chief Priests and the Scribes sought how they might take Him by craft, and put Him to death. But they said, Not on the Feast Day, lest there be an uproar of the people" (Mk. 14:1-2).

(14:1-2) It was the time of the Feast of Passover. The word translated *"Passover"* is *pascha,* which means *"a passing over."* The meaning of Passover is very significant. It was one of the most remarkable and beautiful of all the miracles to happen to the Nation of Israel over the ages.

The Paschal lamb was sacrificed by the Israelites when they were instructed to kill a lamb and sprinkle the blood on the doorposts of their dwellings in Egypt. This protected them from the Death Angel who *passed over* their homes, sparing their firstborn. This was during the time of the tenth plague in Egypt, when the firstborn of all the Egyptian families died.

The houses that had their doorposts sprinkled with the blood of the lamb (the Hebrew houses) were passed over. The lamb died in place of the firstborn children. Our Lord is the Paschal Lamb for us, and His Death is accepted by the High Court of Heaven as payment for our sins.

It was during the commemoration of the Passover — which Israel celebrated as a symbol of the passing over by the Death Angel — that the *true* Passover Lamb (Jesus) was entering Jerusalem to fulfill the typology by dying on the Cross. At the exact time they were celebrating the death of the Paschal lamb, the one pointed to by Moses and the Prophets as the Lamb of God was to die on the Cross. Of course, the religious leaders had no idea of the irony of the situation. The Chief Priests, the Scribes, the Elders, and the members of the Sanhedrin assembled themselves to see how they might accomplish the murder of Jesus — the Lamb of God.

They assembled themselves in the house of Caiaphas to cement their plans and to determine exactly how to hand Jesus over to the Roman authorities. They reasoned that, due to the popularity of Jesus, they could not do it at the exact time of the Passover Feast lest there be an uproar from the people.

MARY ANOINTS JESUS

"And being in Bethany in the house of Simon the leper, as He sat

SELF-HELP
STUDY NOTES

at meat, there came a woman having an alabaster box of ointment of spikenard very precious; and she broke the box, and poured it on His Head. And there were some who had indignation within themselves, and said, Why was this waste of the ointment made? For it might have been sold for more than three hundred pence, and have been given to the poor.

"And they murmured against her. And Jesus said, Let her alone; why trouble ye her? She has wrought a good work on Me. For you have the poor with you always, and whensoever you will you may do them good: but Me you have not always. She has done what she could: she is come aforehand to anoint My Body to the burying. Verily I say unto you, Wheresoever this Gospel shall be preached throughout the whole world, this also that she has done shall be spoken of for a memorial of her" (Mk. 14:3-9).

(14:3) Jesus was in Bethany (a suburb city of Jerusalem and the place where Mary, Martha, and Lazarus lived) at the house of Simon the leper. Simon was one that Jesus healed and perhaps was a man of some means. This event is also recorded in Matthew and John. In John's Gospel, reference is made to Mary, Martha, and Lazarus; and Mary is revealed as the woman with the ointment (Jn. 12:2-8). Lazarus, whom Jesus had raised from the dead, was also there along with Mary and Martha, special friends of the Lord Jesus Christ.

Mary had an alabaster box of ointment, and it is described by Mark with three words: the first is *nardos,* which refers to a perfume that came from India; the second is *pistikos,* indicating that it was genuine and not an imitation of some type; and thirdly, *poluteles,* which indicates that it was very costly. Mary broke the container and poured the contents on our Lord's Head.

(14:4-5) Objection was made to the use of this ointment. John indicates that it was Judas who raised the objection, and Mark points out that the other Disciples *"had indignation within themselves."*

The ointment was extremely costly, possibly worth about a year's average wages. The substance was probably in a flask or bottle, as she broke off the top and poured out the valuable contents as a sacrifice. The bottle was not to be used again.

Mary's dedication to the Master was total. It was she who always desired to worship the Lord. Martha had once upbraided Mary for not helping her prepare for their guests, but Jesus said that Mary had chosen the better part — as she had sat at His Feet, listening to Him. He said further that this better way would not be taken from her. Martha was encumbered with many of the cares of the world, but Mary's life was focused on worshiping the Lord. She knew He was the Son of God. As

Mary worshiped the Lord here, she demonstrated her devotion with a donation of great value.

A probable factor in the discussion of waste among the Disciples was that they were unaccustomed to luxury and this seemed extremely profligate. It also suggests that the Passover season was a time when alms were given to the poor (Jn. 13:29). There were many needy people gathered in Jerusalem at this time. This could well have been in *their* thoughts, but Judas — who *voiced* the question — was not concerned about the poor.

Judas, the treasurer of the group, carried the money bag and had, no doubt been stealing from it. His concern lay in finding additional monies. Though the other Disciples joined with Judas in the complaint, they didn't fully realize the implications. Their senses were dull and they didn't understand what was about to take place — that Judas would betray Jesus in just a few hours.

(14:6-9) SHE HAS WROUGHT A GOOD WORK ON ME. The word translated *"good"* is *kalos* and means a goodness that is apparent. It strikes the eye and is beautiful and pleasing. This act was one of true moral beauty. Undoubtedly, Mary didn't realize the tremendous significance of what was to take place. She *did* recognize that He was the Son of God and had lingered close to Him to learn as much as possible. She may or may not have comprehended what was about to occur.

She did, however, have a sense of foreboding and willingly gave up everything to honor and worship the Lord. She anointed Him here with a costly ointment. It was a sacrifice of great love for Him, and this should have been a special moment. However, the others grumbled and complained while in a few hours Jesus would die on the Cross.

Although some might be critical of the Disciples for their comments, there are many today complaining about money used to support spiritual causes. What Mary did was an act of true worship, and true worship always involves sacrifice. It is always costly to *truly* worship and serve the Lord. Not only did Mary *give* something that cost her a great deal, but she was then criticized by those about her. All too often, serving the Lord means criticism and persecution. Truly Mary had done *"a good work."*

Next, Jesus went on to say that the poor would always be with them but He would not. He was *not* suggesting that the poor were unimportant, because Jesus *had* concern for the poor. But the priority at this point involved a significant spiritual question. Mary was anointing the Body of Jesus with costly ointment prior to His Sacrificial Death on the Cross — and His Burial in a borrowed tomb. Jesus said that *wherever* the Gospel would be proclaimed, her action would be spoken of as a memorial to her.

All sacrifices made for the Lord are memorials. Mary was unaware that some 2,000 years later, Preachers would share this event over and over again. The point is — whatever is done for our Lord will endure. Money, prayer, worship, sacrifice — the life one lives for the Lord Jesus Christ — will live forever and forever.

JUDAS BARGAINS TO BETRAY JESUS

"And Judas Iscariot, one of the Twelve, went unto the Chief Priests, to betray Him unto them. And when they heard it, they were glad, and promised to give him money. And he sought how he might conveniently betray Him" (Mk. 14:10-11).

Judas, stung by Jesus' rebuke at the feast, went to the Temple rulers to bargain with them. The attitude and spirit of Judas was inherently evil. Even though he had walked with the Lord, had witnessed mighty miracles, and knew personally the Righteousness and sweet spirit of Jesus, Judas turned his back on the very Son of God and betrayed Him.

A better environment will not of itself ensure that an individual will follow the path of Righteousness. Judas had the finest of all experiences, having personally walked with the Master. He had an opportunity few people would ever know, and still he rejected all. He went to the Chief Priests realizing full well that they were the vipers committed to murdering the Lord.

Judas had willfully decided to betray Jesus. The word *"betray"* is *paradidomai,* and literally means *"to hand over or alongside."* The chief priests were, of course, delighted. The word used is *chairo,* and means to express a feeling of inward joy. They had sought a way to dispose of Jesus without alerting the Passover crowds who might attempt to interfere. Judas' position as a Disciple gave him a unique opportunity, and now he sought how to most conveniently and efficiently betray Jesus.

PREPARING THE PASCHAL MEAL

"And the first day of Unleavened Bread, when they killed the Passover, His Disciples said unto Him, Where will You that we go and prepare that You may eat the Passover? And He sent forth two of His Diciples, and said unto them, Go ye into the city, and there shall meet you a man bearing a pitcher of water: follow him. And wheresoever he shall go in, say ye to the goodman of the house, The Master says, Where is the guestchamber, where I shall eat the Passover with My Disciples? And he will shew you a large upper room furnished and prepared: there make ready for us. And His Disciples went forth, and came into the city, and found as He had said unto them: and they made ready the Passover" (Mk. 14:12-16).

(14:12) Preparations were underway for breaking bread at the Passover meal. This was a once-a-year feast, commemorating the deliverance of Israel from Egyptian bondage, and the passage of the Death Angel over Israelite homes. The blood of the slain lamb had been applied to the doorposts as a sign. God said, *"When I see the blood I will pass over you"* (Ex. 12:13).

Every year Israelites would eat the Passover in commemoration of this momentous event. After it was sacrificed, they roasted the lamb, eating it with unleavened bread. For this occasion, the paschal lamb is called *to pascha*, the Passover.

(14:13-15) Jesus instructed Peter and John to go to a place where they would find a man carrying a pitcher of water. This was somewhat unusual since women normally carried water. But perhaps this man was a slave. They were told to talk to the master of the house and request the guestchamber where Jesus and His Disciples could partake of the Passover meal. There is a difference of opinion as to whether Jesus knew the man carrying the water. Undoubtedly, Jesus had a Word of Knowledge in His Heart as the Heavenly Father, through the Holy Spirit, told Him exactly what was to happen.

Peter and John followed the instructions and, just as Jesus had said, they found and followed the man bearing the pitcher of water. As instructed, they spoke to the *oikodespotes, "the master of the house, the householder."* They asked the master of the house, *"Where is the guestchamber where I shall eat the Passover with My Disciples."*

Jesus had told them what to say and they were shown a large upper room, furnished, prepared, and made ready for their use. It was a fairly large, special room, located above ground level and probably on the second floor. Here Jesus would observe His last Passover with the Disciples in private.

(14:16) The Disciples found everything just as Jesus had said, and preparations were made for the Passover. Much was involved in this process. A lamb had to be slain and roasted, unleavened cakes were procured, along with bitter herbs, fruit of the vine, and other foods. Some of the food was made into a paste as a reminder of the mortar used in the laying of bricks in Egypt. It was a special occasion, and everything was now ready for their observance of the Passover Feast.

JESUS PARTAKES OF THE PASCHAL MEAL WITH HIS DISCIPLES

"And in the evening He cometh with the Twelve. And as they sat and did eat, Jesus said, Verily I say unto you, One of you which eats

with Me shall betray Me. And they began to be sorrowful, and to say unto Him one by one, Is it I? And another said, Is it I? And He answered and said unto them, It is one of the Twelve, who dips with Me in the dish. The Son of Man indeed goeth, as it is written of Him: but woe to that man by whom the Son of man is betrayed! good were it for that man if he had never been born" (Mk. 14:17-21).

As evening fell, Jesus and His Disciples came to partake of their last meal together. They had been together for the better part of three and one-half years. It was an occasion the Disciples should have approached with great insight, but they apparently comprehended little of what was happening and what was about to occur.

The Heavenly Father revealed Judas' activities to the Lord. He knew Judas was about to betray Him and also the damage that had already been done. When the Disciples sat down at the Passover table, Jesus said that one of them would betray Him. Each one of the Disciples began to ask, *"Is it I?"* The type of expression used in the original Greek is one which calls for a negative answer.

Jesus said it was the one who dipped with Him in the dish. This probably had reference to a sauce made of dates, raisins, and vinegar, into which the master of the house would dip pieces of unleavened bread.

Jesus said that the Son of Man would indeed go, as it was written. In Psalm 41:9 it says, *"Yea, my own familiar friend, in whom I trusted, which did eat of my bread, has lifted up his heel against me."* This prophesied Judas' betrayal and was written one thousand years before Judas actually acted out his calamitous role.

Can you imagine what must have gone on in Judas' mind and heart when he heard the Master say that one of them would betray Him? Judas even asked, *"Is it I?"* Some may think that Judas had no choice — that he was predestined for death and Hell. There is no hint in the Word of God that such was the case. Jesus had called him His own familiar friend. Scripture tells us that God is not willing that *any* should perish, but that all should come to Repentance. If Judas had confessed to the Lord and asked forgiveness, he would have been forgiven.

When Jesus stated that one would betray Him, the Disciples sorrowed. Certainly, to betray the Master was unthinkable and a dreadful thing to do.

Jesus also stated that it would be better if that person had not been born. It is such a tragedy for a person to choose a course in life that leads to Hell for eternity.

Judas dipped with Jesus in the dish as they were eating. They were probably dipping the unleavened bread (the bread or cakes the Lord had blessed) in the sauce of bitter herb.

As Judas was identified, it seems apparent (from the parallel Gospels) that he left. It says that Judas went out. It was night — in more ways than one. There was total darkness in his soul, and he went directly to perpetrate what would be the most terrible deed in all of history. He had already consulted with the High Priests and religious leaders. Now he went out to complete the betrayal of the Son of God.

THE LORD'S SUPPER IS INSTITUTED

"And as they did eat, Jesus took bread, and blessed, and broke it, and gave to them, and said, Take, eat: this is My Body. And He took the cup, and when He had given thanks, He gave it to them: and they all drank of it. And He said unto them, This is My Blood of the New Testament, which is shed for many. Verily I say unto you, I will drink no more of the fruit of the vine, until that day that I drink it new in the Kingdom of God" (Mk. 14:22-25).

(14:22) It was at this Passover Feast that our Lord instituted what is today known as *"the Lord's Supper."* As the meal proceeded, Jesus took bread and blessed it, broke it and gave thanks. He said, *"Take, eat: this is My Body."*

He was comparing His Body and Flesh with the bread He was breaking. He was about to endure the great sacrifice of His Crucifixion. The words He was using were symbolic. When Jesus said (earlier) that He was the door of the sheep, He didn't mean He was a literal door, but rather that He was the means of entry or *"the way."* Now, when He spoke of the bread as His broken Body, He didn't mean the bread had actually *become* His Body, He meant that the bread *represented* Him — as spiritual nourishment — upon which the sinner might feed and have Eternal Life. He said to take and eat because it *symbolized* His Body — broken for the sins of all mankind.

(14:23-25) Then Jesus took the cup and, when He had given thanks, He gave it to them to drink. He then said to them, *"This is My Blood of the New Testament, which is shed for many."*

Here He was saying that He would pay the price for all mankind as the Lamb that was slaughtered for the Atonement of sin. John the Baptist had said, *"Behold the Lamb of God, which takes away the sin of the world"* (Jn. 1:29).

The fruit of the vine was a symbol of Jesus' shed Blood, His Death. Paul, through special revelation from the Lord, gave instructions concerning the Lord's Supper as he told what Jesus had done (I Cor. 11:23-30).

The bread and the cup are to be partaken of regularly. It doesn't say how often; it only says *"as oft as you drink it."* This can be done very often with complete propriety. The same reference indicates that when it *is* done, it shows the Lord's Death *"till He come."* This means in effect that you are reenacting, in remembrance, Jesus' great Sacrifice on the Cross as a memorial to Him. It also looks forward to His soon return. Hallelujah!

When a person partakes of the Lord's Supper, he is to examine himself. One's life is to be cleansed by the Blood of Christ, and he or she is to walk clean and pure in the Lord. If there is sin in one's life, it is to be dealt with and forgiveness sought — which *will* be granted — so one can go on and observe the Lord's Supper.

Paul went on to point out that if one *did* eat and drink unworthily, they would eat and drink damnation to themselves. Because of this, he noted that some in the Church at Corinth were sick — and some had died premature deaths. Obviously, if a person is not right with the Lord and his fellowman, he should not partake of the Lord's Supper. Partaking of the Lord's Supper unworthily can incur illness and difficulties for the individual. On the other hand, as one comes in full commitment to the Lord, seeking to walk *with* Him at all times, this memorial can be a healing experience for the person's *body,* as well as the soul.

Many promises and provisions relate to the Atonement. They include healing, deliverance, and God's Blessings. Some of these are experienced while observing the Lord's Supper, when one comes worthily. The person must not consider himself worthy *within himself,* however. Only when we are redeemed by the Blood of Christ and committed to Him, can we be counted worthy.

The bread and grape juice seen in the Lord's Supper are symbols, and they are a memorial. It is, of course, a very significant event and one to be observed exactly as our Lord commanded.

Jesus said His Blood was the *New Testament,* which was shed for many. The *first* testament refers to the Levitical system of sacrifices (Heb. 8:7). The New Testament (our Lord's Sacrifice on the Cross) *fulfilled the original testament,* and is indeed the New Testament (Heb. 8:8). Where Jesus is quoted as saying *"is shed,"* it literally states *"which is **being** shed."* He was looking ahead to His imminent Sacrifice on the Cross.

Then Jesus said He would not drink of the fruit of the vine again until He drank it new in the Kingdom of God. This has its fulfillment in the Messianic Kingdom — when the Messiah, and His cleansed and restored Israel, will drink in a new and glorious way. There Jesus will reign as King upon the Throne of His father, David. This is coming. It is still future, but at the time Jesus was speaking, they were preparing to murder Him. He was soon to hang on a tree. This was to be Satan's hour, but the time is soon coming when he will be bound and locked away for a thousand years. Israel will then be re-gathered and accept Jesus as the Messiah, the King of kings and Lord of lords.

Two thousand years have passed, and that prophecy has not yet been fulfilled, but it soon will be. Each remembrance of the Lord's Supper looks *back* to what Jesus sacrificed, while it also looks *forward* to His triumphant return.

GOING TO GETHSEMANE

"And when they had sung an hymn, they went out into the Mount of Olives" (Mk. 14:26).

After they finished eating the Paschal lamb and breaking bread, they sang a hymn. It was customary for songs to be sung following a meal. The verb *"to sing"* is *humneo*, and means, *"to sing the praise of, sing hymns to."* It is the word from which we get our word *"hymn."*

If one wonders how they were able to sing under the ominous circumstances, one is reminded of Paul and Silas as they sang in their prison cell at midnight. The Bible says the prisoners all heard them. Their backs had been cut with lashes and they were restrained in stocks, yet they had a song in their hearts. This epitomizes the Child of God. The Christian life is not always easy. There are problems, afflictions, and difficulties for the righteous to surmount, but the Lord supports them through all. There is a song in the heart of the Believer regardless of the situation — and Jesus and His Disciples could sing a hymn.

Then they went out to the Mount of Olives. Jesus was moving relentlessly toward Gethsemane. The Disciples had been spending their nights on the Mount of Olives, so they had made no provisions for remaining in Jerusalem overnight. Jesus knew full well what would occur in the Garden, but He marched resolutely toward His destiny.

JESUS PREDICTS THE DISCIPLES WILL BE OFFENDED

"And Jesus said unto them, All you shall be offended because of Me this night: for it is written, I will smite the Shepherd, and the sheep will be scattered. But after that I am risen, I will go before you into Galilee. But Peter said unto Him, Although all shall be offended, yet will not I. And Jesus said unto him, Verily I say unto you, That this day, even in this night, before the cock crow twice, you shall deny Me thrice. But he spoke the more vehemently, If I should die with you, I will not deny You in any wise. Likewise also said they all" (Mk. 14:27-31).

(14:27-28) Jesus predicted that all the Disciples would be offended because of Him as confirmation of an Old Testament prophecy (Zech. 13:7). The Disciples *did* desert their Lord just when He needed them most. The word translated *"offended"* is *skandalizo*, which means, *"to find occasion of stumbling."* This was *their* occasion for stumbling due to the fact that Jesus' arrest and torture could involve them in the same treatment. Their first consideration was for themselves.

Jesus quoted Zechariah's statement that the shepherd would be smitten and the sheep scattered. Then He went on to say that after He was risen He would go before them into Galilee.

(14:29) Again Peter interrupts. He said that even if all the rest were offended he certainly wouldn't be. He spoke as if it might be that the *others* could be offended, but there could be no cause for stumbling in *his* case.

(14:30) Peter no more than finished this boast when a prophecy was given as to his downfall. The Master turned to Peter and told him directly that *"even in this (very) night, before the cock crow twice, you shall deny me thrice."* Jesus pointed out the precise time of Peter's denial — that very night — three times before the cock would crow twice.

(14:31) Peter went on declaring even more vehemently that he would *not* deny Him. The expression used in the Greek is, *"He kept on speaking."* The word *"vehemently"* is from *ekperissos*, which means *"in abundance and with vehemence and reiteration."* Peter protested and repeatedly said that he would *not* deny the Lord.

JESUS SUFFERS GREAT AGONY IN GETHSEMANE

"And they came to a place which was named Gethsemane: and He said to His Disciples, Sit ye here, while I shall pray. And He took with Him Peter and James and John, and began to be sore amazed, and to be very heavy; And said unto them, My Soul is exceeding sorrowful unto death: tarry you here, and watch. And He went forward a little, and fell on the ground, and prayed that, if it were possible, the hour might pass from Him.

"And He said, Abba, Father, all things are possible unto You, take away this cup from Me: nevertheless not what I will, but what You will.

"And He comes, and finds them sleeping, and said unto Peter, Simon, sleepest thou? could not you watch one hour? Watch ye and pray, lest you enter into temptation. The Spirit truly is ready, but the flesh is weak. And again He went away, and prayed, and spoke the same words. And when He returned, He found them asleep again, (for their eyes were heavy,) neither wist they what to answer Him. And He cometh the third time, and said unto them, Sleep on now, and take your rest: it is enough, the hour is come; behold, the Son of Man is

betrayed into the hands of sinners. Rise up, let us go; lo, he who betrays Me is at hand" (Mk. 14:32-42).

SELF-HELP
STUDY NOTES

(14:32-34) They came to Gethsemane, which is a beautiful spot today. Jesus was about to endure one of the most poignant, difficult, and agonizing moments in His Life and Ministry. The Disciples were with Him, and He told them to sit while He went to pray. He took Peter, James, and John with Him a little further.

He *"began to be sore amazed, and to be very heavy."* Jesus was overwhelmed with sorrow. He was facing the most agonizing torture the mind can conceive of. The word translated *"sore amazed"* is *ekthambeo,* which means, *"to throw into amazement or terror, to alarm, to be struck with terror." "To be heavy"* is from *ademoneo,* and it means to be ill at ease. It projects the idea of facing an experience with which one is neither familiar nor comfortable.

EXCEEDINGLY SORROWFUL. This is from *perilupos.* The word *lupos* means grief and *peri* means *"around."* He was therefore encompassed about with grief — very sad. The horror and terror of the experience He was about to undergo descended as a pall upon Him. For the spotless Lamb of God to bear the sins of the world was shocking and terrifying. The Bible says, He was *"sorrowful unto death,"* and the idea projected is that the stress and grief brought Him almost to the point of death.

Jesus had been tempted in all points like as we are, yet He was without sin. He never failed in any way, and no sin was found in Him. Even though Jesus was perfect, He was going to be forced to die on the Cross to take the sins of the world upon His Shoulders — a devastating and degrading act. The terrible mental anguish was so oppressive that it is difficult to picture. He told Peter, James, and John to remain where they were and watch.

(14:35) Jesus went forward a little and fell to the ground. He fell under the weight of the agony He was bearing. He would get up and, in weakness and terror, stagger and fall again. The tense of the verb indicates that the Disciples were watching, and that He fell *repeatedly* to the ground. All the time He continued praying. It was an agonizing prayer as Jesus anticipated the agony of the Cross and dreaded it. He prayed that, if it were possible, the hour might pass from Him.

(14:36) The Bible says He cried, *"Abba, Father."* The word *"Abba"* is an Aramaic word meaning *"father."*

ALL THINGS ARE POSSIBLE UNTO YOU. As our Lord cried out to God the Father, He said, *"All things are possible unto You."* He asked that the cup be taken away. The next moment, however, in one of the most awesome decisions in all of history, He amended His prayer and said, *"Nevertheless not what I will, but what You will."* Divine Power is unlimited, but God's *will* is an expression of His Divine Righteousness and Love. God *limits* the exercise of His Divine Power. There is a necessary limitation and balance to what one might expect and claim from and Omnipotent God.

Even though Jesus said that *all* things are possible, He clearly indicates that limitations have to be placed on the *individual's* desires. God is Righteous and Holy, and in love there are limitations to the exercise of power. There are many things God *wants* that are not accomplished. He wants the whole world to be saved, but no one is *forced* into conformity. God will never go *too* far in exercising power, for there is a limitation imposed by Divine Love and Righteousness.

Jesus went on to say, *"Nevertheless, not what I will, but what You will."* Jesus was submitting to the Will of God though He humanly shrank from the horror of the events about to befall. He — Who knew no sin — was about to be made sin for us. Jesus was to take upon Himself every bit of filth, rot, and dirt — every loathsome, horrifying, degrading, hellish perversion that could possibly come to mind.

He was to suddenly become a murderer, a rapist, the lowest imaginable form of humanity. And He bore all this, in combination with such *"ordinary"* sins as jealousy, envy, malice, bitterness, and so forth. He was made sin and was charged, in the place of mankind, by the High Court of Heaven with the guilt of all human sin. Is it surprising, therefore, that He did not *want* to drink of that cup?

In addition to all this, while He endured this agony, He knew He would be deprived of fellowship with His Father. On the Cross He was to cry out, *"My God, My God, why have You forsaken Me?"*

This is what He was to face, and the pressure and agony of it were virtually indescribable. There was a dread in His Heart of the price to be exacted. The loss of that fellowship with the Father meant infinite suffering, but Jesus said, *"Not what I Myself desire, but what You desire."*

This was the mission for which Jesus had come to Earth. He came to die; no man *took* His Life from Him. He laid it down freely. This was His whole purpose, but He asked God to relieve Him of the responsibility — *if there were some other way.* Unfortunately, there wasn't, and He had to go through all the suffering, including that of having fellowship with His Father broken. This was all part of the price to be exacted for substituting as *man's* sacrifice for sin. It was a terrible thing, but Jesus did it willingly.

(14:37-38) Jesus came and found His Disciples asleep, even after He had told them to watch with Him. He spoke to Simon Peter and asked if he were sleeping. Peter, who had said he was ready to die for the Master and who would never deny Him, had fallen asleep during the time Jesus had asked Him to watch. Perhaps the Three Disciples were exhausted. By the use of the name *"Simon,"* the Lord was mildly rebuking Peter for weakness.

Peter had been elevated during the preceding three years to a place and position where Jesus had called him Peter — which meant a piece of rock. Now He called him Simon, his original name, perhaps indicating that he was weakening and loosing his commitment. It was a rebuke. Then Jesus told all of them to watch and pray, lest they enter into temptations. The flesh is often weak and prone to failure. It is frail and mortal and impure, while the spirit is the vital force of man.

(14:39-40) Jesus again went away, but, returning, found them asleep again. Scripture suggests that their eyes were heavy. They experienced an overpowering drowsiness. They did not know what to say when He spoke to them. They were speechless and acted almost drugged.

(14:41-42) When Jesus came back a third time and found them asleep, He told them to sleep on and take their rest. There was a bit of irony in what He said. He told them to just go on and sleep, because they could not be aroused out of their lethargy. He really needed them, but they did not stand by Him.

Then Jesus said, *"It is enough."* He wouldn't expose their faults or any of the other difficulties further, for His hour had come. With the Disciples still lying about on the ground and our Lord standing, Judas and his party approached. The Son of Man was about to be betrayed and the betrayer was at hand.

JESUS IS BETRAYED, ARRESTED, AND FORSAKEN

"And immediately, while He yet spoke, cometh Judas, one of the Twelve, and with Him a great multitude with swords and staves, from the Chief Priests and the Scribes and the Elders. And he who betrayed Him had given them a token, saying, Whomsoever I shall kiss, that same is He; take Him, and lead Him away safely. And as soon as he was come, he went straightway to Him, and said, Master, Master; and kissed Him. And they laid their hands on Him, and took Him. And one of them who stood by drew a sword, and smote a servant of the High Priest, and cut off his ear.

"And Jesus answered and said unto them, Are you come out, as against a thief, with swords and with staves to take Me? I was daily with you in the Temple teaching, and you took Me not: but the Scriptures must be fulfilled. And they all forsook Him, and fled. And there followed Him a certain young man, having a linen cloth cast about his

naked body; and the young men laid hold on him: And he left the linen cloth, and fled from them naked" (Mk. 14:43-52).

(14:43) While Jesus was talking to His Disciples and telling them that His betrayer was at hand, Judas and his crowd arrived. The crowd with Judas was not the Temple throng, which had come to love Jesus, but individuals from the Sanhedrin, some members of the Temple police, and some hangers-on willing to perform any service for a price. Some of the people in this crowd were personal servants of the High Priests and of members of the Sanhedrin. They had gathered quickly and armed themselves with sharp swords, knives, staves, and sticks. They were all members of the conspiracy to perpetrate a travesty of justice as they came to arrest the Lord Jesus Christ and put Him to death.

(14:45-46) Judas went to Jesus, addressed Him as Rabbi, and then kissed Him. The verb *"kissed"* is *kataphileo*. This indicates an affectionate, fervent kiss. It was the most hypocritical act the traitor could impose on our Lord.

Judas had received much. He had seen miracles performed by Jesus — and the loving service He had extended to mankind. To whom much is given, much is required, so one wonders how Judas could do such a despicable thing. There are, however, *many* ways to betray the Lord. Many who are piously involved in church activities betray Him by their actions and activities.

Immediately they laid hands on Jesus, seizing Him.

(14:47) One of those with Jesus *"took his sword"* and cut off the ear of a servant of the High Priest. John (18:10) gives the name of this servant as Malchus. Luke indicates that Jesus touched the man's severed ear and instantly restored it. Little is said of this incident, or of this man, but one can imagine his gratitude toward the Lord's action. No doubt his life was never the same after this miraculous meeting with the Son of God.

Most feel it was Peter who struck the servant, for he stood close by and was always impetuous in his actions. He didn't intend to cut off the man's ear to frighten him, but undoubtedly intended much more dramatic results in his effort to defend the Master.

Of course, there was no real need for this. It was not the Master's way. Jesus had been telling the Disciples for months that He was going to die. He had said that if His Kingdom was of this world, He would have defended it. Of course, His Kingdom is not of this world, so there was no *need* to defend it by brawling. Peter, whose name had been given to him by the Lord, had slipped spiritually. In a few hours he would deny the Lord three times. Now he was fighting physically, intending to do the servants of the High Priests harm, as he reverted back to his old nature and old ways.

(14:48) Jesus spoke to the crowd. He objected to being treated as a robber. He was a religious leader and had been involved in spiritual work. There was no excuse for coming out as they did and for treating Him in such a manner. Jesus asked why they were coming against Him as a thief, with swords and staves.

(14:49) Jesus then went on to protest that He had been in the Temple regularly, but they hadn't seized Him then. The secrecy and treachery of the arrest was the fulfillment of Prophecy.

(14:50-52) All the Disciples fled just as Jesus had said they would. They simply ran away.

Reference is made to a young man, without identifying him specifically, who had a linen cloth cast about him. When they tried to seize him, they grabbed his linen cloth as he ran away — leaving the cloth and fleeing naked. It was nighttime and this young man had probably been asleep. He jumped up, grabbed his linen cloth, and threw it about his body. While not identified, it is felt this was Mark, the author of this Gospel. There was, of course, great fear, for even the more mature Disciples abandoned Jesus and fled.

JESUS IS CONDEMNED BY CAIAPHAS AND THE SANHEDRIN

"And they led Jesus away to the High Priest: and with Him were assembled all the Chief Priests and the Elders and the Scribes. And Peter followed Him afar off, even into the palace of the High Priest: and he sat with the servants and warmed himself at the fire. And the Chief Priests and all the Council sought for witness against Jesus to put Him to death; and found none. For many bear false witness against Him, but their witness agreed not together. And there arose certain, and bear false witness against Him, saying, We heard Him say, I will destroy this Temple that is made with hands, and within three days I will build another made without hands. But neither so did their witness agree together.

"And the High Priest stood up in the midst, and asked Jesus, saying, Answerest Thou nothing? what is it which these witness against You? But He held His peace, and answered nothing. Again, the High Priest asked Him, and said unto Him, Are You the Christ, the Son of the Blessed? And Jesus said, I am: and you shall see the Son of Man sitting on the Right Hand of Power, and coming in the clouds of Heaven. Then the High Priest rent his clothes, and said, What need we any further witnesses? Ye have heard the blasphemy: what do you think? And they all condemned Him to be guilty of death.

"And some began to spit on Him, and to cover His Face, and to buffet Him, and to say unto Him, Prophesy: and the servants did strike Him with the palms of their hands" (Mk. 14:53-65).

(14:53-54) Jesus was led away to the High Priest. With Him were assembled all the Chief Priests, together with the Elders and Scribes. The word *"assembled"* is *sunerchomai,* and it portrays the assemblage as flocking together. They gathered in the court about the house of the High Priest. The word for *"servants"* is *huperetes,* and it means *"the members of the Levitical guard."*

Peter followed afar off. There were charcoal braziers burning about to supply heat and light, for the early morning air is very cool at this time of the year in Palestine. It was now *early* in the morning, before daylight, as Peter slipped about and ventured nearer and nearer until he finally drew close enough to the brazier to be warmed by it. Unfortunately, the flames also revealed his features to the servants warming themselves by the fire. Peter had wandered deeper and deeper into the trap set by Satan — which would result in his denial of the Lord.

(14:55-56) The word translated *"council"* is from *sunedrion.* This means *"a sitting together."* It could refer to any assembly of magistrates, judges, ambassadors, or others meeting to make decisions and to pass judgments. Here the word refers specifically to Sanhedrin. This was a seventy-one-member council of the Jews at Jerusalem consisting of Scribes, Elders, and members of the high priestly families, together with the High Priests. They were somewhat analogous to a Supreme Court, or a super city council.

They sought witnesses against Jesus, but they could find no two witnesses agreeing on the central points. They tried over and over again to bring testimony against Jesus which would result in a conviction. Many bore *false* witness against Him, but their testimonies were not in harmony.

According to Levitical Law (as given in Deut. 19:15), the testimony of *two* witnesses was required for conviction, but since no two witnesses could be found agreeing on all points, the council decided to go contrary to the Law. They *ignored* the Law in their obsession to accuse, condemn, and kill Jesus. Legally and morally they could find no fault with Him.

(14:57-59) There were those who bore false witness against Jesus. One reported having heard Jesus say, *"I will destroy this Temple made with hands."* Jesus *had* said — as recorded in John 2:19 — *"You destroy this Temple, and in three days I will raise it up."*

Jesus had not used the first person singular, but rather the second person plural. He had meant *"You"* (referring to the Priests, Scribes, and Pharisees) *"destroy this Temple"* (referring to His Body) *"and in three days I will raise it up"* (from the grave).

He was *not* talking about the massive Temple standing in Jerusalem but was referring instead to the Temple of His Body. He told them they could kill His Body, but in three days He would rise again. They twisted these words and added the phrase *"that is made with hands"* — to refer specifically to the Temple in Jerusalem. Scripture states that their witnesses did not agree together. They lied and twisted the words of Jesus with no agreement among their various testimonies.

(14:60) THE HIGH PRIEST STOOD UP IN THE MIDST. The High Priest in charge of the gathering arose and advanced within the semicircle of the council toward Jesus. The High Priest was irritated and baffled. He had tried to make Jesus' actions sound dangerous. Now, as the council began to look ridiculous, he tried blustering his way through to mask the fact that no evidence existed.

(14:61) BUT HE HELD HIS PEACE. The Greek expression says that Jesus, in the midst of the trial, maintained silence. He refused to deny the charges or to confirm the quotations attributed to Him. In all honesty, there was no one He could properly address. By responding to their charges He would impute to them authority they did not have. Also, these men were so influenced by Satan that whatever defense He might have made would have fallen on deaf ears. This was an unjust arrest, contrary to Levitical Laws, and further corrupted by perjured witnesses. Jesus could not respond, due to the very nature of the situation He was caught up in. This situation was precisely prophesied in Isaiah 53:7 which says, *"He was oppressed, and He was afflicted, yet He opened not His Mouth: He is brought as a lamb to the slaughter, and as a sheep before her shearers is dumb, so He opens not His Mouth."*

ARE YOU THE CHRIST? They asked Him if He was the Messiah, the one awaited by Israel. The question stated was, *"As for you, are you the Anointed One, the Son of the Blessed?"*

(14:62) The religious leaders of the Nation of Israel had put our Lord on oath with the question and Jesus declared with emphasis that He *was* the Christ, the Anointed, the Messiah. The literal translation of this expression is, *"As for myself, in contradistinction to all others, I am!"*

These words of Jesus also imply a *warning* to these judges of the position He will later occupy. Some day these same judges will be judged by the very Lord they condemned.

(14:63-65) Jesus was on trial. It was an unjust and illegal trial. They held the session at night — which was unlawful for the Sanhedrin. They conducted it without formal procedure — which was unlawful. No one was allowed to stand in Jesus' defense — which was unlawful. Any word of accusation must come from at least two witnesses. They did not have these, so the trial was utterly unlawful within the existing Laws.

When the High Priest asked Jesus if He was the Christ, Jesus said, *"I am."*

THE HIGH PRIEST RENT HIS CLOTHES. When Jesus replied that He *was* the Messiah, the High Priest standing before Him tore his clothes. The Greek word is *diarregnumi,* and means, *"to tear asunder."* He tore asunder his *chitonas*: his tunics or undergarments. A person of high position wore two tunics. The tearing of these garments was a sign of mourning or grief and is mentioned first in Genesis 37:29. He tore his clothes to document the fact that he considered Jesus' statement blasphemous. It should be noted that they did *not* tear their garments over their *own* sins, but confronted with anything they considered blasphemous they would do so as a sign of total repudiation.

They had been trying to find witnesses willing and able to successfully bring accusation against Jesus, and their lack of success was extremely embarrassing. Now, however, they felt they finally had Him. He had *"fallen"* into their hands, and out of His own Mouth He had uttered a statement qualifying Him (in their opinion) for the death penalty.

THEY ALL CONDEMNED HIM AS GUILTY OF DEATH. No attempt was made to evaluate Jesus' claim before condemning Him. They agreed immediately that He was worthy of death. They considered Him guilty of blasphemy and, unanimously, condemned Him to death.

All those present seized on the charge of blasphemy. There were outstanding men on the Council who were *not* present who were sympathetic to Jesus. Perhaps they had not been informed of the meeting. Joseph of Arimathaea and Nicodemus were two among those *not* present. All who *were* present, however, agreed to His Death. It was a decision arrived at with almost no thought or discussion, but the consequences were to follow them to the grave — and beyond.

BEGAN TO COVER HIS FACE. First they spat on Jesus, and then covered His Face. The word translated *"to cover"* is *perikalupto,* and it means to *"cover all around, to cover up."* They covered our Lord's Head and then asked Him to reveal who struck Him.

The servants referred to here were the Temple guards or soldiers. As they observed the indignities heaped on our Lord by members of the Sanhedrin, they joined in. They struck Him with their fists and the palms of their hands.

Isaiah had a vision of our Lord's face 700 years before and described His suffering and torment at the hands of a vicious mob (Isa. 52:14, see also Mat. 26:67-68 and 27:27-30). Jesus was subjected to inhuman brutalities and loathsome indignities. The evil treatment that began in the garden at His arrest was now intensifying and would continue unabated until

His Death on the Cross. The vile treatment is difficult to describe, and it was suffered for *our* Salvation.

PETER DENIES JESUS

"And as Peter was beneath in the palace, there cometh one of the maids of the High Priest: And when she saw Peter warming himself, she looked upon him, and said, And you also was with Jesus of Nazareth. But he denied, saying, I know not, neither understand I what you say. And he went out into the porch; and the rooster crowed. And a maid saw him again, and began to say to them who stood by, This is one of them. And he denied it again. And a little after, they stood by said again to Peter, Surely you are one of them: for you are a Galilaean, and your speech agrees thereto. But he began to curse and to swear, saying, I know not this man of whom you speak. And the second time the rooster crowed. And Peter called to mind the word that Jesus said unto him, Before the rooster crowed twice, you shall deny Me thrice. And when he thought thereon, he wept." (Mk. 14:66-72).

(14:66-68) Peter was in the High Priest's palace, in the outer portico. The Verses state that Peter was *"beneath the palace,"* or on the ground level, while the Lord was with the Sanhedrin on an upper level where the trial was held. The maid referred to is one of the servants employed by the High Priest. It was unusual that she should be on duty at this hour of the day, before sunrise. Obviously, something unusual was taking place.

The maid *"looked upon him."* The Greek words are *emblepsasa autoi.* This means, *"to gaze on intently."* She stared at Simon Peter. Undoubtedly, she had seen him many times while he was in Jerusalem with Jesus. Possibly Peter had become quite well known in his own right. He answered her and said, *"I know not, neither understand I what you say."* He was trying to deny her statement and imply that it made no sense. He tried to *"brush her off"* and discourage her from talking further about it.

Peter's insistent denial before a nondescript maid reveals a lack of moral courage on his part. Even though, at the trial, the Lord Jesus did not ask Peter to give his life for Him, it is quite possible Peter would have done so if requested.

Peter's only avenue of service at that moment was to *stand up* for Jesus, but instead he denied the Lord. There are times when it is easier to die for the Lord than to stand up and live for Him. In every activity of life, and in every place, the Christian is to *live* for Christ. Peter denied his relationship to the Lord and went out into the porch as *"the rooster crowed."*

(14:69-71) Once again, Peter was charged with being a Follower of Jesus. The maid doing the charging at this point told those nearby that *"This is one of them."*

After his denial, others standing near said, *"Surely you are one of them: for you are a Galilaean, and your speech agrees thereto."*

Now Peter became desperate in his denials. Mark says he began to curse and to swear, saying, *"I know not this man of whom you speak."* The word curse is *anathematizo*. This means *"to declare anathema or cursed."*

Peter wasn't speaking profanity, but following the Jewish practice of laying one's self under a curse if one were lying. In Galatians 1:8-9, Paul calls for a Divine curse to come upon any who preach a different gospel. Peter, in this case, is doing something similar, as he declares himself subject to a Divine curse if he is not telling the truth.

Of course, Peter *was* lying. He disclaimed all knowledge of Jesus although he had walked closely with Him for three and one-half years and had been His confidant. Jesus loved him, but Peter emphatically denied any relationship with the Lord. While it wasn't profanity or cursing that he used, it was no doubt much worse.

(14:72) Then the rooster crowed a second time and Peter remembered the Words of Jesus. He had said that before the rooster crowed twice, Peter would deny Him thrice (three times). When this happened, the realization of what he had done struck Peter and he began to weep. Matthew's account states that Peter literally *"burst into tears."*

Notes

Chapter 15

The Sanhedrin Deliver Jesus To Pilate

SUBJECT	PAGE
JESUS SENTENCED TO DIE	222
THE ROMAN SOLDIERS MOCK JESUS	224
JESUS ON THE WAY TO THE CROSS	225
THE FIRST THREE HOURS ON THE CROSS	226
THE LAST THREE HOURS ON THE CROSS	227
UNUSUAL EVENTS FOLLOW	228
THE BURIAL OF JESUS	230

CHAPTER 15

THE SANHEDRIN DELIVER JESUS TO PILATE

"And straightway in the morning the Chief Priests held a consultation with the Elders and Scribes and the whole Council, and bound Jesus, and carried Him away, and delivered Him to Pilate. And Pilate asked Him, Are You the King of the Jews? And He answering said unto him, You say it. And the Chief Priests accused Him of many things: but He answered nothing. And Pilate asked Him again, saying, Answerest Thou nothing? behold how many things they witness against You. But Jesus yet answered nothing; so that Pilate marvelled" (Mk. 15:1-5).

(15:1-2) Jesus was subjected to more than one trial. During the night the Sanhedrin questioned Him and condemned Him for blasphemy. Then they reassembled in the morning and confirmed the night's decision. The questions Pilate asked Jesus provide an insight into their craftiness and deceit. He asked Jesus if He were the King of the Jews.

The members of the Sanhedrin had obviously placed a political construction on Jesus' admission of being the Messiah. Jesus had confessed that He was the Christ. By twisting His response to suggest political motives, it appeared to contain a threat to Rome. This would, of course, interest Pilate. In actuality, of all the charges brought by the Priests, this was the only one addressed by Pilate.

The Sanhedrin wanted this to sound like a threat to the throne of the Caesars, suggesting that Jesus was promoting Himself as a *political* leader, in opposition to Rome. Pilate, of course, represented Rome, and his *primary* duty and responsibility was to quell any disturbance that seemed a threat to the authority of Caesar. There were a number of Jewish Zealots anxious to break the bondage of the Roman yoke. Jesus, however, was not trying to assume any political position.

(15:3-5) As Jesus stood before Pilate, the Chief Priests accused Him of many things, but the Lord preserved a strict silence. Neither had He answered the false witnesses who had given contradictory evidence against Him. Pilate marvelled at the self-restraint the Lord exercised for he had never seen a prisoner like this before. Pilate also didn't consider Jesus a political pretender — as one who was trying to usurp the throne.

He was impressed with Jesus and considered Him remarkable. Jesus had answered only once — when Caiaphas asked if He was the Son of

God. Then Jesus said, *"I am."*

Now this was a similar question put to the Lord by Pilate, and again He gave a simple answer, *"You say it."* Beyond this He remained silent.

He lent no dignity or credence to the accusations by answering or acknowledging their insulting lies. Pilate was amazed that Jesus, with His Life in jeopardy, would not speak up to defend Himself. While He was fated to end up on the Cross, Jesus made no effort to escape the series of events that would result in His serving as mankind's Atonement for sin. *"Pilate marvelled."*

JESUS SENTENCED TO DIE

"Now at that Feast he released unto them one prisoner, whomsoever they desired. And there was one named Barabbas, which lay bound with them who had made insurrection with him, who had committed murder in the insurrection. And the multitude crying aloud began to desire him to do as he had ever done unto them. But Pilate answered them, saying, Will you that I release unto you the King of the Jews? For he knew that the Chief Priests had delivered Him for envy. But the Chief Priests moved the people, that he should rather release Barabbas unto them. And Pilate answered and said again unto them, What will you then that I shall do unto Him whom you call the King of the Jews? And they cried out again, Crucify Him. Then Pilate said unto them, Why, what evil has He done? And they cried out the more exceedingly, Crucify Him. And so Pilate, willing to content the people, released Barabbas unto them, and delivered Jesus, when he had scourged Him, to be crucified" (Mk. 15:6-15).

(15:6-8) The Feast of the Passover was observed in commemoration of the release of the Hebrews from Egyptian bondage. Apparently, the governor routinely released one prisoner, as a symbolic gesture to commemorate the freeing of Israel, at that feast each year. The tense of the verb *"released"* indicates a repeated, customary action. It would also make the Roman authority seem less oppressive if they periodically released a prisoner to the people.

THERE WAS ONE NAMED BARABBAS. Literally, in the Greek, it says, *"Now there was one named Barabbas."* He was a brigand who had been involved with others in an insurrection against Rome. Barabbas had committed murder during the incident. From the expression used in the original Text, it indicates that he had been a powerful and well-known man in Jerusalem. He had demonstrated an enormous hatred for the authority of Rome.

The multitude cried aloud, calling for the release of a prisoner. As mentioned, this was a customary practice, and they now demanded it be done again. The crowd was a rabble from the offscourings of society, easily swayed by demonic spirits. They began to scream for the release of the murderer Barabbas.

(15:9-10) Pilate suggested that Jesus be released, calling Him *"King of the Jews."* He had realized that envy motivated the Chief Priests. When he used the term *"King of the Jews,"* Pilate didn't fully understand the implications of his words.

Jesus is, indeed, the King of the Jews, in addition to being King of kings and Lord of lords. To Pilate it was probably a frivolous matter as he made sport of the situation, perhaps in the hope that the crowd might catch the irony and cease their demands. He realized that Jesus did not have political aspirations and was guiltless. He was no insurrectionist planning to overthrow Pilate, or even the High Priests. The church structure hated Jesus because the Master had performed so many impressive miracles that the crowds were beginning to realize He was, indeed, the Messiah. Additionally, Jesus had demonstrated time and again that He saw right through the hypocrisy of the *"spiritual leaders."* Jesus and the High Priests could not *both* survive in Jerusalem. Either Jesus or the religious hierarchy had made their decision that Jesus must die.

(15:11-12) A period of time elapsed during which the Chief Priests moved among the people. It is not known just how long this took, but the implication in the Greek language is that there was an interval during which the Priests brought their influence to bear on the crowd. The people were divided on the question of who should be released, so the High Priests quickly rallied the crowd to demand that Barabbas be released.

Then Pilate asked, *"What will you then that I shall do unto Him whom you call the King of the Jews?"*

(15:13-15) There was no hesitation in their reply. Immediately the demon-influenced and priest-controlled mob screamed, *"Crucify Him."* They shouted it over and over again, *"Crucify Him, crucify Him."*

Pilate thought that surely it would be enough to just torture Him — but the crowd continued their shout to crucify Him. It is recorded in Matthew that the people, in demanding the death of Jesus, said that His Blood would be upon them and on their children (Mat. 27:25). The words screamed at that moment were to bring horror, sorrow, heartache, and agony upon the Jews for generation after generation. They were words tossed off carelessly during an emotional moment, but they were some of the most portentous words ever uttered.

The centuries of persecution oppressing the Jews are not the result of any desire on God's part to *destroy* the Jews. But the oppression has resulted because their statement *removed* them from God's unique protection. They rejected God's continuing help and released themselves over to Satan. It is Satan who steals, kills, and destroys. This hysterical mob, motivated by a demonic hatred and the influence of the Priests, called for the death of Jesus while exposing *themselves* to centuries of indescribable persecution.

In response to the screams and chants of the crowd, Pilate reluctantly acceded to their demands. Barabbas was released and Jesus was sentenced to scourging and Crucifixion.

Scourging was a cruel and barbaric punishment in itself. Normally the victim was stripped to the waist with the hands bound to a pole as he was scourged with an instrument consisting of a handle with several leather thongs attached, weighted with jagged pieces of bone, metal, or rock. Victims lost eyes and teeth, were frequently disemboweled, were always horribly disfigured, and often died. For Jesus to endure *both* scourging and Crucifixion is an unimaginable form of punishment.

Pontius Pilate merely responded to the crowd, feeling that no one really cared what happened to this lowly carpenter from Nazareth. He sadly declared that he would have no more to do with this just man, and *"washed his hands"* of the sordid affair.

THE ROMAN SOLDIERS MOCK JESUS

"And the soldiers led Him away into the hall, called Praetorium; and they call together the whole band. And they clothed Him with purple, and platted a crown of thorns, and put it about His Head, And began to salute Him, Hail, King of the Jews! And they smote Him on the head with a reed, and did spit upon Him, and bowing their knees worshipped Him" (Mk. 15:16-19).

The soldiers led Jesus away to the hall called Praetorium, the soldier's barracks. Having brought Jesus there, they called all the soldiers together and *"clothed Him with purple."* Traditionally, this was the color worn by royalty, but this was no royal garment. It was faded and torn. It was probably a cast-off rag, and, together with it, they plaited a crown of thorns for His Head. The word used for *"crown"* is *stephanos,* and is known as *"the victor's wreath."* It was presented to royalty in recognition of military achievement. The soldiers apparently had this in mind as they mocked Him. These men had observed Jesus' interview with Pilate. They had heard Him referred to as *"King of the Jews,"* and they were making sport of Him.

They also intensified His suffering as they pushed the crown of thorns down on His Head. The Blood ran over His Forehead and into His Eyes. His Head swelled because of the sharp points pushing into His Scalp.

Then they began to salute Him saying, *"Hail, King of the Jews."* In addition, they smote Him on the Head with a reed, driving the thorns into the Bones of His Skull, and they spat upon Him, mocking Him cruelly. All this was done repeatedly, as it appears there was a large number of soldiers present.

Isaiah indicates that the Son of God was so damaged, beaten, and torn that He no longer looked human. It is no wonder after the treatment He experienced. The cruelty, the mocking, the indignities He suffered were all for us. He stripped Himself of heavenly glory and endured ultimate shame in order to redeem fallen humanity.

JESUS ON THE WAY TO THE CROSS

"And when they had mocked Him, they took off the purple from Him, and put His own clothes on Him, and led Him out to Crucify Him. And they compel one Simon, a Cyrenian, who passed by, coming out of the country, the father of Alexander and Rufus, to bear His Cross. And they bring Him unto the place Golgotha, which is, being interpreted, The place of a skull. And they gave Him to drink wine mingled with myrrh: but He received it not" (Mk. 15:20-23).

(15:20) When they finished mocking Jesus, they replaced the purple robe with His own garments. Then they led Him out to crucify Him.

(15:21) They compelled a passerby, Simon a Cyrenian, to bear Jesus' Cross. The word *"compelled"* is *aggareuo.* This word means, *"to press into service."* This Simon was a native of Cyrene, a city of Libya, a country on the northern coast of Africa. It is not known why Simon was in Jerusalem, but he was pressed into service to bear the Cross of Christ.

(15:22-23) THEY BRING HIM. The word *"bring"* is *phero,* and it means, *"to carry a burden, to move by bearing."* It appears that Jesus was so weak (after the strain of the last few days and the horrible scourging) that He was unable to bear the Cross and even had to be supported to the place of the Crucifixion. The word used here in Mark is *pherousin,* and means, *"they bring,"* implying that the Lord needed support.

Jesus was brought to the place called Golgotha. The word *"Golgotha"* is from a Hebrew word and means *"the place that is skull-shaped."* The place was given that name to emphasize the shape of the hill on which Jesus was crucified. The word translated *"skull"* (*kranion*) appears four times in the New Testament. In one place it is translated *"Calvary"* (Lk. 23:33), and in three places it is translated *"skull"* (Mk. 15:22, Mat. 27:33, and Jn. 19:17).

THEY GAVE HIM. The *offered* Jesus wine mingled with myrrh, a stupifying drink offered to criminals about to be crucified. It is said that some of the women of Jerusalem provided this as a service, and it was intended to deaden the pain. However, Jesus refused the drink. He chose rather to face clearheaded all that might befall, in order to experience all He was fated to endure as man's Substitutionary Sacrifice.

THE FIRST THREE HOURS ON THE CROSS

"And when they had crucified Him, they parted His garments, casting lots upon them, what every man should take. And it was the third hour, and they crucified Him. And the superscription of His accusation was written over, THE KING OF THE JEWS.

"And with Him they crucify two thieves; the one on His right hand, and the other on His left. And the Scripture was fulfilled, which said, And He was numbered with the transgressors.

"And they who passed by railed on Him, wagging their heads and saying, Ah, You Who destroyed the Temple, and build it in three days, Save Yourself, and come down from the Cross.

"Likewise also the Chief Priests mocking said among themselves with the Scribes, He saved others; Himself He cannot save. Let Christ the King of Israel descend now from the Cross, that we may see and believe. And they who were crucified with Him reviled Him" (Mk. 15:24-32).

The Bible simply states that they crucified Him. They nailed His Hands and Feet to the Cross and dropped the Cross into a hole between two crucified thieves. His garments were removed, and the soldiers cast lots for them. They gambled beneath the Cross for the clothing for our Lord. Gambling involves covetousness, seeking something belonging to someone else, or getting something the easy way — without effort. Gambling causes untold sorrow and heartache. It can take children's food off the table and clothes off their backs. As it was at the crucifixion, gambling is wrong, and the soldier's actions were despicable.

The time of the Crucifixion was 9 a.m., *"the third hour of the day."* On the basis of that expression, their accounting had begun at 6 a.m. Jesus hung on the Cross until approximately 3 p.m.

Pilate commanded a superscription be written and placed over the head of Jesus. It said *"the King of the Jews."* This was done in irony and mockery. Pilate was making fun of the Jews and the entire Nation of Israel. He was saying, *"You can consider the man hanging here as your king, but in reality Caesar is king."*

The Bible states that two thieves were crucified with Jesus. There is the possibility that even more might have been crucified at this time, but

Jesus and the two thieves were crucified in that particular spot at the same time.

Jesus was put to death with evil men — *"numbered with the transgressors."* Jesus came to die for sinners, bearing the sins of the world. What a terrible price the Master paid for *our* Redemption. But we can rejoice and shout because of the great victory accomplished through His suffering on the Cross at Calvary. He died as our substitute.

(15:29-32) As Jesus hung on the Cross, there were those who passed by and *"railed at Him."* The word *"railed"* is *blasphemeo,* which means to speak reproachfully, to rail at, to revile. People taunted and mocked Him and told Him to save Himself by coming down from the Cross. They laughed that He had said He would rebuild the Temple in three days if they destroyed it. The Chief Priests and Scribes also mocked Jesus saying, *"He saved others, Himself He cannot save."* Of course, their statement was a lie. They *should* have said, *"He saved others, Himself He **would** not save."*

All these circumstances were prophesied in minute detail in Psalms, Chapter 22, written some thousand years before the event by David. To those who today scoff at the Bible and say it *isn't* the Word of God, it would be interesting to hear how David could have seen the *precise* events of the Crucifixion (not to occur for another thousand years) if God *didn't* inspire the Writings.

AND THEY WHO WERE CRUCIFIED WITH HIM DID ALSO REVILE HIM. Two thieves are specified as being crucified with Christ, though it is possible there were more. We know that one was — or least *became* — sympathetic to Jesus and requested mercy as he hung on the Cross. This thief turned to the Lord for help and was assured that he would be with Jesus in Paradise.

THE LAST THREE HOURS ON THE CROSS

"And when the sixth hour was come, there was darkness over the whole land until the ninth hour. And at the ninth hour Jesus cried with a loud voice, saying, Eloi, Eloi, lama sabachthani? which is, being interpreted, My God, My God, why have You forsaken Me? And some of them who stood by, when they heard it, said, Behold, he calls Elijah (Elias). And one ran and filled a spunge full of vinegar, and put it on a reed, and gave Him to drink, saying, Let alone; let us see whether Elijah (Elias) will come to take Him down. And Jesus cried with a loud voice, and gave up the ghost" (Mk. 15:33-37).

During the last three hours of Jesus' suffering, a supernatural darkness descended over the land. This began at the sixth hour (about 12 noon), and lasted until the ninth hour (3 p.m.). This was not just a local condition, as ancient documents found in Rome describe an unnatural darkness covering Rome at this precise time.

Jesus cried out with a loud voice that He had been forsaken by God. *"Forsaken"* is, in the Greek, *egkataleipo,* and it conveys the idea of someone being deserted in a situation over which he has no control. He had been forsaken, deserted, or abandoned, as one who is left completely helpless.

The consequences of Jesus' terrible cry are more far-reaching than any mortal can fathom. Jesus, having been with the Father from eternity and enjoying the Presence of Divine Glory, was now forsaken. This was essential if the Covenant of Redemption were to be accomplished between Father and Son. As Jesus uttered this cry, He was experiencing severe agony and the cumulative weight of universal sin placed upon Him. He had to bear this in order that Redemption might be realized.

It is hard to imagine the terrible price paid for our Redemption. Sin separates us from God, and Jesus took our place. God turned His Back upon the Lord as Jesus accepted the sins of the world on His Shoulders. The words He cried out with a loud voice were, *"Eloi, Eloi, lama sabachtani?"*

Mark gives the interpretation of this as, *"My God, My God, why have You forsaken Me?"*

There was some discussion among the onlookers as to what Jesus had said and the language used. People standing at the foot of the Cross did not understand. Some said He called for Elijah. One ran to get a sponge dipped in vinegar. Then they said: Hold off. Let's see whether Elijah *will* come to take Him down.

But Jesus gave a final cry and *gave up the ghost."* This literally means, in the original, that *"He breathed out His Life."* As recorded by Luke and John, He said, *"It is finished,"* and *"Father, into thy hands I commend my spirit"* (Jn. 19:30 and Lk. 23:46).

UNUSUAL EVENTS FOLLOW

"And the Veil of the Temple was rent in twain from the top to the bottom. And when the centurion, which stood over against Him saw that He so cried out, and gave up the ghost, he said, Truly this man was the Son of God. There were also women looking on afar off: among whom was Mary Magdalene, and Mary the mother of James the less and of Joseph (Joses), and Salome; (Who also, when He was in Galilee, followed Him, and ministered unto Him;) and many other women which came up with Him unto Jerusalem" (Mk. 15:38-41).

Josephus, the respected Jewish historian who some say became a Follower of Jesus after He (Jesus) died and rose from the dead, said that the Veil of the Temple weighed over two thousand pounds and was some four inches thick. He went on to say that four yoke of oxen could not pull it apart. The Veil separated the Holy of Holies from the Holy Place. No man could enter the Holy of Holies except the High Priest, who went in only once a year to make Atonement for the sins of the people.

If the High Priest went in unclean, he would immediately be struck dead. The separation between God and man that the Veil represented was now removed. The Bible says it was rent from top to bottom, for God tore it asunder. If human instruments had been involved, it would have been torn from bottom to top as they couldn't *reach* the top. Instead, it tore from top to bottom in an act of God. Direct access to God was now available to every sinner through Christ, and a mortal High Priest was no longer necessary. The Temple Veil shielded the Holy of Holies from mortal invasion. Now, being torn asunder, the way is open into God's Presence for all who come through Christ.

Jesus Christ paid the price for man's Redemption by fulfilling all the Levitical Laws. There is no longer any need for lambs, turtledoves, or blood sacrifices to be made. The Lamb that was slain from the foundation of the world had now fulfilled His eternal Mission. He opened the way so whosoever will may come and drink of the Water of Life freely.

Whosoever! The bond, the free; the great, the small; the rich, the poor; the sick, the well; the black, the white, the brown, the red, and the yellow. *All* may come and find rest in Him who said, *"Come unto Me, all you that labor and are heavy laden, and I will give you rest. Take My yoke upon you, and learn of Me; for I am meek and lowly in heart: and ye shall find rest unto your souls. For My yoke is easy, and My burden is light"* (Mat. 11:28-30).

The Roman centurion who stood by when Jesus died said, *"Truly this man was the Son of God."* This centurion probably didn't know the Messianic claims of the Lord Jesus Christ, but at that moment he caught a glimpse of Redemption. He declared, concerning Jesus, *"He was the Son of God."*

A number of women watched from a distance where they would be safe from the unruly crowd. Among this group was Mary Magdalene — from whom Jesus had cast seven devils. She loved Him deeply. Mary the mother of Jesus was there, and others from Galilee who had been Followers of Jesus. They had come to Jerusalem for the Passover celebration. These women had ministered to Jesus in the past in a number of ways — preparing food, giving of financial support, or just being friends.

A number of people from Galilee had come to Jerusalem for the

Passover, and some of them came to the Crucifixion. Jesus had given them new life, new status, and new purpose in their existence.

THE BURIAL OF JESUS

"And now when the even was come, because it was the preparation, that is, the day before the Sabbath, Joseph of Arimathaea, an honourable counselor, which also waited for the Kingdom of God, came, and went in boldly unto Pilate, and craved the Body of Jesus. And Pilate marvelled if He were already dead: and calling unto him the centurion, he asked him whether He had been any while dead. And when he knew it of the centurion, he gave the Body to Joseph. And he bought fine linen, and took Him down, and wrapped Him in the linen, and laid Him in a sepulchre which was hewn out of a rock, and rolled a stone unto the door of the sepulchre. And Mary Magdalene and Mary the mother of Joseph (Joses) beheld where He was laid" (Mk. 15:42-47).

It was a short time before the Sabbath. Their new day began at sundown, about 6 p.m., instead of at midnight, as we mark the start of a new day. There is disagreement over the day on which Jesus was crucified. Good Friday is celebrated by religious groups all over the world, but the period of sunset Friday to sunrise Sunday scarcely fulfills His Prophecy that He would be in the grave three days and three nights.

Some scholars feel that any part of a day would be considered as a day, but this would not provide three nights. Some hold to Thursday as the day of the Crucifixion, and some favor Wednesday as the most likely day. Reference to the Sabbath does not necessarily imply that it was the Saturday *weekly* Sabbath which is referred to. There were other special days referred to as the Sabbath. The Feast of the Passover was being celebrated at this time, so in all probability it was *not* the Saturday Sabbath indicated. While there is no agreement as to the exact day on which Jesus died, the important fact is that He *was* crucified, died for our sins, and rose again.

Joseph of Arimathaea was an honorable man, and he, along with Nicodemus, was a member of the Sanhedrin. These men were apparently not informed of the nighttime meeting of the council to try Jesus. Joseph was, undoubtedly, heartbroken when informed of the farcical trial that had taken place without his presence. Also, he was not a member of the screaming mob thirsting for Jesus' Blood. The Bible says he *"waited for the Kingdom of God,"* believing that Jesus was the Messiah. Joseph went *boldly* unto Pilate, unconcerned with the possible reaction of the Sanhedrin. He was not concerned for his reputation or the vengeance they might exact. At the time of Jesus' Crucifixion the city was in an uproar. The religious leaders and their hired rabble had been plotting His execution. They were victorious and now He was dead. Joseph was unconcerned about all this as he took his stand for Christ. This is what every person should do when they choose to follow Jesus.

But Joseph of Arimathaea laid down his reputation, his fortune, his name, and his work. Everything was placed on the line. Jesus had warned that if any would come after Him, they would need to deny themselves, take up their cross, and follow Him.

This is always costly. We are not to hide our lights under a bushel. When a person takes a stand for Christ, it could mean his business, career, fortune, family, or even his life. To follow the call of the Lord is to commit one's *total* life to Him willingly and without reservation.

(15:44-45) Pilate marvelled that Jesus was already dead. Very often the victims of crucifixion lingered on the cross for several days before dying. Some deaths actually resulted from starvation rather than the wounds.

Not believing Joseph, Pilate inquired of the centurion, asking whether or not He had died. Jesus had suffered greatly and died quickly. Despite the physical suffering, He died basically of a broken heart.

When the centurion confirmed that Jesus was dead, Pilate permitted removal of His Body. The word *"body"* is not from *soma*, which is the word generally used for the human body; but from *ptoma*, which means *"a corpse."* Pilate gave the corpse to Joseph. The word for *"give"* is *doreo*, and means *"to freely give."* It was not out of any sense of generosity that he did so, but because he wanted to be finished with this inconvenient and troublesome affair.

Pilate had been deeply disturbed by the proceedings. His wife had come to him during the trial pleading with him to have nothing to do with condemning Jesus. After Jesus died there had been darkness, and an earthquake, and the Roman centurion had perceived Jesus as the Son of God. Pilate was anxious to be rid of the Body and to finally put the incident behind him.

(15:46-47) On the way to Golgotha to retrieve the Body of Jesus, Joseph provided himself with linen. The word used is *sindon*, and refers to a bolt of linen (not a garment) fresh and unused. Then Joseph had to remove Jesus' Body from the Cross. He could not do this alone, and his friend from the Sanhedrin, Nicodemus, was probably already at the spot waiting with a large supply of spices used for embalming the dead. Together they would take Jesus down from the Cross.

It was not a pleasant sight to view the lifeless form that had been so badly battered and bruised and hung upon the Cross. They took Jesus, wrapping His Body in the fresh, clean linen, and placed Him in the sepulchre prepared by Joseph for his own burial. It was in the garden near the place of Crucifixion. The opening to such a tomb was usually closed with a stone when the tomb contained a body. A stone was rolled into the opening of this sepulchre. But at least two of the women, *"Mary Magdalene and Mary the mother of Joseph (Joses),"* attentatively observed where Jesus was laid.

Chapter 16

The Visit Of The Women To The Tomb Of Jesus

SUBJECT	PAGE
JESUS APPEARS TO MARY MAGDALENE	236
JESUS APPEARS TO OTHERS	236
THE GREAT COMMISSION GIVEN	237
THE ASCENSION OF JESUS	239

CHAPTER 16

THE VISIT OF THE WOMEN TO THE TOMB OF JESUS

"And when the Sabbath was past, Mary Magdalene, and Mary the mother of James, and Salome, had bought sweet spices, that they might come and anoint Him.

"And very early in the morning the first day of the week, they came unto the sepulchre at the rising of the sun. And they said among themselves, Who shall roll us away the stone from the door of the sepulchre? And when they looked, they saw that the stone was rolled away: for it was very great.

"And entering into the sepulchre, they saw a young man sitting on the right side, clothed in a long white garment; and they were affrighted. And He said unto them, Be not affrighted: You seek Jesus of Nazareth, Who was crucified: He is risen; He is not here: behold the place where they laid Him. But go your way, tell His Disciples and Peter that He goes before you into Galilee: there shall you see Him, as He said unto you. And they went out quickly, and fled from the sepulchre; for they trembled and were amazed: neither said they any thing to any man; for they were afraid" (Mk. 16:1-8).

(16:1-2) The Sabbath was past and it was *"very early in the morning"* on the first day of the week which was Sunday. It was just about daylight as the sun crept over the eastern horizon. This was to be the greatest day in the annals of human history.

Mary Magdalene and Mary, the mother of James, and Salome had brought sweet spices to anoint the Body of Jesus. Joseph of Arimathaea had already anointed Him and prepared the Body for burial, but they wished to add more spices. This would have been an external application of fragrant oils.

They loved Jesus dearly. Mary Magdalene is mentioned often in events concerning the Ministry of Jesus. She had followed Jesus into Jerusalem and was present at His Death. She was the first to arrive at the tomb on this Resurrection morning.

Since they had brought spices to anoint the Body, they obviously did not believe He would be raised from the dead. Undoubtedly these women, together with the others, had experienced deep grief and sorrow. Mary Magdalene, anxious to get to the tomb early on the first day of the week, probably slept very little. It was perhaps still dark when she left Bethany, which is about two miles from Jerusalem, to arrive there *"at the rising of the sun."*

(16:3-4) THEY SAID AMONG THEMSELVES. The imperfect tense of the verb is literally translated, *"they kept on saying among themselves."* The main topic discussed as they approached the tomb was how to roll the stone away from the entrance. The stone was large, certainly, weighing hundreds of pounds, perhaps more than a ton.

The tomb had been hewn out of solid rock and the recessed opening was covered by this boulder. It would have taken several men to put it in place. Therefore, the two women wondered how to roll back the stone so they could anoint the Body of Jesus with the spices they had purchased.

WHEN THEY LOOKED. When they arrived at the tomb, they saw that the stone had already been rolled away. The verb translated *"they looked"* is *anablepo,* and means to *"look up."* They had been walking with downcast eyes as they approached the tomb, so *"looking up"* they saw that the boulder had been rolled away.

(16:5) As they entered the sepulchre, they saw a young man sitting on the right, wearing an unusual garment. The word translated *"garment"* is *stole.* It had reference to a long, stately robe reaching to the feet. It also indicates a special solemnity, richness, or beauty. It was not a garment common to men of the Earth. Rather, it was different from anything the women had ever seen, and the Bible states as they saw this long, white garment on the young man, they were *"affrighted."* The word *"affrighted"* is *ekthambeo.* A good translation is *"amazed."* It was more wonder than fright, and the literal translation is, *"they were utterly amazed."*

(16:6-8) The Angel told the women not to be *"utterly amazed,"* because Jesus whom they sought was risen. He told them to observe the place where they had lain Jesus. It was empty.

Then he instructed them to tell Peter and the Disciples that they would soon see Jesus, as He had said. One might wonder why Peter had been specifically named. Peter's denial of the Lord had been forceful and deliberate, followed by overwhelming grief and remorse. His very heart was shattered and broken and, no doubt, he felt all was lost. Certainly, Peter needed encouragement and a reminder of Jesus' love for him. What marvelous news they were to bring to the other Disciples, especially Peter. Jesus was risen.

Even though Jesus declared repeatedly that He would rise from the dead, none of His Disciples or Followers had really comprehended the import of His Words. None of them *believed* He would rise from the dead. What an amazing, glorious, phenomenal event! They went out quickly from the sepulchre, trembling in amazement and astonishment. They were reluctant to tell anyone because they were fearful.

JESUS APPEARS TO MARY MAGDALENE

"Now when Jesus was risen early the first day of the week, He appeared first to Mary Magdalene, out of whom He had cast seven devils. And she went and told them who had been with Him, as they mourned and wept. And they, when they had heard that He was alive, and had been seen of her, believed not" (Mk. 16:9-11).

Jesus, having risen early on the first day of the week, appeared first to Mary Magdalene, who had been delivered of seven demons and was filled with gratitude to the Lord. She informed the others as they mourned and wept.

The Disciples were completely despondent, for their world had been turned upside down. For three and one-half years they had followed Jesus faithfully and had seen miracles beyond description. But now He was apparently dead, and it was difficult, almost impossible, for them to understand. They wondered why He hadn't used His Power to thwart His murderers. They mourned and wept in a state of shock and deep depression.

When Mary Magdalene told them that Jesus was risen and alive, and that she had seen Him, they dismissed her account as wishful thinking.

JESUS APPEARS TO OTHERS

"After that He appeared in another form unto two of them, as they walked, and went into the country. And they went and told it unto the residue: neither believed they them. Afterward He appeared unto the Eleven as they sat at meat, and upbraided them with their unbelief and hardness of heart, because they believed not them which had seen Him after He was risen" (Mk. 16:12-14).

Two Disciples were on the road to Emmaus, located about seven and one-half miles northwest of Jerusalem. One of them was named Cleophas (Lk. 24:13-32), but no indication is given as to the name of the other Disciple. Some people think it was Luke because of the detailed description in his Gospel.

In this brief account it simply mentions that Jesus appeared to them in another form. The words "another form" do not mean He took on a totally different appearance, but that they did not recognize Him. He appeared as a fellow-traveler.

Luke gives a more detailed account of the discussion they had with Jesus. He called them foolish men and slow to believe what the Prophets had spoken. When Jesus sat down with them to eat, He took bread, blessed it, broke it, and gave it to them, and then their eyes were opened and He vanished out of their sight. They had not recognized Him because of their unbelief. But He did manifest Himself to them and only then did they recall that, while they had been talking, their hearts had burned within them.

These Disciples reported to the others, and once again the remainder could not believe nor comprehend that Jesus had truly been raised from the dead. The group was so mired in a state of unbelief, after the shock of the horrible Crucifixion, that they didn't know Who He was.

Later Jesus appeared to the Eleven as they *"sat at meat."* He appeared suddenly to His grief-stricken Disciples. They had not believed the report of those that had seen the risen Lord. He reproached and reprimanded them for their unbelief and also for not believing those who had seen Him after He was risen.

THE GREAT COMMISSION GIVEN

"And He said unto them, Go ye into all the world, and preach the Gospel to every creature. He who believes and is baptized shall be saved; but he who believes not shall be damned. And these signs shall follow them who believe; In My Name shall they cast out devils; they shall speak with new tongues; They shall take up serpents; and if they drink any deadly thing, it shall not hurt them; they shall lay hands on the sick, and they shall recover" (Mk. 16:15-18).

Jesus' commission to the Disciples was to go into all the world and preach the Gospel. This is the Great Commission and involves proclaiming the Message to *"every creature."* Jesus had told them prior to His Crucifixion that there would be great natural catastrophes, disasters, and wars, but nothing should hinder the spreading of the Gospel to the world. The Great Commission involves delivering the Good News to *all* men.

The Good News is that Jesus saves. He died to save the lost, to redeem them and to deliver them from eternal Hell. The concern of this Ministry and the concern of every dedicated Christian should be to get the Gospel Message out to the whole world and every living being.

HE WHO BELIEVES. He who believes — that is, he who *accepts* the Lord Jesus Christ — shall be saved. A single Scripture in John (3:16) summarizes the Gospel, *"For God so loved the world, that He gave His Only Begotten Son, that whosoever believes in Him should not perish, but have Everlasting Life."*

In Mark's Text it says that Jesus declared, *"He who believes and is baptized shall be saved."* The word *"believe"* is a very strong term. It is more than just mental agreement or acceptance. It implies total commitment to Christ. One is to seek Him with the whole heart and to strive only to please and serve Him.

Reference is also made to Baptism here. It does *not* state that he who is *not* baptized shall be damned. Condemnation rests on disbelief. Salvation rests on belief, not Baptism. When a person believes and trusts Christ, he is saved. Baptism is then a physical confirmation of the new attitude and new life, and *not* the means of *securing* it. Water Baptism is extremely important, but it is still just a representation of a new life. It is not the essential element in *acquiring* Salvation and Redemption. The simplest expression of Salvation in the Scriptures is, *"Believe on the Lord Jesus Christ and you shall be saved."* While following the Lord's precedent of Water Baptism is an example of Christian submission, the water itself does not save. Baptism is referred to as a Sacrament or an Ordinance — just as is the Lord's Supper — but these Ordinances do not save a person. It must be emphasized that a person is saved by believing and is damned by disbelief. And the Greek word used here is a *strong* term, defining belief as a *life-changing* commitment to completely trust in the Lord.

(16:17-18) Some have questioned the authenticity of these Verses because they are not in the earliest manuscripts. However, some accurate manuscripts *do* contain them, and they *are* in harmony with the rest of the Gospel. A good case has been made for their authenticity by some who have made in-depth studies, and there is no need to delete them.

SIGNS SHALL FOLLOW THEM. Some of the signs mentioned have to do with the casting out of demons and manifestations of the mighty infilling of the Holy Spirit. There is much demon activity today, and the Christian is to take command over the powers of demon spirits in Jesus' Name. We have authority in the Name of Christ. We are involved in constant spiritual warfare and wrestle not against flesh and blood — but against spiritual powers (Eph. 6:12).

THEY SHALL TAKE UP SERPENTS. This is not to suggest that we should test God by picking up venomous snakes. The Greek word used here is *airo*, and means to *"take up, to remove, to take away, to destroy, to do away with."* It is not referring to a sideshow of serpent-handling or of anything of this nature.

There are snake charmers in India and other places who handle cobras and other poisonous snakes, but they are in no way demonstrating Faith in God. This is not what is referred to in this Scripture. In Luke 10:19 we read, *"Behold, I give unto you power to tread on serpents and scorpions, and over all the power of the enemy: and nothing shall by any means hurt you."* God's Holy Spirit is referring to *demon activity* and the *powers of the Devil* (who is called *"that old serpent"*). Christians are to take authority over demonic forces, bind them, and cast them out in order to liberate and free the oppressed.

There is much demonic activity in our world today, and the Gospel is often impeded. Many evil events are occurring in the world that are demon-directed. There are countries whose leaders are *completely controlled* by demonic forces. This, of course, creates great suffering. We, as Believers, are to exercise authority over demon powers.

It also states that if Believers drink any deadly thing it shall not hurt them. Here again, a person is *not* to take some deadly poison and demonstrate his Faith by drinking it. However, Christians have been *forced* to drink poisonous substances by evil men and they *have* marvelously and miraculously escaped any adverse effects. There are historic cases of Christians being forced to drink deadly poisons and surviving unharmed.

People are never to pick up snakes or ingest deadly substances to demonstrate their Faith. Rather than *proving* their Faith, this would actually be tempting God and is Scripturally prohibited. If one *accidentally* ingests a poison, or is *forced* to do so, the Lord will grant His protection for that particular individual and that situation, if He wills to do so.

This Passage also states that *"Believers shall lay hands on the sick and they shall recover."* Millions have been healed by the Power of Almighty God and there has been a growing emphasis on healing in Christian circles for several decades. Christians *should* ask the Lord to heal them. Believers can minister to others and agree together in trusting God for healing.

However, this does not mean that we should be opposed to doctors, hospitals, or medicine, for they are working to help people. We receive healing in various ways, and the Holy Spirit can work *through* capable medical personnel. But one thing needs to be understood, and that is that there *is* Divine healing. And as Believers lay hands on the sick, as they believe, they *will* experience recovery. (The subject of Divine healing is an extensive subject within itself and is covered more fully in other publications available through this Ministry.)

THE ASCENSION OF JESUS

"So then after the Lord had spoken unto them, He was received up into Heaven, and sat on the Right Hand of God. And they went forth, and preached everywhere, the Lord working with them, and confirming the Word with signs following. Amen" (Mk. 16:19-20).

After the Lord spoke to the Disciples, He was received up into Heaven. He sits today at the Right Hand of God and will come again.

The Disciples went forth and preached everywhere. In effect, this is a one-sentence synopsis of the Book of Acts. The Disciples and Believers went everywhere as the Lord commanded them. As the Word of God was declared, signs and wonders followed, confirming His Word. Thus it was in the First Century, and it is the same today. Lives are changed and made new by the Power of God.

And event that happened in the Twentieth Century which mirrors events of the Book of Acts is related by a Minister friend of mine. He was preaching in Africa when one night thousands of black-skinned Africans filled the crude, makeshift, open-sided tabernacle in which he was speaking. The people came and sang to the Glory of God, and he preached.

In response to the Message, and elderly, aged, and haggard African woman walked up the aisle to find new life in Christ. She had been a demon worshiper and a high priestess in a demonic cult. She had not only killed people, but had actually eaten human flesh.

She had sunk to the depths of sin, but this night, instead of coming to ridicule the things of God, she accepted Jesus as her Saviour. The Minister stated that a few minutes later the woman began to speak in perfect English and thanked God for the Blood of Jesus. She declared her freedom in rolling phrases glorifying the Lord Jesus Christ. They said her face literally shone.

The Pastor went into an ecstasy of joy. He said, *"Do you hear her?"*

The Minister said, *"Yes, I hear. But what is so remarkable? I've heard **many** people praise the Lord."*

The local Pastor stared at him for a moment. *"But she can't speak a single **word** of English. To my knowledge she doesn't even know one **syllable** of English."*

Listening to her, my friend said she expressed praise in perfectly constructed and pronounced phrases. She was gloriously and wonderfully filled with the Holy Spirit and was speaking in tongues. What made the event so startling was that the tongue given to her was *English*.

These events occurred over a period of about thirty minutes. This is how the Power of God transforms a life and changes a person in a moment's time.

Jesus brought Redemption to a lost and dying world. The Message declared in the First Century is still valid in the Twentieth Century. This is the Power that saves from sin and transforms lives. Jesus paid the price. His Promises are sure, and His Word never fails.

Amen!